Readings
in
American Criticism

Readings

in

American Criticism

Edited with an Introduction by

THOMAS ELLIOTT BERRY

West Chester State College

THE ODYSSEY PRESS

Acknowledgments

The author is grateful to the following publishers and literary agents for permission to use the materials listed below.

E. P. Dutton & Co., Inc. For passage from the book *On Literature Today* by Van Wyck Brooks. Copyright 1941 by Van Wyck Brooks. Reprinted by permission of E. P. Dutton & Co., Inc.

Harcourt, Brace & World, Inc. For "Tradition and the Individual Talent" from *Selected Essays*, New Edition, by T. S. Eliot, copyright 1932, 1936, 1950 by Harcourt, Brace & World, Inc.; copyright 1960, 1964 by T. S. Eliot. Reprinted by permission of the publishers.

Holt, Rinehart and Winston, Inc. For "Dust of Snow" from *Complete Poems of Robert Frost*. Copyright 1923 by Holt, Rinehart and Winston, Inc. Copyright 1951 by Robert Frost. Reprinted by permission of Holt, Rinehart and Winston, Inc.

The Houghton Mifflin Company. For "Standards in Criticism" from *Masters of Modern French Criticism* by Irving Babbitt. Copyright 1940 by Dora D. Babbitt. Reprinted by permission of The Houghton Mifflin Company.

The Hudson Review. For "Theatre Chronicle" by John Simon. Vol. XXI, No. 4 (Winter 1968-69) of *The Hudson Review;* pp. 703–712. Copyright © 1969 by The Hudson Review, Inc. Reprinted by permission of the author and *The Hudson Review.*

Alfred A. Knopf, Inc. For "Footnote on Criticism" from *Prejudices: Third Series* by H. L. Mencken. Copyright © 1922 by Alfred A. Knopf, Inc. and renewed 1950 by H. L. Mencken. Reprinted by permission of the publisher.

New Directions Publishing Corporation. For Chapter XI, "Vorticism," from *Gaudier Brzeska* by Ezra Pound. All Rights Reserved. Reprinted by permission of New Directions Publishing Corporation.

The New York Review of Books. For "William Carlos Williams" by Kenneth Burke from *The New York Review of Books*. Copyright © 1963 The New York Review.

Princeton University Press. For "The Historical Interpretation of Literature" by Edmund Wilson and "Criticism as Pure Speculation" by John Crowe Ransom in *The Intent of the Critic*, ed. D. A. Stauffer (Copyright 1941 by Princeton University Press). Reprinted by permission of Princeton University Press.

The Ronald Press Company. For foreward by Cleanth Brooks from *Critiques and Essays in Criticism, 1920–1948*, selected by Robert Wooster Stallman. Copyright © 1949 The Ronald Press Company, New York.

The Swallow Press. For "Understanding Modern Poetry" by Allen Tate from *Essays of Four Decades:* Swallow Press, Chicago; Copyright © 1968.

The University of Chicago Press. For "Questions and Answers in the Teaching of Literary Texts" from *The Idea of the Humanities*, p. 176 of Vol. 2 by Ronald Crane. Copyright © 1967 The University of Chicago Press.

The Viking Press. For introduction from *The Portable Faulkner*, edited by Malcolm Cowley. Copyright 1946 by The Viking Press, Inc. Reprinted by permission of The Viking Press, Inc.

The Wayne State University Press. For "Against 'The Great Gatsby," by Gary J. Scrimgeour, pp. 75–86 from *Criticism*, Vol. VIII.1 (Winter 1966). Copyright © 1966 The Wayne State University Press. Reprinted by permission of the author and publisher.

Preface

This book is essentially a short anthology of American critical thought. It presents the critical theories of a selection of personalities who, with varying degrees of competence and success, have made an impact on American criticism.

In assembling this collection, the editor met an initial problem in the matter of types of criticism. American criticism encompasses everything from the esoteric criticism that can be comprehended only by the knowledgeable few to the newspaper reviews that daily judge for the mass audience books, poetry, drama, and other endeavors usually termed "literary." To present representative selections of all critical thought, therefore, would require much more than a single volume. Nonetheless, some attempt toward all-inclusiveness had to be made.

Then, too, the editor naturally encountered difficulties in choosing selections for each critic to be presented. What essay, for instance, properly reflects the critical theories of T. S. Eliot? Like most other important critics, Eliot modified his views from time to time. He also, in effect, repudiated some of his earlier pronouncements. How, then, can one choose the essay which most accurately exhibits the "true" Eliot? At best, one can proceed only from the realization that any selection must be considered in the context of date of composition.

As the reader peruses this book he must remember that many of the selections are actually only excerpts from longer and hence more extensively developed works. Consequently, the reader may feel that some of the arguments are strangely truncated, or he may tend to judge the critic's case on the basis of incomplete evidence. This situation can be overcome, of course, by seeking out the full work.

In preparing this book, the editor received assistance from many persons—all of whom merit recognition in print. However, because of limitations of space, listing all becomes unrealistic. The editor, therefore, must restrict himself to thanking Ruth C. Wright, Allen C. Budd, and his colleagues at West Chester State College for many valuable suggestions; and he must extend his gratitude to the members of his family who, with characteristically good humor, withstood the many inconveniences occasioned by the typing, editing, proofreading, and other details involved in producing a book.

T. E. B.

Contents

Readings
in
American Criticism

Introduction

I

The term "criticism" as commonly employed in the study of
literature defies concise definition. The word encompasses
so broad a field, so wide a diversity of attitudes, and so great a
range of subtleties that no single sentence—or indeed any relatively small number of sentences—can delineate the total situation.

Nonetheless, despite this basic problem of definition, one
can understand the nature of criticism by isolating for consideration the procedures associated with the critical process. Initially,
one should think of the entire critical act in terms of examination
and conclusion. One person, the critic, examines the work of a
second person, the artist, and makes decisions or conclusions
regarding the work. These conclusions are essentially of one of
two kinds—evaluative or explicative.

Evaluative conclusions are by far the more common. To make
an evaluative conclusion, the critic examines the work (novel,
poem, short story, etc.) with the aim of assessing its final value.
He strives to determine, in essence, the nature of the respect to
be accorded the work; that is, he strives to place the work in
its proper place on the scale between the extremes of true greatness and mere hack production. Thus a given critic may evaluate
Edmund Spenser's "Prothalamion" as the greatest marriage hymn
of all time while naming many similar works that never rise
above the commonplace. By the same process, another critic may
evaluate Herman Melville's *Moby Dick* as monumental achievement while categorizing Frank Norris' *The Octopus* as routine
craftsmanship.

Explicative criticism, as the name implies, is criticism designed

1

to explain; it is criticism which examines parts or all of a work in order to establish precise meaning. The most striking example of explicative criticism in literature is textual criticism. In this process, a competent person examines the text of a particular work and explains its meaning, line by line. The medievalist, for example, studies the manuscript copies of *The Ormulum* (*c.* 1200) and discusses its meaning. He settles the implications of words, he clarifies references, and he elucidates ideas inherent in the work itself. In each instance, his function is to explain.

Explicative criticism has assumed great importance within the recent past in the field of poetry.[1] Some critics advocate a searching analysis of each line of a poem as the most effective approach for settling all questions—including final merit—of the particular work. Hence they stress proficiency in determining meaning as the essence of criticism.

The value of explicative criticism is also evident in its role in modern scholarship, where it has served to resolve many questions heretofore treated subjectively. A representative tribute is that of Professor Mark Schorer, who has written, "Modern criticism, through its exacting scrutiny of literary texts, has demonstrated with finality that in art, beauty and truth are indivisible and one."[2]

In thinking of evaluative and explicative criticism, however, one must observe a special caution: they are not completely separable. All evaluative criticism possesses an element of explication, while all explicative criticism is partially an evaluation.

When, for instance, one attempts to evaluate a novel, he must first determine, among other things, the nature of the novel's theme. Thereafter, he discusses the novelist's success in handling that theme. Hence the critic explicates as a foundation for evaluating. Then, too, when one attempts to explicate meaning, he passes, at the least, an implied judgment on the author's ability to establish his meaning. Hence he is making an evaluation.

---

[1] See page 249.
[2] "Technique as Discovery," *Hudson Review* I (1948), 67–87. For an interesting challenge to this statement, see page 243.

After one has comprehended thoroughly the nature of evaluative and explicative criticism, he should think of criticism in terms of attitude. This procedure is especially important because the critic always works with a series of attitudinal concepts that comprise his "critical theory." A critic's theory is composed of his ideas concerning the nature and function of literature, his standards for judging literature, and his sensitivities to the particular work of literature involved. All of these matters are primarily, of course, matters of attitude; and as a reading of the selections in this book demonstrates, the attitudes of some major critics are frequently quite different from those of other, equally important critics.

In applying his theory, one critic may invoke one set of demands upon a drama while another may endorse a sharply different set. Similarly, one critic of poetry may demand certain qualities in a particular kind of poem (e.g., dignified restraint in a love lyric) while another may endorse diametrically opposed ones (e.g., uninhibited expression in a love lyric). Hence one critic may regard a given work as a paragon while a second may consider it barely adequate achievement.

As one examines the theories of well-known critics, he can discern rather clearly the basis for their judgments. Among other requirements, Henry James insists on a finely wrought novel; Edgar Allan Poe demands a clearly pronounced rhythmical pattern in poetry; I. A. Richards emphasizes intellectual challenge.

Another basic point regarding criticism is that the critical act represents a completely natural reaction. Anyone who examines a literary work invariably finds himself rendering a critical judgment—however tentative or superficial it may be—because he cannot escape the process. T. S. Eliot, one of the greatest critics of the present century, says that "criticism is as inevitable as breathing," that it is the natural result of "articulating what passes in our minds when we read a book and feel an emotion about it."[3]

The fact that criticism is inescapable underscores the sig-

[3] "Tradition and the Individual Talent." See page 221.

nificance of the whole critical act. If criticism is inescapable and if it is as important as most critics contend, then anyone making a serious study of literature must develop thoroughly his critical faculties. He must ever strive to learn the precise value he assigns to a given work; but equally important, he must know the reasons for assigning that particular value.

II

By virtue of its fundamental nature, the act of criticism involves the confrontation of two personalities, that of the artist and that of the critic. The artist creates in terms of his personality—his emotions, his visions, his reactions, his understandings. Similarly the critic—however much he may strive for objectivity—is influenced by these same qualities within himself. Therefore, in the critical act, two personalities meet in a situation that may range from highly compatible to distinctly incompatible; and, naturally, any critical judgment is affected accordingly.

The fact that every act of criticism involves two personalities brings another truism into focus: every man, and hence every critic, is the prisoner of his own limitations and the beneficiary of his own special insights.

This truism has many implications. Perhaps most important, it largely explains the ineptitude and the excellence of critics. Many would-be critics are simply not equal to the responsibility involved.[4] They lack the mind to follow the particular work, or they lack the necessary background of knowledge. More often, however, they suffer from short-ranged horizons, deficiencies in handling ideas, or a tendency to make rash statements.

In contradistinction, the success of a given critic frequently arises from the special insights which are peculiarly his. A critic like Edmund Wilson, for example, is often able to delve beneath the surface of a work to discover some unusual strength or flaw;

[4] For a thoughtful treatment of this matter, see "What Is a Good Review?" by Joseph Wood Krutch, *The Nation*, CXLIV (April 17, 1937).

he seems to possess an uncanny ability to see where others do not. As a result, he can discern heretofore undiscovered qualities in great literary figures—as he does with Yeats, Valéry, Eliot, Proust, Joyce, and Gertrude Stein in his *Axel's Castle* (1931)—and, fortunately, he can explain those qualities to the admiration of competent judges everywhere.

This truism that every man is a prisoner of his limitations and the beneficiary of his insights also provides a point of departure for evaluating many artists. In adjudging novels, for instance, it becomes an especially helpful instrument. Critics can demonstrate that Mark Twain possessed truly remarkable perceptive powers in explaining the adolescent boy; yet he lacked any real perception of the nature of happiness for the middle-aged man. They have found that Theodore Dreiser understood the man imprisoned by a particular brand of economic and social force; but he did not really understand the man of fine sensibility who successfully meets life on its own terms. They have found that Norman Mailer comprehends the stress and the anguish of soldiering; meanwhile, he does not comprehend the little nuances of the workaday world. In judging these writers, therefore, critics have relied on this truism to assess, in part, the achievement of these novelists.

Another implication of the truism is that it undergirds the argument that criticism is an art rather than a science; that is, it strengthens the contention that the successful critic relies on the visions, the interpretative powers, and the aesthetic sensitivities of the artist rather than on the formally acquired, impersonal techniques of the scientist. Otherwise, he could not appreciate—and hence could not evaluate properly—the work of the artist.

This significant fact then supports the conclusion that criticism cannot be reduced to a set of tight rules which, if mastered, enables one to designate himself a "critic." Rather, the critic is one who, through a rigid course of practice, develops and polishes natural abilities into the techniques that enable him to make the competent, perceptive judgments that are known as "sound criticism." In this regard, he is like a singer who, endowed with a naturally pleasing voice, improves that gift through proper study and practice.

III

One of the most subtle relationships is that of criticism and actual artistic production. The immediate tendency is to think of literary production and literary criticism as things apart, as separate activities in the same general area of endeavor. One tends to think of the literary artist as a man off in one corner of the world writing his novel, his short story, his poem, his play, or his essay while off in another corner the critic waits, silently and menacingly, for the opportunity to pass his judgment on the work. In actuality, however, every literary artist is deeply affected by principles of criticism from his first thoughts regarding composition to his final glance of satisfaction at the completed task.

The short story writer, for example, has a set of critical dicta in mind, however nebulously framed, from his earliest planning. He has a definite concept of a "good" story, and he has firm convictions regarding procedures and criteria for writing that story. Thus he is actually two persons: he is the critic, and he is the artist creating in terms of his critical percepts. He also employs critical principles thereafter as he examines his writing, makes revisions, and attempts generally to cast his work into a more finely wrought creation.

The inter-workings of the artist and the critic have cast some interesting sidelights on the study of literature. William Wordsworth and Samuel Taylor Coleridge have aired their agreements and disagreements on poetry. Henry James and William Dean Howells have written extensively on the place, purpose, and evaluation of the novel. T. S. Eliot and Ezra Pound were first close and then rather far apart, critically speaking, as they discussed their poetry with each other. The many poets and novelists who fill writer-in-residence roles in colleges and universities are often quite revealing as they discuss their work as artist-critics.

Another aspect of the relationship of criticism to actual literary production is an entity commonly termed "critical climate." This phrase designates the critical dicta and the general philosophical concepts that pervade the literary atmosphere of a given time and place. When, for example, James Fenimore Cooper was writing, he worked in a climate that was largely romantic. It was an atmosphere conducive to the romantic novel, to the kind of novel that he could write. When Henry Wadsworth Longfellow composed his "Evangeline" and shorter poems, he worked in an atmosphere highly favorable to his literary modes and material. His audience was there waiting—sympathetic, encouraging, receptive. When Bret Harte published his "Luck of Roaring Camp," he was obviously catering to a reading public that liked his sentimental, melodramatic stories of local color.

To appreciate the importance of climate for each of these authors, one need only imagine the difficulty which an unknown writer would encounter in attempting to place a similar work with a publisher today. The material, he would soon learn, is hopelessly inappropriate for current literary tastes.

Not all writers, of course, have produced work in harmony with prevailing critical dicta; but they have suffered accordingly. Poe's beautiful "To Helen" received only the scantest of praise for many years. Walt Whitman did not begin to receive the critical acclaim during his lifetime that his great achievement merits. Stephen Crane, writing before the turn of the century, had to wait until the 1920's for anything approaching proper recognition. Each of these writers suffered from the prevailing critical climate. Each was writing in an era in which the dicta to appreciate him were absent. Therefore, each suffered until his work was reappraised by the measuring rods of another kind of criticism.

Critical climate also accounts for one of the most interesting and surprising of phenomena—the alternate rising and falling in favor of established figures. John Donne and the other metaphysicals had been relegated to the background when T. S. Eliot's pronouncements on their stature returned them to front-center stage.

The two Victorian giants, Alfred, Lord Tennyson and Robert Browning, are currently in the shadows because, among other reasons, ours is an age that derides the name "Victorian." Yet, if critical history repeats itself, these once widely acclaimed poets are certain to rise to prominence once more.

IV

What attributes must the successful critic possess? Although this question can scarcely be answered with a single flat statement, it can be answered broadly.

As already shown, the critic, above all else, must have the knowledge, the insight, and the overall ability to understand the work itself. He must be able to read the particular poem, novel, or other literary work with competence and comprehension. He must be able, in short, to grasp every thought and to relate it to every other. Otherwise he is in no position to analyze or evaluate.

The critic, of course, can usually strengthen himself in this respect through formal study and self-training. By working sufficiently hard, he can generally obtain through reading and direct experience the knowledge and background needed to evaluate capably many kinds of literary works. Therefore, he can prepare himself to assess competently a wide range of literary productions.

In addition, he can fortify himself by a careful observation of life. In fact, he must learn to observe and study life in full dimension in order to analyze character depictions. He must also observe and study life as a basis for understanding the events, emotions, ideas, and similiar subjects commonly treated in literature. How sound, for instance, is Ernest Hemingway in his depiction of women? Hemingway presents some of his men quite convincingly—his Jake Barnes, his Nick Adams, his Robert Jordan— but his women, most critics agree, lack genuine depth of portraiture; they are mere figures who, at best, serve only to provide a cohesiveness for the story. How sound is Henry David Thoreau in his oft-quoted "The mass of men live lives of quiet desperation"? How sound is Edwin Arlington Robinson when he says in "The Man Against the Sky" that life for most people is a genuinely difficult experience? Obviously, in making judgments on these matters, the critic must rely on his knowledge of life.

Observation of life has been especially important in creating criteria for measuring novelists. A striking example is evident in recent reevaluations of Nathaniel Hawthorne. Although most critics still regard Hawthorne as a major novelist, they tend to agree with the judgment of Richard Chase that Hawthorne's characters lack a lifelike ring.[5]

There is a further caution to be observed regarding the understanding of a literary work: in some situations a critic may be baffled, despite an extensive background of knowledge and a penetrating insight into life. This condition is especially common in modern poetry, in which many poems admit of no final solution.

An example is T. S. Eliot's widely known "The Love Song of J. Alfred Prufrock." This poem is filled with such subtle references, it relies so heavily upon a special brand of impressionism to achieve its purpose, and it evokes such a depth of understanding that the best of critics cannot agree on its final meaning. Hence they can base their conclusions only on the meanings which they discern. As a result, one finds such statements as the following made, each of which attempts to give the central thought of the poem:

"J. Alfred Prufrock is a name plus a Voice. He isn't a 'character' cut out of the rest of the universe and equipped with a history and a little necessary context, like the speaker of a Browning monologue."

—Hugh Kenner[6]

In "The Love Song of J. Alfred Prufrock," Eliot presents "the

---

[5] See *The American Novel and Its Tradition.*
[6] "Bradley," *The Invisible Poet,* Ivan Obolensky, Inc., New York, 1959.

futilities and the boredom of the middle-aged unsuccessful Prufrock."

—Muriel Clara Bradbrook[7]

"Prufrock is the personification of an unredeemed life . . . and if there is any affirmation in the poem it is that Prufrock is lost."

—Raymond Tschumi[8]

"Prufrock is a middleaged man . . . his world outlook is romantic. The realities of life have not yet made their impact on him."

—A. S. George[9]

"the poem is a dialogue between 'you' and 'I', between the inner and outer or the private and public selves of a reticent middle-aged man who still has stirrings and aspirations outside the normal patterns of the polite society to which he is accustomed."

—Philip R. Headings[10]

A second attribute of the successful critic is a familiarity with the major works similar to that being evaluated. The critic must know these works as a basis for comparison; he must know them to determine the relative place of the work under consideration in its particular field. The critic evaluating a poem that defines love, for instance, must know Shakespeare's famous sonnet CXVI ("Let me not to the marriage of true minds admit impediment"). He must know this particular sonnet because it is generally considered to be the greatest poem of its kind. Therefore, it becomes an invaluable criterion.

The necessity of using other well-known works as a basis for comparison has been made popular by Matthew Arnold's term "touchstones." Arnold contends that just as the ancient dealer in gems always carried stones of predetermined value to use as

[7] *T. S. Eliot,* Longmans, Green and Co., Ltd., London, 1960, p. 10.
[8] *Twentieth Century Poetry,* Routledge and Kegan Paul, Ltd., London, 1951, p. 127.
[9] *T. S. Eliot, His Mind and His Art,* Asia Publishing House, New York, 1962, p. 104.
[10] *T. S. Eliot,* Twayne Publishers, Inc., New York, 1964, p. 17.

standards, so must the critic of literature possess a stock of lines of poetry and great poems to employ as standards when criticizing.

The third ability required of the competent critic is generally summarized in the all-inclusive and hence vague phrase "critical ability." This phrase refers to the proficiency of the critic fortunate enough to be blessed with the insights and other abilities necessary to understand a work, fortified by the wide reading necessary for background, and sufficiently skilled to handle the devices of criticism. It is, in its essence, a competence acquired by developing one's basic talent through a rigorous program of proper practice.

An important factor in developing critical judgment is the acquisition of a critical vocabulary. As the student of language soon learns, the function of language and the function of thought are interactive. Before one can think in abstract terms, he must have a command of the necessary vocabulary. Hence before one can reflect on virtue or integrity or loyalty, he must have terms to assign to those abstract ideas. Similarly, before one can criticize, he must have words and phrases to assign to the ideas upon which he cogitates and then writes.

Frequently, critics have had to invent their own critical terminology. T. S. Eliot, for instance, has given to criticism the expression "objective correlative." In "Hamlet and His Problems," he maintains that the "only way of expressing emotion in the form of art is by finding an 'objective correlative'; in other words, a set of objects, a situation, a chain of events which shall be the formula of that *particular* emotion; such that when the external facts, which must terminate in sensory experience, are given, the emotion is immediately evoked."[11]

In providing valuable terminology, Eliot and other critics are moving in an old tradition. From Classical antiquity onward, im-

[11] From *Selected Essays, New Edition*, Harcourt, Brace and Company, New York, 1950, p. 124. This essay was originally published in 1919. One should also note that the phrase "objective correlative" was used before Eliot employed the term, but it failed to gain wide currency.

portant critics have made contributions in this area. Horace, for example, has given the statement, now worn thin from constant quoting, that the function of literature is "to entertain and to delight." From the last century, one can recall immediately Coleridge's famous insistence upon the "willing suspension of disbelief" as a requisite for proper reading of poetry.

V

In seeking to discover the foundation for all critical theory, one can invoke profitably a distinction made by W. H. Abrams, who, in *The Mirror and the Lamp*,[12] maintains that in any consideration of a work of art, one must recognize the presence of four elements: (1) the work itself, (2) the creator (i.e., the artist) of the work, (3) the universe (i.e., the nature) to be imitated or drawn, and (4) the audience. One then develops his theory of criticism by concentrating on one element to the exclusion of the others or by combining two or more of the elements in various patterns.

If one bases his approach on the work of art itself—that is, if he elects to see the work as a self-contained entity—he is then employing the *objective* theory of criticism.

This particular approach has received considerable acceptance within the recent past by critics and by college teachers of literature.[13] Many individuals within these groups insist that poems and other literary works must be considered solely in terms of facts within the work itself. One must not probe into the author's life or into contemporary events for answers; neither must he rely on hypothesis or conjecture. Instead, he must concentrate on the work, deriving all answers and judgments from the work alone.

The great advantage of this approach is, of course, that it tends to remove extraneous considerations. Ezra Pound's alleged treason during World War II is certainly not a pertinent consideration

[12] Oxford University Press, New York, 1953.
[13] See page 242.

in adjudging the artistry of "Hugh Selwyn Mauberley." Neither is William Faulkner's refusal of a dinner invitation by President John F. Kennedy a significant fact in criticizing *Light in August*. Each event, of course, tells something of the author years after he wrote the work cited. Yet such events often tend to color critical judgments in instances where they have little, if any, bearing on the work itself.

The most serious disadvantage of the purely objective approach is that it ignores the instances where pertinent considerations exist outside the work itself. Certainly John Keats' deep commitment to poetry, his frail health, and his thoughts about an early death are pertinent matters in discussing his sonnet "When I have fears that I may cease to be." Similarly, one can appreciate more thoroughly the humor in James Russell Lowell's "Fable for Critics" by knowing the work of Poe, Emerson, Whittier, and the others whom he discusses.

If one chooses to consider the work of art in terms of the second consideration cited above—that is, if he chooses to concentrate on the artist—he is then employing the *expressive* theory.

Under this approach, one thinks of the artist as a personality expressing a message which is peculiarly his own. If, for example, one employs the expressive theory in considering Emily Dickinson's "I never saw a moor," he makes critical judgments in the light of the author's religious conviction. If one employs this same theory in considering Edgar Allan Poe's "Fall of the House of Usher," he reaches conclusions in terms of the author's reactions in that particular house under those particular circumstances.

This approach has great merit in examining such intensely personal poems as Walt Whitman's "Song of Myself" and Robert Frost's "After Apple Picking." Clearly, the basic appeal of these poems lies in the reflections of their authors. This approach, however, has discernible limitations in considering writings of an impersonal nature; that is, it has little value in assessing many formal essays, short stories, and poems which treat their subjects objectively.

If one elects to consider the work in terms of the third consideration—the consideration of the universe or world to be drawn—he is said to be employing the *mimetic* theory.

Under this approach, one measures the author's successes and failures in depicting the world of the work itself. Hence one can say that Thomas Wolfe is strikingly successful in capturing the atmosphere of his native Asheville in many of his works; and that James T. Farrell has caught interesting reflections of the Chicago he knows first hand—with all its idiom, its mores, its peculiar brand of realistic philosophy. Also, one can question Sinclair Lewis' understanding of people by demonstrating that Lewis never really comprehends human motives; and that Lloyd C. Douglas, who was popular in the 1930's and the 1940's, relies on surface observation rather than depth of perception in depicting great events.

If one chooses to consider the work in terms of the fourth consideration—the consideration of the audience—he is said to be employing the *pragmatic* theory.

This particular theory has received a strong emphasis—although in varying forms—down through the years. One of the earliest and most widely accepted pronouncements has already been cited. It is that of Horace (65–8 B.C.), who holds that the basic aim of literature must be "to entertain and to delight." Literature, therefore, is to be created and evaluated with impact on audience as the dominant consideration. During the Middle Ages, however, the pragmatic theory was given more narrow delineations. With the ascendancy of the great body of religious literature of the time, the primary aim became that of instructing and edifying. Literature, in short, was to exist principally to chart the way to the higher life. Hence literature was, once again, to be produced and assessed in terms of its effect upon the audience. Currently, one can see the pragmatic theory employed by such literary artists as novelists and playwrights who produce works with a social or political argument; and one can see the pragmatic theory invoked by those critics who denounce a particular creation as "disgusting," "obscene," or otherwise objectionable—basing their statement, of course, on the effect of the work on the beholder.

Undoubtedly, the most significant thought regarding the pragmatic theory is its inevitable presence as one evaluates. Each of us has a natural tendency to weigh a piece of literature, in part at least, according to its appeal to our aesthetic sensitivities. Quite often, in fact, we assign such terms as "great," "marvelous," "fair," "pedestrian"—purely on the basis of initial reactions. Then we seek round for the evidence to support our judgments.

VI

In establishing an evaluative judgment, one will find that three familiar questions serve effectively as guidelines. The questions are: (1) What is the author attempting? (2) How well has he succeeded? (3) Was his work worth doing? As the answers emerge, one finds that he has formulated largely his opinion of the work.

The first question is far more deceptive than is commonly realized. In fact, quite often one cannot be certain of the fundamental aim of a given work. What, for example, is the controlling purpose of John Steinbeck's *Grapes of Wrath?* Is it to depict the hardships of a family group forced to leave its Oklahoma home to press westward in search of a livelihood? Is it a plea for recognition of an entire group—the economically oppressed farm workers—of which the Joads are representative? Is it propaganda for a distinctly liberal political philosophy? Or if not, precisely what is it? Obviously, before one can judge this work competently, he must know its central purpose.

Then, too, one must remember that the central thought of some works can never be cast into a phrase or a sentence; the basic idea, of necessity, must remain fluid. The aim of much modern impressionistic and expressionistic writing, for instance, is not to convey a message so much as to create a dominant impression. The author seeks to establish a mood, an atmosphere, or a response rather than to present a clearly etched thought.

As one probes for the basic aim of a work, he must beware of a common misconception: it is the belief that the author can always supply the supposedly final statement on any controversy regarding meaning. One frequently hears the question, "What does the author say about the meaning?" uttered in tones of finality. The questioner implies by his very inflection that the author can settle any dispute whatever.

One of the most interesting refutations of this belief is the fact that, strange though it may seem, authors have sometimes achieved meanings which they neither intended nor recognized. A few examples can illustrate the point. Jonathan Swift produced a brilliant satire in *Gulliver's Travels*. However, he also produced unknowingly an excellent story for children. Lewis Carroll, all evidence seems to indicate, wrote his *Alice in Wonderland* purely as a child's story. Yet modern scholarship has discovered and explained an intricate pattern of symbolic meaning. Many novelists have written straightforward narratives, only to find later that their character depictions have influenced legislation, behavior patterns, and conclusions held by society in general.

The second of the three questions—How well has the author succeeded?—obviously encompasses more than a brief treatment can explain. Around this question, some of the greatest controversies in literature revolve. One critic, for example, feels that an author has been brilliantly successful; another feels that he has been only moderately successful; and another feels that he has failed dismally. Meanwhile, of course, each offers evidence to substantiate his conclusion.

Because of the different answers to this question, scholars, literary historians, and others devoted to a study of literature engage in polite and spirited arguments. Is Dickens or Thackeray the greater novelist? Is Edith Wharton overrated or underrated? Does Jack London merit any respect as an "important" novelist? Has anything worth reading appeared within the last year? These and similar questions contribute substantially to the fascination of the study of literature in general and the study of criticism in particular.

The third question—Was the work worth doing?—is only

slightly less controversial than the second. As one considers this question, several pertinent matters arise.

One of the most obvious and yet most complex is that of the literary artist's responsibility, if any, to the society in which he lives. Stated more specifically, does the artist have any responsibility to try to improve the world; does he have a right to live completely apart from the world; does he have a right to praise or disparage the religion, the values, the institutions, or anything else within his society? One's answers to these and similar questions indicate, of course, his reactions to the basic question— Was the work worth doing?

The entire question is further complicated by the factor of personal taste. Because taste is a subjective matter, one can scarcely identify and defend his viewpoints objectively. Yet, his taste seriously influences his answers to questions in this area. Is Henry Miller's *Tropic of Cancer* obscene or not? Is the modern novelist justified in searching into every corner of his subject's life? How objectionable must a word be to be excluded from literature? Or should any words be excluded at all? Once again, therefore, one finds considerations so significant that they cannot be cast aside but so subjective that they cannot be handled with any genuine impartiality.

VII

In any critical consideration of a literary work, one should recognize the three areas into which the question of meaning is divided: (1) the area of indisputable fact, (2) the area of logical deduction, and (3) the area of subjective reaction.

The area of indisputable fact comprises all the data from a given poem, novel, or other literary work upon which competent readers can agree. To illustrate, a little poem by Robert Frost can be cited.

> The way a crow
> Shook down on me
> The dust of snow
> From a hemlock tree

Has given my heart
A change of mood
And saved some part
Of a day I had rued.

Among the indisputable facts in this poem are the following: (1) typographically speaking, the poem is eight lines long; (2) the author is speaking in the first person; (3) the speaker has had a generally unpleasant day; (4) the speaker is pleased that the crow shook the snow down on him.

The area of logical deduction comprises all the data which one can advance and defend logically. For example, one can defend the conclusion that the weather is cold enough to have snow; but it is not cold enough for the snow to be frozen solidly on the trees. One can also defend logically the conclusion that the speaker is a person who can be delighted by the behavior patterns of some birds.

The area of subjective reaction is simply the experiences which one feels, but is unable to defend or even explain, as he reads the literary work. For instance, is this particular poem too short? Is the situation of having snow shaken down on one a pleasant or an unpleasant experience? If it is pleasant, is it as pleasant as the author seems to think? Naturally, a reader can supply only personal answers because only subjective reactions are involved.

In considering these three areas, one should recognize two basic points: (1) the reader must not mistake one area for another and (2) modern criticism places a heavy emphasis on attitude and subjective reaction.

The danger of mistaking these areas is almost self-evident. For example, one can easily mistake personal opinion for fact and, in the process, make an unsound conclusion. When one adjudges a novel as "unpleasant" or a poem as "sentimental" or a drama as "stilted," he is invariably offering a subjective judgment rather than fact. Similarly, when the teacher of literature "reads into" a poem facts that no textual analysis can support, he is mistaking the area of subjective reaction for the area of indisputable fact.

The emphasis that modern criticism places on the third area arises from necessity. Much modern writing employs impressionism, expressionism, and similar devices beyond the range of objective analysis and discussion. These devices aim primarily to create a mood or an impression rather than to present facts. Therefore, any critical approach must consider them in terms of the subjective impression which they create.

VIII

Just what is the practical function of criticism? Or stated more directly, why should one bother to learn about criticism or to develop his critical faculties? There are several answers to this question.

Above all else, one develops his critical faculties in order to appreciate properly. One of the truisms of aesthetics is that one appreciates in direct proportion to his ability to criticize. If, for instance, one is to follow meaningfully Leo Tolstoy's *War and Peace,* he must read with a well-developed background of knowledge and critical ability. He must be able to comprehend the philosophical perspectives, the magnificent sweep, and the excellent character depictions. Further, he must be able to discern clearly the vast panorama of events and their interrelationships in order to perceive Tolstoy's understandings. In short, he must be able to appraise this great work. Otherwise, the book becomes just another novel—perhaps even at times a long and tedious one filled with actions that halt and grind.

Inability to criticize is unquestionably the reason that many people do not read more great works of literature. For all too many readers, many of the descriptive passages in Melville's *Moby Dick* seem unnecessary. Also, these same readers are often unable to discern symbolic meaning in the pursuit of the whale; or they conclude that the action is too drawn out and too laden with extraneous detail. Some even consider Melville a careless craftsman, one who introduces material that impedes the flow of

the story. Actually, of course, this material often contributes substantially toward making the book a truly great novel.

Another significant function of criticism is to provide a structure for the study of a national literature. If one were to assemble
all the American prose and poetry published annually, he would
have a forbidding assignment to create a framework upon which
to trace the development of American literature. Naturally, all are
not equally significant. Most are mere routine productions, lacking any intrinsic or historical importance. Hence the historian of
American literature—like the historian of any other literature—
must make selections; he must classify; and he must examine. In
these processes, he naturally relies on critical judgments to plot
his course.

The value of this critical function is not to be readily underestimated. Criticism tells us, for example, that Charles Brockden
Brown is the first American novelist of any genuine stature; that
William Cullen Bryant was the first American poet to draw any
appreciable critical approval from abroad; that Edgar Allan Poe
has exerted a far reaching significance in the fields of poetry, the
short story, and critical dicta. Thus the critic locates the important points upon which to plot the story of American literature, thereby creating a basis for the understanding of our
literature. In this regard, he is, of course, like the political
historian who selects the significant events, personalities, and
movements of a given time and interprets as a basis for explaining.

IX

As one reflects on the history of criticism within the confines
of American literature, he finds that until well into the last
century, American criticism was largely English criticism. The
trends, the concepts, the ideas that prevailed in England during
the seventeenth, eighteenth, and early nineteenth century also
prevailed in America. Dryden, Pope, Johnson, Wordsworth, and
Coleridge dominated both British and American critical thought;

and consequently no basic differences existed between the critical precepts of the two nations.

With the emergence of Emerson and Poe, however, the qualities which characterize American thought and hence American criticism made their appearance. Thereafter, American criticism not only asserted itself at home but began to radiate its influence abroad, eventually ranking favorably within the great body of critical dicta of the world.

In the following pages, writers who have earned a significant place in American criticism are treated. In each instance, representative selections are presented to demonstrate the critical attitude and the reasoning of the particular critic. Naturally, every selection is not of equal merit, but each has had an importance for a wide following of readers.

William Cullen Bryant

(1794–1878)

From the Calvinism, the austerity, and the solemnity of eighteenth-century New England, William Cullen Bryant emerged to become a genuinely significant figure in American letters and American life. Best known as the author of "Thanatopsis," one of America's most widely read poems, Bryant also had a long and distinguished career as lawyer, newspaper publisher, champion of public causes, and critic.

Bryant's critical views were strongly influenced by his sense of nationalism. Like Emerson, he believed firmly in the power of America to produce great literature: he always maintained that the subject matter and the ability required for great writing were present in the new nation. As a consequence, he often railed against the opinion dominant in Great Britain and tacitly approved at home that true art was indigenous only to the Old World. His indictment of this concept became a familiar quotation: "We do not praise a thing until we see the seal of transatlantic approbation upon it."

Other discernible influences on Bryant's thought and therefore on his critical judgments are the deep love of nature developed in his hometown of Cummington, Massachusetts, and his all-encompassing faith in personal liberty and democracy. His convictions regarding freedom were omnipresent in his work as a trial lawyer in Massachusetts and as a newspaper publisher in New York.

Bryant is generally regarded as the first American critic to devise a thoroughly systematic study of poetry. Through a long span of critical writings, he enunciated the ideas which reveal *a movement from the classicism of his earliest years to the romanticism with which his work is associated. He feels, above all else, that poetry must be essentially romantic in that it must be from the heart to the heart. Further, it must be the product of the creative imagination, and it must induce the reader to travel the "path which the poet only points out." Bryant is also the true romantic in his emphasis on clarity and simplicity of style. The "luminous style," he states, is "one of the most important requisites for a great poet." Meanwhile, however, he endorses an element of the didactic. He contends that poetry must present "direct lessons of wisdom"—which to him meant overtones of religion and an atmosphere of lofty morality.*

The passage below is representative of Bryant's views. Especially noteworthy are his pronouncements on the relationship of the poet to the poetic tradition, a relationship that has received the thoughtful consideration of numerous poets and critics.

From Lecture to New York Athaenaeum Society [1825]

I propose in this lecture to say a few words to the true use and value of imitation in poetry. I mean not what is technically called the imitation of nature, but the studying and copying of models of poetic composition. There is hardly any praise of which writers in the present age, particularly writers in verse, are more ambitious than that of originality. This ambition is a laudable one, for a captivating originality is everything in the art. Whether it consists in presenting familiar things in a new and striking yet natural light, or in revealing secrets of emotion and thought which have lain undetected from the birth of literature, it is one of the most abundant and sure sources of poetic delight. It strikes us with the same sort of feeling as the finding of some beautiful spot in our familiar walks which we had never observed before, or the exhibition of some virtue in the character of a friend which we were ignorant that he possessed. It is of itself a material addition to the literary riches of the country in which it is produced; and it impresses something of its character upon that literature, which lasts as long as the productions in which it is contained are read and remembered.

Nor does it lose its peculiar charm with the lapse of time, for there is an enduring freshness and vividness in its pictures of nature, of action and emotion, that fade not with years. The poetry of Shakespeare, for instance, maintains its original power over the mind, and no more loses its living beauty by the lapse of ages than the universe grows dim and deformed in the sight of men.

It is not at all strange that a quality of so much importance to the poet should be sought after with great ardor, and that, in the zeal of pursuit, mistakes should sometimes be made as to that characteristic of it which alone is really valuable. Poets have often been willing to purchase the praise of it at the sacrifice of what is better. They have been led, by their overeagerness to attain it, into puerile conceits, into extravagant vagaries of imagination, into overstrained exaggerations of passion, into mawkish and childish simplicity. It has given birth to outrages upon moral principle, upon decency, upon common sense; it has produced, in short, irregularities and affectations of every kind. The grandiloquous nonsense of euphuism, which threatened to overlay and smother English literature in its very cradle, the laborious wit of the metaphysical poets who were contemporaries of Milton, the puling effeminacy of the cockney school, which has found no small favor at the present day—are all children of this fruitful parent.

It seems to me that all these errors arise from not paying sufficient attention to the consideration that poetry is an art; that, like all other arts, it is founded upon a series of experiments—experiments, in this instance, made upon the imagination and the feelings of mankind, that a great deal of its effect depends upon the degree of success with which a sagacious and strong mind seizes and applies the skill of others, and that to slight the experiences of our predecessors on this subject is a pretty certain way to go wrong. For, if we consider the matter a little more narrowly, we shall find that the most original of poets is not without very great obligations to his predecessors and his contemporaries. The art of poetry is not perfected in a day. It is brought to excellence, by slow degrees, from the first rude and imperfect attempts at versification to the finished productions of its greatest masters.

Genius, therefore, with all its pride in its own strength, is but a dependent quality, and cannot put forth its whole powers nor claim all its honors without an amount of aid from the talents and labors of others which it is difficult to calculate. In those fortunate circumstances which permit its most perfect exercises, it takes, it is true, a pre-eminent station; but, after all, it is elevated upon the shoulders of its fellows. It may create something in literature, but it does not create all, great as its merit may be. What it does is infinitely less than what is done for it; the new treasures it finds are far less in value than the old of which it makes use. There is no warrant for the notion maintained by some, that the first poets in any language were great poets, or that, whatever their rank, they did not learn their art from the great poets in other languages. It might as well be expected that a self-taught architect would arise in a country whose inhabitants live in caves, and, without models or instruction, raise the majestic Parthenon and pile up St. Peter's into the clouds.

At the present day, however, a writer of poems writes in a language which preceding poets have polished, refined, and filled with forcible, graceful, and musical expressions. He is not only taught by them to overcome the difficulties of rhythmical construction, but he is shown, as it were, the secrets of the mechanism by which he moves the mind of his reader; he is shown ways of kindling the imagination and of interesting the passions which his own sagacity might never have discovered; his mind is filled with the beauty of their sentiments, and their enthusiasm is breathed into his soul. He owes much, also, to his contemporaries as well as to those who have gone before him. He reads their works, and whatever excellence he beholds in them, inspires him with a strong desire to rival it—stronger, per-

haps, than that excited by the writings of his predecessors; for
such is our reverence for the dead that we are willing to concede
to them that superiority which we are anxious to snatch from
the living. Even if he should refuse to read the writings of his
brethren, he cannot escape the action of their minds on his
own. He necessarily comes to partake somewhat of the character
of their genius, which is impressed not only on all contemporary
literature, but even on the daily thoughts of those with whom he
associates. In short, his mind is in a great degree formed by
the labors of others; he walks in a path which they have made
smooth and plain, and is supported by their strength.

But when once a tame and frigid taste has possessed the tribe
of poets, when all their powers are employed in servilely copying
the works of their predecessors, it is not only impossible that
any great work should be produced among them, but the period
of a literary reformation, of the awakening of genius, is postponed
to a distant futurity. It is the quality of such a state of literature,
by the imposing precision of its rules and the ridicule it throws
on everything out of its own beaten track, to perpetuate itself
indefinitely. The happy appearance of some extraordinary genius,
educated under different influences than those operating on the
age, and compelling admiration by the force of his talents; or,
perhaps, some great moral or political revolution, by unsettling
old opinions and familiarizing men to daring speculations—can
alone have any effect to remove it. The mind grows indolent, or,
at least, enfeebled, by the want of those higher exercises to which
it was destined. At the same time, the spirit of poetry, as seen in
its power of elevating the mind, of humanizing the affections, and
expelling sordid appetites, is no longer felt, or only felt by a few,
who conceal in their own bosoms the secret of its power over
them.

Ralph Waldo Emerson

(1803–1882)

The high reputation which Ralph Waldo Emerson once held
as a literary critic resulted largely from the audience which
he attracted as lecturer, poet, and essayist. Because of his fame
in these areas, he was given a receptive and attentive hearing
on whatever topic he chanced to speak. Hence his views on
literature and standards for judging literature became widely
known—as did his appraisals of individual writers. As one examines these many pronouncements, he can see the elements of
Emerson's critical theories.

The statement has often been made that Emerson was not
original in his critical concepts. However, despite the essential
truth of this charge, it is somewhat severe in its overtones. It
tends to overlook the fact that Emerson displayed originality
as he reexamined and reappraised the tenets of established
critics. An example is evident in the essay "The Poet" which is
presented, in part, below. Herein he couples the originality of
thought and presentation of "Self-Reliance" with the best of
critical dicta—as he discerns those dicta—from both Classical
antiquity and contemporary English and American critics.

Emerson was especially perceptive in his recognition of the
interrelationships of all art with nature; and using this point
as a base, he argued that true expression in art represents man's
loftiest endeavor. Further, he held that the literary artist possesses unusual powers of observation and expression. Consequently he must use these powers to depict the true essence of
his experience, his vision, or his thought.

Like so many other eclectic critics, Emerson reflects an

interesting combination of tenets. Especially appealing is the manner in which he explains the need of a warm, understanding imagination with which to tread a path worn by carefully executed thought. The poet must be the child of the creative impulse, but he must also be the disciplined thinker.

Ralph Waldo Emerson was born in Boston, Massachusetts, and remained in that area throughout his life. After graduating from Harvard in 1821, he taught school briefly and pursued further study at the Harvard Divinity School. In 1829, he became pastor of the Second Church (Unitarian) in Boston, a post which he held until 1832 when he resigned because of his views regarding the communion service. In 1836, he published his first book, Nature, *a slim volume of essays, and in 1837, he delivered his most famous speech, the monumental* American Scholar *address. For the remainder of his life he lectured and wrote poetry and essays, achieving a fame that has made his name one of the most respected in all Americana.*

The essay below was widely read and quoted in Emerson's time. Now, although primarily of historical interest, it still possesses the charm of an essentially romantic writer's thoughts on poetry.

From The Poet [1844]

Those who are esteemed umpires of taste are often persons who have acquired some knowledge of admired pictures or sculptures, and have an inclination for whatever is elegant; but if you inquire whether they are beautiful souls, and whether their own acts are like fair pictures, you learn that they are selfish and sensual. Their cultivation is local, as if you should rub a log of dry wood in one spot to produce fire, all the rest remaining cold. Their knowledge of the fine arts is some study of rules and particulars, or some limited judgment of color or form, which is exercised for amusement or for show. It is a proof of the shallowness of the doctrine of beauty as it lies in the minds of our amateurs, that men seem to have lost the perception of the instant dependence of form upon soul. There is no doctrine of forms in our philosophy. We were put into our bodies, as fire is put into a pan to be carried about; but there is no accurate adjustment between the spirit and the organ, much less is the latter the germination of the former. So in regard to other forms, the intellectual men do not believe in any essential dependence of the material world on thought and volition. Theologians think it a pretty air-castle to talk of the spiritual meaning of a ship or a cloud, of a city or a contract, but they prefer to come again to the solid ground of historical evidence; and even the poets are contented with a civil and conformed manner of living, and to write poems from the fancy, at a safe distance from their own experience. But the highest minds of the world have never ceased to explore the double meaning, or shall I say the quadruple or the centuple or much more manifold meaning, of every sensuous fact; Orpheus, Empedocles, Heraclitus, Plato, Plutarch, Dante, Swedenborg, and the masters of sculpture, picture, and poetry. For we are not pans and barrows, nor even porters of the fire and torch-bearers, but children of the fire, made of it, and only the same divinity transmuted and at two or three removes, when we know least about it. And this hidden truth, that the fountains whence all this river of Time and its creatures floweth are intrinsically ideal and beautiful, draws us to the consideration of the nature and functions of the Poet, or the man of Beauty; to the means and materials he uses, and to the general aspect of the art in the present time.

The breadth of the problem is great, for the poet is representative. He stands among partial men for the complete man, and apprises us not of his wealth, but of the common wealth. The young man reveres men of genius, because to speak truly, they are more himself than he is. They receive of the soul as he also receives, but they more. Nature enhances her beauty, to the eye of loving men, from their belief that the poet is beholding her shows at the same time. He is isolated among his contemporaries by truth and by his art, but with this consolation in his pursuits, that they will draw all men sooner or later. For all men live by truth and stand in need of expression. In love, in art, in avarice, in politics, in labor, in games, we study to utter our painful secret. The man is only half himself, the other half is his expression.

Notwithstanding this necessity to be published, adequate expression is rare. I know not how it is that we need an interpreter, but the great majority of men seem to be minors, who have not yet come into possession of their own, or mutes, who cannot report the conversation they have had with nature. There is no man who does not anticipate a super-sensual utility in the sun and stars, earth and water. These stand and wait to render him a peculiar service. But there is some obstruction or some excess of phlegm in our constitution, which does not suffer them to yield the due effect. Too feeble fall the impressions of nature on us to make us artists. Every touch should thrill. Every man should be so much an artist that he could report in conversation what had befallen him. Yet, in our experience, the rays of appulses have sufficient force to arrive at the senses, but not enough to reach the quick and compel the reproduction of themselves in speech. The poet is the person in whom these powers are in balance, the man without impediment, who sees and handles that which others dream of, traverses the whole scale of experience, and is representative of man, in virtue of being the largest power to receive and to impart.

For the Universe has three children, born at one time, which reappear under different names in every system of thought, whether they be called cause, operation, and effect; or, more poetically, Jove, Pluto, Neptune; or, theologically, the Father, the Spirit, and the Son: but which we will call here the Knower, the Doer, and the Sayer. These stand respectively for the love of truth, for the love of good, and for the love of beauty. These three are equal. Each is that which he is, essentially, so that he cannot be surmounted or analyzed, and each of these three has the power of the others latent in him, and his own, patent.

The poet is the sayer, the namer, and represents beauty. He is a sovereign, and stands on the centre. For the world is not painted or adorned, but is from the beginning beautiful; and God has not made some beautiful things, but Beauty is the creator of the universe. Therefore the poet is not any permissive potentate, but is emperor in his own right. Criticism is infested with a cant of materialism, which assumes that manual skill and activity is the first merit of all men, and disparages such as say and do not, overlooking the fact that some men, namely poets, are natural savers sent into the world to the end of expression, and confounds them with those whose province is action but who quit it to imitate the sayers. But Homer's words are as costly and admirable to Homer as Agamemnon's victories are to Agamemnon. The poet does not wait for the hero or the sage, but, as they act and think primarily, so he writes primarily what will and must be spoken, reckoning the others, though primaries also, yet, in respect to him, secondaries and servants; as sitters or models in the studio of a painter, or as assistants who bring building-materials to an architect.

For poetry was all written before time was, and whenever we are so finely organized that we can penetrate into that region where the air is music, we hear those primal warblings and attempt to write them down, but we lose ever and anon a word or a verse and substitute something of our own, and thus miswrite the poem. The men of more delicate ear write down these cadences more faithfully, and these transcripts, though imperfect, become the songs of the nations. For nature is as truly beautiful as it is good, or as it is reasonable, and must as much appear as it must be done, or be known. Words and deeds are quite indifferent modes of the divine energy. Words are also actions, and actions are a kind of words.

The sign and credentials of the poet are that he announces that which no man foretold. He is the true and only doctor; he knows and tells; he is the only teller of news, for he was present and privy to the appearance which he describes. He is a beholder of ideas and an utterer of the necessary and causal. For we do not speak now of men of poetical talents, or of industry and skill in metre, but of the true poet. I took part in a conversation the

other day concerning a recent writer of lyrics, a man of subtle
mind, whose head appeared to be a music-box of delicate tunes
and rhythms, and whose skill and command of language we could
not sufficiently praise. But when the question arose whether he
was not only a lyrist but a poet, we were obliged to confess that
he is plainly a contemporary, not an eternal man. He does not
stand out of our low limitations, like a Chimborazo[1] under the
line, running up from a torrid base through all the climates of
the globe, with belts of the herbage of every latitude on its high
and mottled sides; but this genius is the landscape-garden of a
modern house, adorned with fountains and statues, with well-
bred men and women standing and sitting in the walks and ter-
races. We hear, through all the varied music, the ground-tone of
conventional life. Our poets are men of talents who sing, and
not the children of music. The argument is secondary, the finish
of the verses is primary.

For it is not metres, but a metre-making argument that makes
a poem,—a thought so passionate and alive that like the spirit of
a plant or an animal it has an architecture of its own, and adorns
nature with a new thing. The thought and the form are equal in
the order of time, but in the order of genesis the thought is prior
to the form. The poet has a new experience to unfold; he will tell
us how it was with him, and all men will be the richer in his
fortune. For the experience of each new age requires a new
confession, and the world seems always waiting for its poet. I
remember when I was young how much I was moved one morning by tidings that genius had appeared in a youth who sat near
me at table. He had left his work and gone rambling none knew
whither, and had written hundreds of lines, but could not tell
whether that which was in him was therein told; he could tell
nothing but that all was changed,—man, beast, heaven, earth and
sea. How gladly we listened! how credulous! Society seemed to
be compromised. We sat in the aurora of a sunrise which was to
put out all the stars. Boston seemed to be at twice the distance
it had the night before, or was much farther than that. Rome,—

---

[1] Chimborazo is a peak in the Andes.

what was Rome? Plutarch and Shakespeare were in the yellow leaf, and Homer no more should be heard of. It is much to know that poetry has been written this very day, under this very roof, by your side. What! that wonderful spirit has not expired! These stony moments are still sparkling and animated! I had fancied that the oracles were all silent, and nature had spent her fires; and behold! all night, from every pore, these fine auroras have been streaming. Everyone has some interest in the advent of the poet, and no one knows how much it may concern him. We know that the secret of the world is profound, but who or what shall be our interpreter, we know not. A mountain ramble, a new style of face, a new person, may put the key into our hands. Of course the value of genius to us is in the veracity of its report. Talent may frolic and juggle; genius realizes and adds. Mankind in good earnest have availed so far in understanding themselves and their work, that the foremost watchman on the peak announces his news. It is the truest word ever spoken, and the phrase will be the fittest, most musical, and the unerring voice of the world for that time.

All that we call sacred history attests that the birth of a poet is the principal event in chronology. Man, never so often deceived, still watches for the arrival of a brother who can hold him steady to a truth until he has made it his own. With what joy I begin to read a poem which I confide in as an inspiration! And now my chains are to be broken; I shall mount above these clouds and opaque airs in which I live,—opaque, though they seem transparent,—and from the heaven of truth I shall see and comprehend my relations. That will reconcile me to life and renovate nature, to see trifles animated by a tendency, and to know what I am doing. Life will no more be a noise; now I shall see men and women, and know the signs by which they may be discerned from fools and satans. This day shall be better than my birthday: then I became an animal; now I am invited into the science of the real. Such is the hope, but the fruition is postponed. Oftener it falls that this winged man, who will carry me into the heaven, whirls me into mists, then leaps and frisks about with me as it were from cloud to cloud, still affirming that he is bound heavenward: and I, being myself a novice, am slow in perceiving that he does not know the way into the heavens, and is merely bent that I should admire his skill to rise like a fowl or a flying fish, a little way from the ground or the water; but the all-piercing, all-feeding, and ocular air of heaven that man shall never inhabit. I tumble down again soon into my old nooks, and lead the life of exaggerations as before, and have lost my faith in the possibility of any guide who can lead me thither where I would be.

But, leaving these victims of vanity, let us, with new hope, observe how nature, by worthier impulses, has insured the poet's fidelity to his office of announcement and affirming, namely by the beauty of things, which becomes a new and higher beauty when expressed. Nature offers all her creatures to him as a picture-language. Being used as a type, a second wonderful value appears in the object, far better than its old value; as the carpenter's stretched cord, if you hold your ear close enough, is musical in the breeze. "Things more excellent than every image," says Jamblichus, "are expressed through images." Things admit of being used as symbols because nature is a symbol, in the whole, and in every part. Every line we can draw in the sand has expression; and there is no body without its spirit or genius. All form is an effect of character; all conditions, of the quality of the life; all harmony, of health; and for this reason a perception of beauty should be sympathetic, or proper only to the good. The beautiful rests on the foundations of the necessary. The soul makes the body, as the wise Spenser teaches:—

> "So every spirit, as it is more pure,
> And hath in it the more of heavenly light,
> So it the fairer body doth procure
> To habit in, and it more fairly dight,
> With cheerful grace and amiable sight.
> For, of the soul, the body form doth take,
> For soul is form, and doth the body make."

Here we find ourselves suddenly not in a critical speculation but in a holy place, and should go very warily and reverently. We stand before the secret of the world, there where Being passes into Appearance and Unity into Variety.

The Universe is the externization of the soul. Wherever the life is, that bursts into appearance around it. Our science is sensual, and therefore superficial. The earth and the heavenly bodies, physics, and chemistry, we sensually treat, as if they were self-existent; but these are the retinue of that Being we have. "The mighty heaven," said Proclus, "exhibits, in its transfigurations, clear images of the splendor of intellectual perceptions; being moved in conjunction with the unapparent periods of intellectual natures." Therefore science always goes abreast with the just elevation of the man, keeping step with religion and metaphysics; or the state of science is an index of our self-knowledge. Since every thing in nature answers to a moral power, if any phenomenon remains brute and dark it is because the corresponding faculty in the observer is not yet active.

• • •

But I am not wise enough for a national criticism, and must use the old largeness a little longer, to discharge my errand from the muse to the poet concerning his art.

Art is the path of the creator to his work. The paths or methods are ideal and eternal, though few men ever see them; not the artist himself for years, or for a lifetime, unless he come into the conditions. The painter, the sculptor, the composer, the epic rhapsodist, the orator, all partake one desire, namely to express themselves symmetrically and abundantly, not dwarfishly and fragmentarily. They found or put themselves in certain conditions, as, the painter and sculptor before some impressive human figures; the orator, into the assembly of the people; and the others in such scenes as each has found exciting to his intellect; and each presently feels the new desire. He hears a voice, he sees a beckoning. Then he is apprised, with wonder, what herds of daemons hem him in. He can no more rest; he says, with the old painter, "By God it is in me and must go forth of me." He pursues a beauty, half seen, which flies before him. The poet pours out verses in every solitude. Most of the things he says are conventional, no doubt; but by and by he says something which is original and beautiful. That charms him. He would say nothing else but such things. In our way of talking we say "That is yours, this is mine;" but the poet knows well that it is not his; that it is as strange and beautiful to him as to you; he would fain hear the like eloquence at length. Once having tasted this immortal ichor, he cannot have enough of it, and as an admirable creative power exists in these intellections, it is of the last importance that these things get spoken. What a little of all we know is said! What drops of all the sea of our science are baled up! and by what accident it is that these are exposed, when so many secrets sleep in nature! Hence the necessity of speech and song; hence these throbs and heart-beatings in the orator, at the door of the assembly, to the end namely that thought may be ejaculated as Logos, or Word.

Doubt not, O poet, put persist. Say "It is in me, and shall out." Stand there, balked and dumb, stuttering and stammering, hissed and hooted, stand and strive, until at last rage draw out of thee that dream-power which every night shows thee is thine own; a power transcending all limit and privace, and by virtue of which a man is the conductor of the whole river of electricity. Nothing walks, or creeps, or grows, or exists, which must not in turn arise and walk before him as exponent of his meaning. Comes he to that power, his genius is no longer exhaustible. All the creatures by pairs and by tribes pour into his mind as into a Noah's Ark, to come forth again to people a new world. This is like the stock of air for our respiration or for the combustion of our fireplace: not a measure of gallons, but the entire atmosphere if wanted. And therefore the rich poets, as Homer, Chaucer, Shakespeare, and Raphael, have obviously no limits to their works except the limits of their lifetime, and resemble a mirror carried through the street, ready to render an image of every created thing.

O poet! a new nobility is conferred in groves and pastures,

and not in castles or by the swordblade any longer. The conditions are hard, but equal. Thou shalt leave the world and know the muse only. Thou shalt not know any longer the times, customs, graces, politics, or opinions of men, but shalt take all from the muse. For the time of towns is tolled from the world by funereal chimes, but in nature the universal hours are counted by succeeding tribes of animals and plants and by growth of joy on joy. God wills also that thou abdicate a manifold and duplex life, and that thou be content that others speak for thee. Others shall be thy gentlemen and shall represent all courtesy and worldly life of thee; others shall do the great and resounding actions also. Thou shalt lie close hid with nature, and canst not be afforded to the Capitol or the Exchange. The world is full of renunciations and apprenticeships, and this is thine; thou must pass for a fool and a churl for long season. This is the screen and sheath in which Pan has protected his well-beloved flower, and thou shalt be known only to thine own, and they shall console thee with tenderest love. And thou shalt not be able to rehearse the names of thy friends in thy verse, for an old shame before the holy ideal. And this is the reward; that the ideal shall be real to thee, and the impressions of the actual world shall fall like summer rain, copious, but not troublesome to thy invulnerable essence. Thou shalt have the whole land for thy park and manor, the sea for thy bath and navigation, without tax and without envy; the woods and the rivers thou shalt own, and thou shalt possess that wherein others are only tenants and boarders. Thou true land-lord! sea-lord! air-lord! Wherever snow falls or water flows or birds fly, wherever day and night meet in twilight, wherever the blue heaven is hung by clouds or sown with stars, wherever are forms with transparent boundaries, wherever are outlets into celestial space, wherever is danger, and awe, and love,—there is Beauty, plenteous as rain, shed for thee, and though thou shouldst walk the world over, thou shalt not be able to find a condition inopportune or ignoble.

Edgar Allan Poe

(1809–1849)

Edgar Allan Poe established himself as a major figure in three areas of American literature—the short story, poetry, and criticism.

In the short story, Poe is acclaimed for the mastery of construction and the inventiveness of his detective stories and for the peculiar power which he achieves in narratives like "The Fall of the House of Usher" and "The Tell-Tale Heart." He is also praised highly for the quality of his prose style. His word choice, stylistic devices, and arrangement of detail are paragons of serious prose writing.

His stature in poetry rests on a relatively few poems. Especially notable are his "To Helen," which is generally rated as one of the finest lyrics of its kind in all literature, and his "The Bells," which is considered front-rank achievement in onomatopoeia. However, despite a wide popularity, such poems as "The Raven" and "Annabel Lee" are not regarded highly by critics while some of his other poems—for example, "Ulalume" and "El Araaf"—are so enigmatic as to defy satisfactory explication and hence assessment.

Poe exerted his greatest effect in criticism. Above all, he is designated as the strongest force in the rise of impressionism. This device, which Poe explains in his "Review of Hawthorne's Twice-Told Tales" and his "Philosophy of Composition," is a common technique in modern poetry. Stated briefly, impressionism relies on the creation of a dominant impression or series of impressions to convey the author's message.

Poe advanced the cause of impressionism principally by using impressionistic devices in his poetry and his short stories. However, his impact in this area was not felt immediately in American letters. Rather, he first influenced the French symbolists who, in turn, cast their influence on British and American writers. Poe, therefore, is in the unique position of influencing a foreign literature which then influenced his native literature.

Poe was born in Boston, Massachusetts, of actor parents. Orphaned before he was three, Poe was reared by Mr. and Mrs. John Allan of Richmond, Virginia, whose surname he later used as a middle name, even though the Allan family never legally adopted him. His formal secondary education he acquired in private schools at home and abroad and his limited higher education in brief stays at the University of Virginia and the Military Academy at West Point. Throughout his short and hectic life, Poe worked as a free lance writer, a newspaperman, a short story writer, and a poet. Death came in a Baltimore, Maryland hospital, where he had been taken after being found unconscious on a Baltimore street. As yet, no one has found the real cause of his death nor any firm basis for stories of inebriety and addiction to narcotics which have persisted over the years.

Below are selections from two of Poe's most important critical writings. The first is from the "Review" cited above. The second is from the well-known essay "The Poetic Principle." In each, one can find the elements which lie at the very center of Poe's critical outlook.

Twice-Told Tales, By Nathaniel Hawthorne
A Review

We said a few hurried words about Mr. Hawthorne in our last number, with the design of speaking more fully in the present. We are still, however, pressed for room, and must necessarily discuss his volumes more briefly and more at random than their high merits deserve.

The book professes to be a collection of *tales*, yet is, in two respects, misnamed. These pieces are now in their third republication, and, of course, are thrice-told. Moreover, they are by no means *all* tales, either in the ordinary or in the legitimate understanding of the term. Many of them are pure essays; for example, "Sights from a Steeple," "Sunday at Home," "Little Annie's Ramble," "A Rill from the Town Pump," "The Toll-Gatherer's Day," "The Haunted Mind," "The Sister Years," "Snow-Flakes," "Night Sketches," and "Foot-Prints on the Sea-Shore." We mention these matters chiefly on account of their discrepancy with that marked precision and finish by which the body of the work is distinguished.

Of the essays just named, we must be content to speak in brief. They are each and all beautiful, without being characterized by the polish and adaptation so visible in the tales proper. A painter would at once note their leading or predominant feature, and style it *repose.* There is no attempt at effect. All is quiet, thoughtful, subdued. Yet this repose may exist simultaneously with high originality of thought; and Mr. Hawthorne has demonstrated the fact. At every turn we meet with novel combinations; yet these combinations never surpass the limits of the quiet. We are soothed as we read; and withal is a calm astonishment that ideas so apparently obvious have never occurred or been presented to us before. Herein our author differs materially from Lamb or Hunt or Hazlitt—who, with vivid originality of manner and expression, have less of the true novelty of thought than is generally supposed, and whose originality, at best, has an uneasy and meretricious quaintness, replete with startling effects unfounded in nature, and inducing trains of reflection which lead to no satisfactory result. The Essays of Hawthorne have much of the character of Irving, with more of originality, and less of finish; while, compared with the Spectator, they have a vast superiority at all points. The Spectator, Mr. Irving, and Mr. Hawthorne have in common that tranquil and subdued manner which we have chosen to denominate *repose;* but, in the case of the two former, this repose is attained rather by the absence of novel combination, or of originality, than otherwise, and consists chiefly in the calm, quiet, unostentatious expression of commonplace thoughts, in an unambitious, unadulterated Saxon. In them, by strong effort, we are made to conceive the absence of all. In the essays before us the absence of effort is too obvious to be mistaken, and a strong undercurrent of *suggestion* runs continuously beneath the upper stream of the tranquil thesis. In short, these effusions of Mr. Hawthorne are the product of a truly imaginative intellect, restrained, and in some measure repressed, by fastidiousness of taste, by constitutional melancholy, and by indolence.

But it is of his tales that we desire principally to speak. The tale proper, in our opinion, affords unquestionably the fairest field for the exercise of the loftiest talent, which can be afforded by the wide domains of mere prose. Were we bidden to say how the highest genius could be most advantageously employed for the best display of its own powers, we should answer, without hesitation—in the composition of a rhymed poem, not to exceed in length what might be perused in an hour. Within this limit alone can the highest order of true poetry exist. We need only here say, upon this topic, that, in almost all classes of composition, the unity of effect or impression is a point of the greatest importance. It is clear, moreover, that this unity cannot be thoroughly preserved in productions whose perusal cannot be completed at one sitting. We may continue the reading of a prose composition, from the very nature of prose itself, much longer than we can persevere, to any good purpose, in the perusal of a poem. This latter, if truly fulfilling the demands of the poetic sentiment, induces an exaltation of the soul which cannot be long sustained. All high excitements are necessarily transient. Thus a long poem is a paradox. And, without unity of impression, the deepest effects cannot be brought about. Epics were the offspring of an imperfect sense of Art, and their reign is no more. A poem *too* brief may produce a vivid, but never an intense or enduring impression. Without a certain continuity of effort—without a certain duration or repetition of purpose—the soul is never deeply moved. There must be the dropping of the water upon the rock.

De Béranger has wrought brilliant things—pungent and spirit-stirring—but, like all immassive bodies, they lack *momentum*, and thus fail to satisfy the Poetic Sentiment. They sparkle and excite, but, from want of continuity, fail deeply to impress. Extreme brevity will degenerate into epigrammatism; but the sin of extreme length is even more unpardonable. *In medio tutissimus ibis.*

Were we called upon, however, to designate that class of composition which, next to such a poem as we have suggested, should best fulfil the demands of high genius—should offer it the most advantageous field of exertion—we should unhesitatingly speak of the prose tale, as Mr. Hawthorne has here exemplified it. We allude to the short prose narrative, requiring from a half-hour to one or two hours in its perusal. The ordinary novel is objectionable, from its length, for reasons already stated in substance. As it cannot be read at one sitting, it deprives itself, of course, of the immense force derivable from *totality*. Worldly interests intervening during the pauses of perusal, modify, annul, or counteract, in a greater or less degree, the impressions of the book. But simple cessation in reading would, of itself, be sufficient to destroy the true unity. In the brief tale, however, the author is enabled to carry out the fulness of his intention, be it what it may. During the hour of perusal the soul of the reader is at the writer's control. There are no external or extrinsic influences—resulting from weariness or interruption.

A skilful literary artist has constructed a tale. If wise, he has not fashioned his thoughts to accommodate his incidents; but having conceived, with deliberate care, a certain unique or single *effect* to be wrought out, he then invents such incidents—he then combines such events as may best aid him in establishing this preconceived effect. If his very initial sentence tend not to the outbringing of this effect, then he has failed in his first step. In the whole composition there should be no word written, of which the tendency, direct or indirect, is not to the one pre-established design. And by such means, with such care and skill, a picture is at length painted which leaves in the mind of him who contemplates it with a kindred art, a sense of the fullest satisfaction. The idea of the tale has been presented unblemished, because undisturbed; and this is an end unattainable by the novel. Undue brevity is just as exceptionable here as in the poem; but undue length is yet more to be avoided.

We have said that the tale has a point of superiority even over the poem. In fact, while the *rhythm* of this latter is an essential aid in the development of the poem's highest idea—the idea of the Beautiful—the artificialities of this rhythm are an inseparable bar to the development of all points of thought or expression which have their basis in *Truth*. But Truth is often, and in very great degree, the aim of the tale. Some of the finest tales are tales of ratiocination. Thus the field of this species of composition, if not in so elevated a region on the mountain of Mind, is a table-land of far vaster extent than the domain of the mere poem. Its products are never so rich, but infinitely more numerous, and more appreciable by the mass of mankind. The writer of the prose tale, in short, may bring to his theme a vast variety of modes or inflections of thought and expression—(the ratiocinative, for example, the sarcastic, or the humorous) which are not only antagonistical to the nature of the poem, but absolutely forbidden by one of its most peculiar and indispensable adjuncts; we allude, of course, to rhythm. It may be added here, *par parenthèse*, that the author who aims at the purely beautiful in a prose tale is laboring at a great disadvantage. For Beauty can be better treated in the poem. Not so with terror, or passion, or horror, or a multitude of such other points. And here it will be seen how full of prejudice are the usual animadversions against those *tales of effect*, many fine examples of which were found in the earlier numbers of *Blackwood*. The impressions produced were wrought in a legitimate sphere of action, and constituted a legitimate although sometimes an exaggerated interest. They were relished by every man of genius: although there were found many men of genius who condemned them without just ground. The true critic will but demand that the design intended be accomplished, to the fullest extent, by the means most advantageously applicable.

We have very few American tales of real merit—we may say, indeed, none, with the exception of *The Tales of a Traveller* of Washington Irving, and these *Twice-Told Tales* of Mr. Hawthorne. Some of the pieces of Mr. John Neal abound in vigor and originality; but, in general, his compositions of this class are excessively diffuse, extravagant, and indicative of an imperfect sentiment of Art. Articles at random are, now and then, met with in our periodicals which might be advantageously compared with the best effusions of the British Magazines; but, upon the whole, we are far behind our progenitors in this department of literature.

Of Mr. Hawthorne's tales we should say, emphatically, that they belong to the highest region of Art—an Art subservient to genius of a very lofty order. We had supposed, with good reason for so supposing, that he had been thrust into his present position by one of the impudent *cliques* which beset our literature, and whose pretensions it is our full purpose to expose at the earliest opportunity; but we have been most agreeably mistaken. We know of few compositions which the critic can more honestly commend than these *Twice-Told Tales*. As Americans, we feel proud of the book. . . .

From The Poetic Principle

In speaking of the Poetic Principle, I have no design to be either thorough or profound. While discussing, very much at random, the essentiality of what we call Poetry, my principal purpose will be to cite for consideration some few of those minor English or American poems which best suit my own taste, or which, upon my own fancy, have left the most definite impression. By "minor poems" I mean, of course, poems of little length. And here, in the beginning, permit me to say a few words in regard to a somewhat peculiar principle, which, whether rightfully or wrongfully, has always had its influence in my own critical estimate of the poem. I hold that a long poem does not exist. I maintain that the phrase, "a long poem," is simply a flat contradiction in terms.

I need scarcely observe that a poem deserves its title only inasmuch as it excites, by elevating the soul. The value of the poem is in the ratio of this elevating excitement. But all excitements are, through a psychal necessity, transient. That degree of excitement which would entitle a poem to be so called at all, cannot be sustained throughout a composition of any great length. After the lapse of half an hour, at the very utmost, it flags— fails—a revulsion ensues—and then the poem is, in effect, and in fact, no longer such.

There are, no doubt, many who have found difficulty in reconciling the critical dictum that the "Paradise Lost" is to be devoutly admired throughout, with the absolute impossibility of maintaining for it, during perusal, the amount of enthusiasm which that critical dictum would demand. This great work, in fact, is to be regarded as poetical only when, losing sight of that vital requisite in all works of Art, Unity, we view it merely as a series of minor poems. If, to preserve its Unity—its totality of effect or impression—we read it (as would be necessary) at a single sitting, the result is but a constant alternation of excitement and depression. After a passage of what we feel to be true poetry, there follows, inevitably, a passage of platitude which no critical pre-judgment can force us to admire; but if, upon completing the work, we read it again, omitting the first book—that is to say, commencing with the second—we shall be surprised at now finding that admirable which we before condemned—that damnable which we had previously so much admired. It follows from all this that the ultimate, aggregate, or absolute effect of even the best epic under the sun, is a nullity: and this is precisely the fact.

In regard to the Iliad, we have, if not positive proof, at least very good reason, for believing it intended as a series of lyrics; but, granting the epic intention, I can say only that the work is based in an imperfect sense of Art. The modern epic is, of the supposititious ancient model, but an inconsiderate and blindfold imitation. But the day of these artistic anomalies is over. If, at any time, any very long poem were popular in reality, which I doubt, it is at least clear that no very long poem will ever be popular again.

That the extent of a poetical work is, *ceteris paribus*,[1] the measure of its merit, seems undoubtedly, when we thus state it, a proposition sufficiently absurd—yet we are indebted for it to the Quarterly Reviews. Surely there can be nothing in mere size, abstractly considered—there can be nothing in mere bulk, so far as a volume is concerned, which has so continuously elicited admiration from these saturnine pamphlets! A mountain, to be sure, by the mere sentiment of physical magnitude which it conveys, does impress us with a sense of the sublime—but no man is impressed after *this* fashion by the material grandeur of even "The Columbiad." Even the Quarterlies have not instructed us to be so impressed by it. As yet, they have not insisted on our estimating Lamartine by the cubic foot, or Pollok by the pound— but what else are we to infer from their continued prating about "sustained effort"? If, by "sustained effort," any little gentleman has accomplished an epic, let us frankly commend him for the effort—if this indeed be a thing commendable—but let us forbear praising the epic on the effort's account. It is to be hoped that common sense, in the time to come, will prefer deciding upon a work of Art, rather by the impression it makes—by the effect it produces—than by the time it took to impress the effect, or by the amount of "sustained effort" which had been found necessary in effecting the impression. The fact is, that perseverance is one thing and genius quite another—nor can all the Quarterlies in Christendom confound them. By-and-by, this proposition, with many which I have just been urging, will be received as self-evident. In the meantime, by being generally condemned as falsities, they will not be essentially damaged as truths.

On the other hand, it is clear that a poem may be improperly brief. Undue brevity degenerates into mere epigrammatism. A very short poem, while now and then producing a brilliant or vivid, never produces a profound or enduring effect. There must

[1] *Ceteris paribus:* other things being equal.

be the steady pressing down of the stamp upon the wax. De Béranger has wrought innumerable things, pungent and spirit-stirring; but in general they have been too imponderous to stamp themselves deeply into the public attention, and thus, as so many feathers of fancy, have been blown aloft only to be whistled down the wind.

A remarkable instance of the effect of undue brevity in depressing a poem—in keeping it out of the popular view—is afforded by the following exquisite little Serenade:

> I arise from dreams of thee
>   In the first sweet sleep of night,
> When the winds are breathing low,
>   And the stars are shining bright;
> I arise from dreams of thee,
>   And a spirit in my feet
> Has led me—who knows how?—
>   To thy chamber-window, sweet!
>
> The wandering airs, they faint
>   On the dark, the silent stream—
> The champak odors fail
>   Like sweet thoughts in a dream;
> The nightingale's complaint,
>   It dies upon her heart,
> As I must die on thine,
>   O, beloved as thou art!
>
> O, lift me from the grass!
>   I die, I faint, I fail!
> Let thy love in kisses rain
>   On my lips and eyelids pale.
> My cheek is cold and white, alas!
>   My heart beats loud and fast:
> Oh! press it close to thine again,
>   Where it will break at last!

Very few perhaps are familiar with these lines—yet no less a poet than Shelley is their author. Their warm, yet delicate and ethereal imagination will be appreciated by all—but by none so thoroughly as by him who has himself arisen from sweet dreams of one beloved, to bathe in the aromatic air of a southern mid-summer night.

One of the finest poems by Willis—the very best in my opinion which he has ever written—has, no doubt, through this same de-fect of undue brevity, been kept back from its proper position, not less in the critical than in the popular view.

> The shadows lay along Broadway,
>   'Twas near the twilight-tide—
> And slowly there a lady fair
>   Was walking in her pride.
> Alone walk'd she; but, viewlessly,
>   Walk'd spirits at her side.
>
> Peace charm'd the street beneath her feet,
>   And Honour charm'd the air;
> And all astir looked kind on her,
>   And call'd her good and fair—
> For all God ever gave to her
>   She kept with chary care.
>
> She kept with care her beauties rare
>   From lovers warm and true—
> For her heart was cold to all but gold,
>   And the rich came not to woo—
> But honour'd well are charms to sell,
>   If priests the selling do.
>
> Now walking there was one more fair—
>   A slight girl, lily-pale;
> And she had unseen company
>   To make the spirit quail—
> 'Twixt Want and Scorn she walk'd forlorn,
>   And nothing could avail.

> No mercy now can clear her brow
>   For this world's peace to pray;
> For, as love's wild prayer dissolved in air,
>   Her woman's heart gave way!—
> But the sin forgiven by Christ in Heaven
>   By man is cursed alway!

In this composition we find it difficult to recognize the Willis who has written so many mere "verses of society." The lines are not only richly ideal, but full of energy; while they breathe an earnestness—an evident sincerity of sentiment—for which we look in vain throughout all the other works of this author.

While the epic mania—while the idea that, to merit in poetry, prolixity is indispensable—has for some years past been gradually dying out of the public mind by mere dint of its own absurdity— we find it succeeded by a heresy too palpably false to be long tolerated, but one which, in the brief period it has already endured, may be said to have accomplished more in the corruption of our Poetical Literature than all its other enemies combined. I allude to the heresy of The Didactic. It has been assumed, tacitly and avowedly, directly and indirectly, that the ultimate object of all Poetry is Truth. Every poem, it is said, should inculcate a moral; and by this moral is the poetical merit of the work to be adjudged. We Americans especially have patronized this happy idea; and we Bostonians, very especially, have developed it in full. We have taken it into our heads that to write a poem simply for the poem's sake, and to acknowledge such to have been our design, would be to confess ourselves radically wanting in the true Poetic dignity and force:—but the simple fact is, that would we but permit ourselves to look into our own souls, we should immediately there discover that under the sun there neither exists nor can exist any work more thoroughly dignified—more supremely noble than this very poem—this poem *per se*, this poem which is a poem and nothing more—this poem written solely for the poem's sake.

With as deep a reverence for the True as ever inspired the

bosom of man, I would nevertheless limit, in some measure, its
modes of inculcation. I would limit to enforce them. I would not
enfeeble them by dissipation. The demands of Truth are severe.
She has no sympathy with the myrtles. All *that* which is so indispensable in Song is precisely all that with which she has
nothing whatever to do. It is but making her a flaunting paradox
to wreathe her in gems and flowers. In enforcing a truth, we need
severity rather than efflorescence of language. We must be
simple, precise, terse. We must be cool, calm, unimpassioned. In
a word, we must be in that mood which, as nearly as possible,
is the exact converse of the poetical. *He* must be blind indeed
who does not perceive the radical and chasmal differences between the truthful and the poetical modes of inculcation. He
must be theory-mad beyond redemption who, in spite of these
differences, shall still persist in attempting to reconcile the ob-
stinate oils and waters of Poetry and Truth.

Dividing the world of mind into its three most immediately
obvious distinctions, we have the Pure Intellect, Taste, and the
Moral Sense. I place Taste in the middle, because it is just this
position which, in the mind, it occupies. It holds intimate relations
with either extreme; but from the Moral Sense is separated by so
faint a difference that Aristotle has not hesitated to place some
of its operations among the virtues themselves. Nevertheless, we
find the offices of the trio marked with a sufficient distinction.
Just as the Intellect concerns itself with Truth, so Taste informs
us of the Beautiful while the Moral Sense is regardful of Duty.
Of this latter, while Conscience teaches the obligation, and
Reason the expediency, Taste contents herself with displaying
the charms:—waging war upon Vice solely on the ground of her
deformity, her disproportion, her animosity to the fitting, to the
appropriate, to the harmonious, in a word, to Beauty.

An immortal instinct, deep within the spirit of man, is thus
plainly a sense of the Beautiful. This it is which administers to
his delight in the manifold forms, and sounds, and odors, and
sentiments, amid which he exists. And just as the lily is repeated
in the lake, or the eyes of Amaryllis in the mirror, so is the mere

oral or written repetition of these forms, and sounds, and colors, and odors, and sentiments, a duplicate source of delight. But this mere repetition is not poetry. He who shall simply sing, with however glowing enthusiasm, or with however vivid a truth of description, of the sights, and sounds, and odors, and colors, and sentiments, which greet him in common with all mankind—he, I say, has yet failed to prove his divine title. There is still a something in the distance which he has been unable to attain. We have still a thirst unquenchable, to allay which he has not shown us the crystal springs. This thirst belongs to the immortality of Man. It is at once a consequence and an indication of his perennial existence. It is the desire of the moth for the star. It is no mere appreciation of the Beauty before us—but a wild effort to reach the Beauty above. Inspired by an ecstatic prescience of the glories beyond the grave, we struggle by multiform combinations among the things and thoughts of Time, to attain a portion of that Loveliness whose very elements, perhaps, appertain to eternity alone. And thus when by Poetry—or when by Music, the most entrancing of the Poetic moods—we find ourselves melted into tears—we weep then—not as the Abbate Gravina supposes—through excess of pleasure, but through a certain, petulant, impatient sorrow at our inability to grasp now, wholly, here on earth, at once and forever, those divine and rapturous joys, of which through the poem or through the music, we attain to but brief and indeterminate glimpses.

The struggle to apprehend the supernal Loveliness—this struggle, on the part of souls fittingly constituted—has given to the world all that which it (the world) has ever been enabled at once to understand and to feel as poetic.

The Poetic Sentiment, of course, may develop itself in various modes—in Painting, in Sculpture, in Architecture, in the Dance—very especially in Music—and very peculiarly, and with a wide field, in the composition of the Landscape Garden. Our present theme, however, has regard only to its manifestation in words. And here let me speak briefly on the topic of rhythm. Contenting myself with the certainty that Music, in its various modes of metre, rhythm, and rhyme, is of so vast a moment in Poetry as never to be wisely rejected—is so vitally important an adjunct that he is simply silly who declines its assistance, I will not now pause to maintain its absolute essentiality. It is in Music, perhaps, that the soul most nearly attains the great end for which, when inspired by the Poetic Sentiment, it struggles—the creation of supernal Beauty. It may be, indeed, that here this sublime end is, now and then, attained in fact. We are often made to feel, with a shivering delight, that from an earthly harp are stricken notes which cannot have been unfamiliar to the angels. And thus there can be little doubt that in the union of Poetry with Music in its popular sense, we shall find the widest field for the Poetic development. The old Bards and Minnesingers had advantages which we do not possess—and Thomas Moore, singing his own songs, was, in the most legitimate manner, perfecting them as poems.

To recapitulate, then:—I would define, in brief, the Poetry of Words as The Rhythmical Creation of Beauty. Its sole arbiter is Taste. With the Intellect or with the Conscience, it has only collateral relations. Unless incidentally, it has no concern whatever either with Duty or with Truth.

A few words, however, in explanation. That pleasure which is at once the most pure, the most elevating, and the most intense, is derived, I maintain, from the contemplation of the Beautiful. In the contemplation of Beauty we alone find it possible to attain that pleasurable elevation, or excitement, of the soul, which we recognize as the Poetic Sentiment, and which is so easily distinguished from Truth, which is the satisfaction of the Reason, or from Passion, which is the excitement of the heart. I make Beauty, therefore—using the word as inclusive of the sublime—I make Beauty the province of the poem, simply because it is an obvious rule of Art that effects should be made to spring as directly as possible from their causes:—no one as yet having been weak enough to deny that the peculiar elevation in question is at least most readily attainable in the poem. It by no means follows, however, that the incitements of Passion, or the precepts of Duty, or even the lessons of Truth, may not be introduced into a poem, and with advantage; for they may subserve, incidentally, in various ways, the general purposes of the work:—but the true artist will always contrive to tone them down in proper subjection to that Beauty which is the atmosphere and the real essence of the poem. . . .

Henry David Thoreau

(1817–1862)

Of the dominant qualities in Henry David Thoreau, the most striking is his overriding independence of thought. He worked mightily to free himself from the fetters of conventional ideas by removing himself periodically from society and by invoking an automatic skepticism of everything approved by traditional practice.

Accompanying this strain of individuality was a finely developed sense of evaluation. Thoreau examined evidence with an intense scrutiny and made conclusions only after deliberate thought. Where he found ideas to be sound, he endorsed them. Where he detected flaws, he proclaimed his discoveries with an uninhibited expression. Contrary to popular opinion, he was not an iconoclast for the mere sake of opposing others; he was one who assessed every act, every thought, every philosophical concept in terms of the inherent value he found therein. If his views caused opposition or even consternation among his contemporaries, no one could challenge his fundamental integrity.

Thoreau's literary production was not highly regarded in his day. In fact, his reputation did not rise to any great heights for more than a half century after his death. Now, however, the best parts of his Journals, Walden, A Week on the Concord and Merrimack Rivers, and several assorted essays are considered to be classics of American literature.

Because of the appeal of Thoreau's personality and the merit of his best writings, his thoughts on criticism are well worth reading. One must not look, however, for any detailed critical theory. Thoreau was not interested in theory. He expressed his *critical judgments as he expressed all else—as the observations of a discerning, forthright individual who delights in voicing his views on a topic which chances to interest him.*

Thoreau, who spent the greatest portion of his life within the Concord, Massachusetts region where he was born, never really pursued a specific career. After graduation from Harvard in 1837, he taught school briefly and then worked with his father for a short time making lead pencils. Thereafter he lectured, wrote magazine articles, surveyed properties, whitewashed farm buildings, built fences, tended gardens, and did numerous other jobs— all as his whims and his economic situation dictated. Most of his time, however, he spent studying nature and seeking answers to the eternal questions concerning the meaning of life.

Below are some brief selections which are representative of Thoreau's critical thought.

From Journal

Aug. 22, 1851. It is the fault of some excellent writers—De Quincey's first impressions on seeing London suggest it to me— that they express themselves with too great fullness and detail. They give the most faithful, natural, and lifelike account of their sensations, mental and physical, but they lack moderation and sententiousness. They do not affect us by an ineffectual earnestness and a reserve of meaning, like a stutterer; they say all they mean. Their sentences are not concentrated and nutty. Sentences which suggest far more than they say, which have an atmosphere about them, which do not merely report an old, but make a new, impression; sentences which suggest as many things and are as durable as a Roman aqueduct; to frame these, that is the art of writing. Sentences which are expensive, towards which so many volumes, so much life, went; which lie like boulders on the page, up and down or across; which contain the seed of other sentences, not mere repetition, but creation; which a man might sell his grounds and castles to build. If De Quincey had suggested each of his pages in a sentence and passed on, it would have been far more excellent writing. His style is nowhere kinked and knotted up into something hard and significant, which you could swallow like a diamond, without digesting.

Nov. 1, 1851. It is a rare qualification to be able to state a fact simply and adequately, to digest some experience cleanly, to say 'yes' and 'no' with authority, to make a square edge, to conceive and suffer the truth to pass through us living and intact, even as a waterfowl an eel, as it flies over the meadows, thus stocking new waters. First of all a man must see, before he can say. Statements are made but partially. Things are said with reference to certain conventions or existing institutions, not absolutely. A fact truly and absolutely stated is taken out of the region of common sense and acquires a mythologic or universal significance. Say it and have done with it. Express it without expressing yourself. See not with the eye of science, which is barren, nor of youthful poetry, which is impotent. But taste the world and digest it. It would seem as if things got said but rarely and by chance. As you see, so at length will you say. When facts are seen superficially, they are seen as they lie in relation to certain institutions, perchance. But I would have them expressed as more deeply seen, with deeper references; so that the hearer or reader cannot recognize them or apprehend their significance from the platform of common life, but it will be necessary that he be in a sense translated in order to understand them, when the truth respecting his things shall naturally exhale from a man like the odor of the muskrat from the coat of the trapper. At first blush a man is not capable of reporting truth; he must be drenched and saturated with it first. What was enthusiasm in the young man must become temperament in the mature man. Without excitement, heat, or passion, he will survey the world which excited the youth and threw him off his balance. As all things are significant, so all words should be significant. It is a fault which attaches to the speaker, to speak flippantly or superficially of anything. Of what use are words which do not move the hearer—are not oracular and fateful? A style in which the matter is all in all, and the manner nothing at all.

Jan. 2, 1859. When I hear the hypercritical quarrelling about grammar and style, the position of the particles, etc., etc., stretching or contracting every speaker to certain rules of theirs—Mr. Webster, perhaps, not having spoken according to Mr. Kirkham's rule—I see that they forget that the first requisite and rule is that expression shall be vital and natural, as much as the voice of a brute or an interjection: first of all, mother tongue; and last of all, artificial or father tongue. Essentially your truest poetic sentence is as free and lawless as a lamb's bleat. The grammarian is often one who can neither cry nor laugh, yet thinks that he can express human emotions. So the posture–masters tell you how you shall walk—turning your toes out, perhaps, excessively—but so the beautiful walkers are not made.

From Life Without Principle

This world is a place of business. What an infinite bustle! I am awakened almost every night by the panting of the locomotive. It interrupts my dreams. There is no sabbath. It would be glorious to see mankind at leisure for once. It is nothing but work, work, work. I cannot easily buy a blankbook to write thoughts in; they are commonly ruled for dollars and cents. An Irishman, seeing me making a minute in the fields, took it for granted that I was calculating my wages. If a man was tossed out of a window when an infant, and so made a cripple for life, or scared out of his wits by the Indians, it is regretted chiefly because he was thus incapacitated for—business! I think that there is nothing, not even crime, more opposed to poetry, to philosophy, ay, to life itself, than this incessant business.

Oliver Wendell Holmes

(1809–1894)

Relying on training received in the field of medicine, a reading of important critics, and a carefully developed insistence on objective analysis of fact, Oliver Wendell Holmes employed a critical approach that earned him a high reputation in his time— even though he was a refiner of other's thoughts rather than an original thinker.

The influence of Holmes' medical training is reflected in his use of scientific processes of reasoning and in his careful and deliberate manner of establishing conclusions. For the most part, he probes and studies literary endeavors much as a scientist works in a laboratory. Then he presents his findings in a similarly orderly manner.

The influence of Holmes' acquaintance with important critics is evident mainly in his Classical emphasis on carefully developed form. It is also evident in his contention that poetry represents hard work, accomplished in an atmosphere of rigor and exacting care. Holmes gives short shrift to the concept of poetry as the product of careless spontaneity.

The influence of Holmes' respect for objective analysis of fact is present throughout his critical writings. He seems to have demanded objectivity as a result of a habitual abhorrence of quick judgments. By inclination, Holmes moved slowly and cautiously, examining every fact thoroughly before rendering a conclusion.

One must not think of Holmes, however, exclusively in terms of the scientist or the objectively rational thinker; for he does reflect other philosophical views. Especially significant in this regard is his belief that good or great poetry requires a genuinely fertile imagination. He also subscribes to the argument that poetry attains a loftiness not to be found in the realm of science. Hence he draws a clear line between these activities.

Holmes, born and reared in Cambridge, Massachusetts, was graduated from Harvard College in 1829. Interested at first in law, he soon shifted his attention to medicine, a field wherein he achieved considerable fame in the year 1843 with his discovery that puerperal fever is contagious. Later, he added to this fame in medicine while serving as professor of anatomy at Harvard from 1847 to 1882. Meanwhile, he was building a solid reputation in literature as poet, essayist, and novelist; and he was gaining renown for his calm, deliberate, and soundly based conclusions on important contemporary questions.

The passage below is taken from Holmes' essay "Over the Teacups." Herein one can see the essence of Holmes' views on the subject of poetry and literature in general.

From Over the Teacups [1891]

We got talking on the subject of realism, of which so much has been said of late.

It seems to me, I said, that the great additions which have been made by realism to the territory of literature consist largely in swampy, malarious, ill-smelling patches of soil which had previously been left to reptiles and vermin. It is perfectly easy to be original by violating the laws of decency and the canons of good taste. The general consent of civilized people was supposed to have banished certain subjects from the conversation of well bred people and the pages of respectable literature. There is no subject, or hardly any, which may not be treated of at the proper time, in the proper place, by the fitting person, for the right kind of listener or reader. But when the poet or the story-teller invades the province of the man of science, he is on dangerous ground. I need say nothing of the blunders he is pretty sure to make. The imaginative writer is after effects. The scientific man is after truth. Science is decent, modest; does not try to startle, but to instruct.

The same scenes and objects which outrage every sense of delicacy in the story-teller's highly colored paragraphs can be read without giving offence in the chaste language of the physiologist or the physician.

There is a very celebrated novel, "Madame Bovary," the work of M. Flaubert, which is noted for having been the subject of prosecution as an immoral work. That it has a serious lesson there is no doubt, if one will drink down to the bottom of the cup. But the honey of sensuous description is spread so deeply over the surface of the goblet that a large proportion of its readers never think of its holding anything else. All the phases of unhallowed passion are described in full detail. That is what the book is bought and read for, by the great majority of its purchasers, as all but simpletons very well know. That is what makes it sell and brought it into the courts of justice. This book is famous for its realism; in fact, it is recognized as one of the earliest and most brilliant examples of that modern style of novel which, beginning where Balzac left off, attempted to do for literature what the photograph has done for art. For those who take the trouble to drink out of the cup below the rim of honey, there is a scene where realism is carried to its extreme,—surpassed in horror by no writer, unless it be the one whose name must be looked for at the bottom of the alphabet, as if its natural place were as low down in the dregs of realism as it could find itself. This is the death-bed scene, where Madame Bovary expires in convulsions. The author must have visited the hospitals for the purpose of watching the terrible agonies he was to depict, tramping from one bed to another until he reached the one where the cries and contortions were the most frightful. Such a scene he has reproduced. No hospital physician would have pictured the struggle in such colors. In the same way, that other realist, M. Zola, has painted a patient suffering from delirium tremens, the disease known to common speech as "the horrors. . . ." In describing this case he does all that language can do to make it more horrible than the reality. He gives us, not realism, but super-realism, if such a term does not contradict itself.

In this matter of the literal reproduction of sights and scenes which our natural instinct and our better informed taste and judgment teach us to avoid, art has been far in advance of literature. It is three hundred years since Joseph Ribera, more commonly known as Spagnoletto, was born in the province of Valencia, in Spain. We had the misfortune of seeing a painting of his in a collection belonging to one of the French princes, and exhibited at the Art Museum. It was that of a man performing upon himself the operation known to the Japanese as hara-kiri. Many persons who look upon this revolting picture never get rid of its remembrance, and will regret the day when their eyes fell upon it. I should share the offence of the painter if I ventured to describe it. Ribera was fond of depicting just such odious and frightful subjects. "Saint Lawrence writhing on his gridiron, Saint Sebastian full of arrows, were equally a source of delight to him. Even in subjects which had no such elements of horror he finds the materials of the delectation of his ferocious pencil; he makes up for the defect by rendering with a brutal realism deformity and ugliness."

The first great mistake made by the ultra-realists, like Flaubert and Zola, is, as I have said, their ignoring the line of distinction between imaginative art and science. We can find realism enough in books of anatomy, surgery, and medicine. In studying the human figure, we want to see it clothed with its natural integuments. It is well for the artist to study the *écorché* in the dissecting-room, but we do not want the Apollo or the Venus to leave their skins behind them when they go into the gallery for exhibition. Lancisi's figures show us how the great statues look when divested of their natural covering. It is instructive, but useful chiefly as a means to aid in the true artistic reproduction of nature. When the hospitals are invaded by the novelist, he should learn something from the physician as well as from the patients. Science delineates in monochrome. She never uses high tints and strontian lights to astonish lookers-on. Such scenes as Flaubert and Zola describe would be reproduced in their essential characters, but not dressed up in picturesque phrases. That is the first stumbling block in the way of the reader of such realistic stories as those to which I have referred. There are subjects which must be investigated by scientific men which most educated persons would be glad to know nothing about. When a realistic writer like Zola surprises his reader into a kind of knowledge he never thought of wishing for, he sometimes harms him more than he has any idea of doing. He wants to produce a sensation, and he leaves a permanent disgust not to be got rid of. Who does not remember odious images that can never be washed out from the consciousness which they have stained? A man's vocabulary is terribly retentive of evil words, and the images they present cling to his memory and will not loose their hold. One who has had the mischance to soil his mind by reading certain poems of Swift will never cleanse it to its original whiteness. Expressions and thoughts of a certain character stain the fibre of the thinking organ, and in some degree affect the hue of every idea that passes through the discolored tissues.

This is the gravest accusation to bring against realism, old or recent, whether in the brutal paintings of Spagnoletto or in the unclean revelations of Zola. Leave the description of the drains and cesspools to the hygienic specialist, the painful facts of disease to the physician, the details of the laundry to the washer-woman. If we are to have realism in its tedious descriptions of unimportant particulars, let it be of particulars which do not excite disgust. Such is the description of the vegetables in Zola's "Ventre de Paris," where, if one wishes to see the apotheosis of turnips, beets, and cabbages, he can find them glorified as supremely as if they had been symbols of so many deities; their forms, their colors, their expression, worked upon until they seem as if they were made to be looked at and worshiped rather than to be boiled and eaten.

I am pleased to find a French critic of M. Flaubert expressing ideas with which many of my own entirely coincide. "The great mistake of the realists," he says, "is that they profess to tell the truth because they tell everything. This puerile hunting after details, this cold and cynical inventory of all the wretched conditions in the midst of which poor humanity vegetates, not only do not help us to understand it better, but, on the contrary, the effect on the spectators is a kind of dazzled confusion mingled with fatigue and disgust. The material truthfulness to which the school of M. Flaubert more especially pretends misses its aim in going beyond it. Truth is lost in its own excess."

I return to my thoughts on the relations of imaginative art in all its forms with science. The subject which in the hands of the scientific student is handled decorously,—reverently, we might almost say,—becomes repulsive, shameful, and debasing in the unscrupulous manipulations of the low-bred man of letters.

I confess that I am a little jealous of certain tendencies in our own American literature, which led one of the severest and most outspoken of our satirical fellow-countrymen, no longer living to be called to account for it, to say, in a moment of bitterness, that the mission of America was to vulgarize mankind. I myself have sometimes wondered at the pleasure some Old World critics have professed to find in the most lawless freaks of New World literature. I have questioned whether their delight was not like that of the Spartans in the drunken antics of their Helots. But I suppose I belong to another age, and must not attempt to judge the present by my old-fashioned standards.

[On Whitman]

Thomas Jefferson is commonly recognized as the first to proclaim before the world the political independence of America. It is not so generally agreed upon as to who was the first to announce the literary emancipation of our country.

One of Mr. Emerson's biographers has claimed that his Phi Beta Kappa Oration was our Declaration of Literary Independence. But Mr. Emerson did not cut himself loose from all the traditions of Old World scholarship. He spelled his words correctly, he constructed his sentences grammatically. He adhered to the slavish rules of propriety, and observed the reticences which a traditional delicacy has considered inviolable in decent society.

. . . He was not always so careful as he might have been in the rhythm and rhyme of his verse, but in the main he recognized the old established laws which have been accepted as regulating both. . . .

A stronger claim might be urged for Mr. Whitman. He takes into his hospitable vocabulary words which no English dictionary recognizes as belonging to the language,—words which will be looked for in vain outside of his own pages. He accepts as poetical subjects all things alike, common and unclean, without discrimination, miscellaneous as the contents of the great sheet which Peter saw let down from heaven. He carries the principle of republicanism through the whole world of created objects. He will "thread a thread through his poems," he tells us, "that no one thing in the universe is inferior to another thing." No man has ever asserted the surpassing dignity and importance of the American citizen so boldly and freely as Mr. Whitman. He calls himself "teacher of the unquenchable creed, namely, egotism." He begins one of his chants, "I celebrate myself," but he takes us all in as partners in his self-glorification. He believes in America as the new Eden.

"A world primal again, vistas of glory incessant and branching,
  A new race dominating previous ones and grander far,
  New politics—new literature and religions—new inventions and
    arts."

Of the new literature he himself has furnished specimens which certainly have all the originality he can claim for them. . . .

. . . So far as concerns literary independence, if we understand by that term the getting rid of our subjection to British criticism, such as it was in the days when the question was asked, "Who reads an American book?" we may consider it pretty well established. If it means dispensing with punctuation, coining words at will, self-revelation unrestrained by a sense of what is decorous, declamations in which everything is glorified without being idealized, "poetry" in which the reader must make the rhythms which the poet has not made for him, then I think we had better continue literary colonists. I shrink from a lawless independence to which all the virile energy and trampling audacity of Mr. Whitman fail to reconcile me. But there is room for everybody and everything in our huge hemisphere. Young America is like a three-year-old colt with his saddle and bridle just taken off. The first thing he wants to do is to *roll*. He is a droll object, sprawling in the grass with his four hoofs in the air; but he likes it, and it won't harm us. So let him roll,—let him roll!

Margaret Fuller

(1810–1850)

One of the most widely read and active of the Concord circle, Margaret Fuller (Marchioness Ossoli) was a more highly respected critic in her day than is commonly realized. In fact, only the specialist in the period seems to understand the full force of her impact; others tend to regard her as little more than a dim figure on the critical stage of the time.

Although Miss Fuller concentrated her critical writing primarily on the subject of poetry, where she succeeded in casting some small light of originality, she also wrote extensively about the art of criticism itself and about America and its cultural and intellectual nature.

In evolving her critical theory, Miss Fuller drew from several sources. She was well grounded in the criticism of Classical antiquity—as is evident in her emphasis on a well-ordered literary product, emanating from a carefully disciplined thought. She was also influenced, however, by Coleridge and others who espoused a romantic emphasis on the individual and his reactions. Hence her criticism leans toward the expressionist rather than the objective theory.

In her theory, Miss Fuller recognizes three kinds of critics—the subjective, the apprehensive, and the comprehensive. The subjective critic bases his judgments on the impact of the work on him as an individual. The apprehensive critic attempts to move into the author's personality to explain and evaluate the work. The comprehensive critic possesses all the strengths of the apprehensive critic, but in addition he is able to judge the work objectively.

Miss Fuller dismisses the subjective critic; she endorses the approach of the apprehensive critic; but she designates the comprehensive critic as most worthy of respect. In presenting her case, she employs the tight, orderly pattern of argument that typifies her critical writing. She develops her points slowly and carefully, exhibiting meanwhile a rather nicely balanced judgment.

Sarah Margaret Fuller was born in Cambridge, Massachusetts, on May 23, 1810. An unusually precocious child destined to mature into one of America's most brilliant women, she insisted on being educated at home in order to avoid the strictures of formal schooling. From her earliest years, she was associated with writing, social reform, women's rights, and the study of literature. Between 1840 and 1844, she worked as editor (with Emerson and George Ripley) of The Dial, and between 1844 and 1846, she was on the staff of the New York Tribune.

In 1847, while in Rome, Miss Fuller met and married the Italian nobleman, Angelo Ossoli, thereby becoming Marchioness Ossoli. Marital happiness, however, was short lived. As the result of the siege and eventual capture of Rome by the French, the Ossoli's and their infant sailed for America, only to die in a shipwreck off Fire Island, New York, on July 19, 1850.

Below are two short selections which are illustrative of Miss Fuller's theories and general outlook on the field of literature.

A Short Essay on Critics[1]

An essay on criticism were a serious matter; for though this age be emphatically critical, the writer would still find it necessary to investigate the laws of criticism as a science to settle its conditions as an art. Essays entitled critical are epistles addressed to the public, through which the mind of the recluse relieves itself of its impressions. Of these the only law is, "Speak the best word that is in thee." Or they are regular articles got up to order by the literary hack writer for the literary mart, and the only law is to

[1] First published in the *Dial*, Vol. I, No. 1.

make them plausible. There is not yet deliberate recognition of a standard of criticism, though we hope the always strengthening league of the republic of letters must erelong settle laws on which its amphictyonic council may act. Meanwhile let us not venture to write on criticism, but by classifying the critics imply our hopes and thereby our thoughts.

First there are the subjective class (to make use of a convenient term introduced by our German benefactors). These are persons to whom writing is no sacred, no reverend employment. They are not driven to consider, not forced upon investigation by the fact that they are deliberately giving their thoughts an independent existence, and that it may live to others when dead to them. They know no agonies of conscientious research, no timidities of self-respect. They see no ideal beyond the present hour, which makes its mood an uncertain tenure. How things affect them now they know; let the future, let the whole take care of itself. They state their impressions as they rise of other men's spoken, written, or acted thoughts. They never dream of going out of themselves to seek the motive, to trace the law of another nature. They never dream that there are statures which cannot be measured from their point of view. They love, they like, or they hate; the book is detestable, immoral, absurd, or admirable, noble, of a most approved scope—these statements they make with authority, as those who bear the evangel of pure taste and accurate judgment, and need be tried before no human synod. To them it seems that their present position commands the universe.

Thus the essays on the works of others which are called criticisms are often in fact mere records of impressions. To judge of their value you must know where the man was brought up, under what influences—his nation, his church, his family, even. He himself has never attempted to estimate the value of these circumstances, and find a law or raise a standard above all circumstances, permanent against all influence. He is content to be the creature of his place, and to represent it by his spoken and written word. He takes the same ground with a savage who does not hesitate to say of the product of a civilization on which he could not stand, "It is bad" or "It is good."

The value of such comments is merely reflex. They characterize the critic. They give an idea of certain influences on a certain act of men in a certain time or place. Their absolute, essential value is nothing. The long review, the eloquent article by the man of the nineteenth century, are of no value by themselves considered, but only as samples of their kind. The writers were content to tell what they felt, to praise or to denounce without needing to convince us or themselves. They sought not the divine truths of philosophy, and she proffers them not if unsought.

Then there are the apprehensive. These can go out of themselves and enter fully into a foreign existence. They breathe its life; they live in its law; they tell what it meant, and why it so expressed its meaning. They reproduce the work of which they speak, and make it better known to us in so far as two statements are better than one. There are beautiful specimens in this kind. They are pleasing to us as bearing witness of the genial sympathies of nature. They have the ready grace of love with somewhat of the dignity of disinterested friendship. They sometimes give more pleasure than the original production of which they treat, as melodies will sometimes ring sweetlier in the echo. Besides, there is a peculiar pleasure in a true response; it is the assurance of equipoise in the universe. These, if not true critics, come nearer the standard than the subjective class, and the value of their work is ideal as well as historical.

Then there are the comprehensive, who must also be apprehensive. They enter into the nature of another being and judge his work by its own law. But having done so, having ascertained his design and the degree of his success in fulfilling it, thus measuring his judgment, his energy, and skill, they do also know how to put that aim in its place and how to estimate its relations. And this only the critic can do who perceives the analogies of the universe, and how they are regulated by an absolute, invariable principle. He can see how far that work expresses this principle, as well as how far it is excellent in its details. Sustained by a principle such as can be girt within no rule, no formula, he can walk around the work, he can stand above it, he can uplift it, and try its weight. Finally he is worthy to judge it.

Critics are poets cut down, says someone by way of jeer; but in truth they are men with the poetical temperament to apprehend, with the philosophical tendency to investigate. The maker is divine; the critic sees this divine, but brings it down to humanity by the analytic process. The critic is the historian who records the order of creation. In vain for the maker who knows without learning it, but not in vain for the mind of his race.

The critic is beneath the maker, but is his needed friend. What tongue could speak but to an intelligent ear, and every noble work demands its critic. The richer the work, the more severe should be its critic; the larger its scope, the more comprehensive must be his power of scrutiny. The critic is not a base caviler, but the younger brother of genius. Next to invention is the power of interpreting invention; next to beauty the power of appreciating beauty.

And of making others appreciate it; for the universe is a scale of infinite gradation, and below the very highest every step is explanation down to the lowest. Religion in the two modulations of poetry and music descends through an infinity of waves to the lowest abysses of human nature. Nature is the literature and art of the divine mind; human literature and art the criticism on that; and they too find their criticism within their own sphere.

The critic then should be not merely a poet, not merely a philosopher, not merely an observer, but tempered of all three. If he criticize the poem, he must want nothing of what constitutes the poet except the power of creating forms and speaking in music. He must have as good an eye and as fine a sense; but if he had as fine an organ for expression also, he would make the poem instead of judging it. He must be inspired by the philosopher's spirit of inquiry and need of generalization, but he must not be constrained by the hard-cemented masonry of method to which philosophers are prone. And he must have the organic acuteness of the observer, with a love of ideal perfection which forbids him to be content with mere beauty of details in the work or the comment upon the work.

There are persons who maintain that there is no legitimate criticism except the reproductive; that we have only to say what the work is or is to us, never what it is not. But the moment we look for a principle, we feel the need of a criterion, of a standard; and then we say what the work is *not*, as well as what it *is*; and this is as healthy though not as grateful and gracious an operation of the mind as the other. We do not seek to degrade but to classify an object by stating what it is not. We detach the part from the whole lest it stand between us and the whole. When we have ascertained in what degree it manifests the whole, we may safely restore it to its place and love or admire it there ever after.

The use of criticism in periodical writing is to sift, not to stamp a work. Yet should they not be "sieves and drainers for the use of luxurious readers," but for the use of earnest inquirers, giving voice and being to their objections as well as stimulus to their sympathies. But the critic must not be an infallible adviser to his reader. He must not tell him what books are not worth reading or what must be thought of them when read, but what he read in them. Woe to that coterie where some critic sits despotic, intrenched behind the infallible "We." Woe to that oracle who has infused such soft sleepiness, such a gentle dullness into his atmosphere that when he opes his lips no dog will bark. It is this attempt at dictatorship in the reviewers, and the indolent acquiescence of their readers, that has brought them into disrepute. With such fairness did they make out their statements, with such dignity did they utter their verdicts that the poor reader grew all too submissive. He learned his lesson with such docility that the greater part of what will be said at any public or private meeting can be foretold by anyone who has read the leading periodical works for twenty years back. Scholars sneer at and would fain dispense with them altogether; and the public, grown lazy and helpless by this constant use of props and stays, can now scarce brace itself even to get through a magazine article, but reads in the daily paper laid beside the breakfast plate a short notice of the last number of the long established and popular review, and thereupon passes its judgment and is content.

Then the partisan spirit of many of these journals has made it unsafe to rely upon them as guidebooks and expurgatory indexes. They could not be content merely to stimulate and suggest thought; they have at last become powerless to supersede it.

From these causes and causes like these, the journals have lost much of their influence. There is a languid feeling about them, an inclination to suspect the justice of their verdicts, the value of their criticisms. But their golden age cannot be quite past. They afford too convenient a vehicle for the transmission of knowledge; they are too natural a feature of our time to have done all their work yet. Surely they may be redeemed from their abuses, they may be turned to their true uses. But how?

It were easy to say what they should *not* do. They should not have an object to carry or a cause to advocate, which obliges them either to reject all writings which wear the distinctive traits of individual life or to file away what does not suit them, till the essay, made true to their design, is made false to the mind of the writer. An external consistency is thus produced at the expense of all salient thought, all genuine emotion of life, in short, and all living influence. Their purpose may be of value, but by such means was no valuable purpose ever furthered long. There are those who have with the best intention pursued this system of trimming and adaptation, and thought it well and best to

Deceive their country for their country's good.

But their country cannot long be so governed. It misses the pure, the full tone of truth; it perceives that the voice is modulated to coax, to persuade, and it turns from the judicious man of the world, calculating the effect to be produced by each of his smooth sentences, to some earnest voice which is uttering thoughts, crude, rash, ill-arranged it may be, but true to one human breast and uttered in full faith that the God of Truth will guide them aright.

And here it seems to me has been the greatest mistake in the conduct of these journals. A smooth monotony has been attained, a uniformity of tone, so that from the title of a journal you can infer the tenor of all its chapters. But nature is ever various, ever new, and so should be her daughters, art and literature. We do not want merely a polite response to what we thought before, but by the freshness of thought in other minds to have new thought awakened in our own. We do not want stores of information only, but to be roused to digest these into knowledge. Able and experienced men write for us, and we would know what they think, as they think it not for us but for themselves. We would live with them rather than be taught by them how to live: we would catch the contagion of their mental activity rather than have them direct us how to regulate our own. In books, in reviews, in the senate, in the pulpit we wish to meet thinking men, not schoolmasters or pleaders. We wish that they should do full justice to their own view, but also that they should be frank with us, and, if now our superiors, treat us as if we might sometime rise to be their equals. It is this true manliness, this firmness in his own position, and this power of appreciating the position of others that alone can make the critic our companion and friend. We would converse with him, secure that he will tell us all his thought and speak as man to man. But if he adapts his work to us, if he stifles what is distinctively his, if he shows himself either arrogant or mean, or above all if he wants faith in the healthy action of free thought and the safety of pure motive, we will not talk with him, for we cannot confide in him. We will go to the critic who trusts genius and trusts us, who knows that all good writing must be spontaneous, and who will write out the bill of fare for the public as he read it for himself—

> Forgetting vulgar rules, with spirit free
> To judge each author by his own intent,
> Nor think one standard for all minds is meant.

Such a one will not disturb us with personalities, with sectarian prejudices, or an undue vehemence in favor of petty plans or

temporary objects. Neither will he disgust us by smooth ob-
sequious flatteries and an inexpressive, lifeless gentleness. He
will be free and make us free from the mechanical and distorting
influences we hear complained of on every side. He will teach us
to love wisely what we before loved well, for he knows the difference between censoriousness and discernment, infatuation and
reverence; and while delighting in the genial melodies of Pan,
can perceive, should Apollo bring his lyre into audience, that
there may be strains more divine than those of his native groves.

Three Classes of Literature[1]

The office of literature is twofold. It preserves through ages the
flowers of life which came to perfect bloom in minds of genius.
What bloomed but for a day in the highest epochs of thought or
of love becomes an amaranth if translated into literature. A small
part of literature has a permanent value.

But the office of the larger part is temporary, as affording the
means of interpreting contemporary minds to each other on a
larger scale than actual conversation in words or deeds furnishes.
And the requisites for success in this class are very different from,
in some respects opposite to, those for the other.

Excellence in this kind is not to be held lightly. It is no small
matter to live a full life in the day; it is what those who live for
the ages rarely do. Those who are most geniuses are very commonly least men, and take the total growth of a man, we may well
doubt whether an equable expansion of harmonious growth of
the nature is to be sacrificed to a partial though exquisite result.
What is said fully and pertinently now does its office and cheers
the heart of the world, though it may not pass to posterity with
the name of the speaker. We confess our partiality for those noble
men who lived too full and vigorous a life to have time to set
apart portions of it—those men whose soul was in their eyes, and
whose tongue or pen did justice to the occasion as it came. The

[1] From "English Writers Little Known Here," New York *Daily Tribune*,
March 4, 1845.

mistletoe is a sacred plant, but we must have oaks before mistletoes. It is well that we have both, when he who fulfills the life of the day has such a superfluity besides as to scatter its seed through a wide future. But let the oaks grow first, though their fruit be no larger than the acorn. The common and daily purposes of literature are the most important. It cannot and will not dispense with the prophecies of genius, but the healthy discharge of its functions must not be disparaged to exalt these.

Thus whatever is truly said and forcibly said is valuable in literature as in life, though its pretensions be not the highest as to originality of thought or form. Individuality is sufficient, for every fact is worth knowing and stating. Only we must not dwell too long on what is temporary, nor give to what is but relatively good, absolute praise.

There is a class of writers, midway between geniuses and men of merely healthy energy, who are very valuable also. They are audience to the genius, interpreter to the multitude, cultivated friends for those who need such.

The writers of this class do not enjoy extensive fame. They are not poets nor merely active men; they may be called in distinction gentlemen and scholars. They have not perhaps the deep glow of experience that makes the universal heart thrill at their slight magnetic tokens; they have not the magician's wand to evoke from the realm of shadows forms that in life they have never seen.

Yet they are delightful private companions. We are not their lovers nor their worshipers, but their familiar friendship we prize. We would introduce them to others that they may find and be found by their own. They need to be thus introduced, for they do not command fame, nor make the earth shake with their tread so that all may know where to find them.

James Russell Lowell

(1819–1891)

James Russell Lowell was a widely read, intensely active figure
who earned for himself a high reputation as poet, critic, and
essayist—only to suffer an uneven reception with specialists in
American literature in later times.

Lowell's critical theory arose from a combination of rather
diverse elements. Fundamentally, he was romantic in temperament. He placed great emphasis on the individual expressing himself as a personality—truthfully, sincerely, imaginatively. In fact,
one can see in Lowell's theory certain dominant elements from
Coleridge. He was also influenced, however, by his admiration
for Classicism, especially the critical principles of Plato, Aristotle,
and Horace. From these sources, he drew support for his view
that poetry must be a carefully executed endeavor, regardless of
the type involved.

Lowell, like most other critics, did not develop a theory of
criticism and live by it undeviatingly thereafter. Rather, he altered
his views noticeably over the years. As a young man deeply committed to the cause of abolition, he endorsed a brand of didacti-
cism in poetry. He saw in poetry not only the opportunity but the
necessity to present important precepts to the reader. With the
passing years, however, he moved more toward the idea of pure
literature. He subscribed to the concept that the literary artist is
a man impelled by aesthetic sensitivities as he views and interprets his subject.

In evaluating his contemporaries, Lowell has drawn considerable reproof. Lacking the invaluable perspective which the passing of years provides for a critic, he sometimes missed the mark

rather seriously. He clearly underestimated the achievements of Whitman and Thoreau; and his appraisal of Henry James is too low while his judgment of Henry Wadsworth Longfellow is ludicrously high. In fairness, however, one should note that his critical assessments of Nathaniel Hawthorne, Edgar Allan Poe, and William Dean Howells approximate those accorded by posterity.

Lowell was born in Cambridge, Massachusetts, into a family that had lived in that area from the 1630's onward. Deeply committed to culture and learning at an early age, he was graduated from Harvard in 1838 and thereafter continued a lifelong study of many literatures—but especially those of England and his own nation. In addition to writing poetry and critical essays, Lowell was active in several other fields. Beginning in 1856, he taught for sixteen years as Professor of Modern Languages and Literature at Harvard; he served as editor of the Atlantic Monthly *from 1857 to 1871 and as co-editor of the* North American Review *from 1863 to 1867; and he campaigned actively for abolition for over twenty years before the Civil War. He was also in the foreign service from 1877 to 1885, representing the United States in Spain and later Great Britain.*

The two following selections exhibit important facets of Lowell the critic. The first is an essay in which he evaluates the achievement of Edgar Allan Poe. The second is an extract from his well-known "Fable for Critics," a humorous treatment in verse of important American writers.

Edgar Allan Poe

The situation of American literature is anomalous. It has no center, or, if it have, it is like that of the sphere of Hermes. It is divided into many systems, each revolving round its several sun, and often presenting to the rest only the faint glimmer of a milk-and-watery way. Our capital city, unlike London or Paris, is not a great central heart, from which life and vigor radiate to the extremities, but resembles more an isolated umbilicus, stuck down as near as may be to the center of the land, and seeming rather to tell a legend of former usefulness than to serve any present need. Boston, New York, Philadelphia, each has its literature almost more distinct than those of the different dialects of Germany; and the Young Queen of the West has also one of her own, of which some articulate rumor barely has reached us dwellers by the Atlantic. Meanwhile, a great babble is kept up concerning a national literature, and the country, having delivered itself of the ugly likeness of a paint-dedaubed, filthy savage, smilingly dandles the rag baby upon her maternal knee, as if it were veritable flesh and blood, and would grow timely to bone and sinew.

But, before we have an American literature, we must have an American criticism. We have, it is true, some scores of "American Macaulays," the faint echoes of defunct originalities, who will discourse learnedly at an hour's notice upon matters, to be even a sciolist in which would ask the patient study and self-denial of years—but, with a few rare exceptions, America is still to seek a profound, original, and aesthetic criticism. Our criticism, which from its nature might be expected to pass most erudite judgment upon the merit of thistles, undertakes to decide upon

The plant and flower of light.

There is little life in it, little conscientiousness, little reverence; nay, it has seldom the mere physical merit of fearlessness. It may be best likened to an intellectual gathering of chips to keep the critical pot of potatos or reputation a-boiling. Too often, indeed, with the cast garments of some pigmy Gifford, or other foreign notoriety, which he has picked up at the ragfair of literature, our critic sallies forth, a self-dubbed Amadis, armed with a pen, which, more wonderful even than the fairy-gifts in an old ballad, becomes at will either the lance couched terribly at defiant windmills, or the trumpet for a halfpenny pæan.

Perhaps there is no task more difficult than the just criticism of contemporary literature. It is even more grateful to give praise where it is needed than where it is deserved, and friendship so often seduces the iron stylus of justice into a vague flourish, that she writes what seems rather like an epitaph than a criticism. Yet if praise be given as an alms, we could not drop so poisonous a one into any man's hat. The critic's ink may suffer equally from too large an infusion of nutgalls or of sugar. But it is easier to be generous than to be just, though there are some who find it equally hard to be either, and we might readily put faith in that fabulous direction to the hiding-place of truth, did we judge from the amount of water which we usually find mixed with it.

We were very naturally led into some remarks on American criticism by the subject of the present sketch. Mr. Poe is at once the most discriminating, philosophical, and fearless critic upon imaginative works who has written in America. It may be that we should qualify our remark a little, and say that he *might be,* rather than that he always *is,* for he seems sometimes to mistake his phial of prussic-acid for his inkstand. If we do not always agree with him in his premises, we are, at least, satisfied that his deductions are logical, and that we are reading the thoughts of a man who thinks for himself, and says what he thinks, and knows well what he is talking about. His analytic power would furnish forth bravely some score of ordinary critics. We do not know him personally, but we suspect him for a man who has one or two pet prejudices on which he prides himself. These sometimes allure him out of the strict path of criticism,[1] but, where they do not interfere, we would put almost entire confidence in his judgments. Had Mr. Poe had the control of a magazine of his own, in which to display his critical abilities, he would have been as autocratic, ere this, in America, as Professor Wilson has been in England; and his criticisms, we are sure, would have been far more profound and philosophical than those of the Scotsman. As it is, he has squared out blocks enough to build an enduring pyramid, but has left them lying carelessly and unclaimed in many different quarries.

[1] We cannot but think that this was the case in his review of W. E. Channing's poems, in which we are sure that there is much which must otherwise have challenged Mr. Poe's hearty liking. J. R. L.

Remarkable experiences are usually confined to the inner life of imaginative men, but Mr. Poe's biography displays a vicissitude and peculiarity of interest such as is rarely met with. The offspring of a romantic marriage, and left an orphan at an early age, he was adopted by Mr. Allan, a wealthy Virginian, whose barren marriage bed seemed the warranty of a large estate to the young poet. Having received a classical education in England, he returned home and entered the University of Virginia, where, after an extravagant course, followed by reformation at the last extremity, he was graduated with the highest honors of his class. Then came a boyish attempt to join the fortunes of the insurgent Greeks, which ended at St. Petersburg, where he got into difficulties through want of a passport, from which he was rescued by the American consul and sent home. He now entered the military academy at West Point, from which he obtained a dismissal on hearing of the birth of a son to his adopted father, by a second marriage, an event which cut off his expectations as an heir. The death of Mr. Allan, in whose will his name was not mentioned, soon after relieved him of all doubt in this regard, and he committed himself at once to authorship for a support. Previously to this, however, he had published (in 1827) a small volume of poems, which soon ran through three editions, and excited high expectations of its author's future distinction in the minds of many competent judges.

That no certain augury can be drawn from a poet's earliest lispings there are instances enough to prove. Shakespeare's first poems, though brimful of vigor and youth and picturesqueness, give but a very faint promise of the directness, condensation, and overflowing moral of his maturer works. Perhaps, however, Shakespeare is hardly a case in point, his *Venus and Adonis* having been published, we believe, in his twenty-sixth year. Milton's Latin verses show tenderness, a fine eye for nature, and a delicate appreciation of classic models, but give no hint of the author of a new style in poetry. Pope's youthful pieces have all the sing-song, wholly unrelieved by the glittering malignity and eloquent irreligion of his later productions. Collins' callow namby-pamby died and gave no sign of the vigorous and original genius which he afterward displayed. We have never thought that the world lost more in the "marvelous boy," Chatterton, than a very ingenious imitator of obscure and antiquated dullness. Where he becomes original (as it is called) the interest of ingenuity ceases and he becomes stupid. Kirke White's promises were endorsed by the respectable name of Mr. Southey, but surely with no authority from Apollo. They have the merit of a tradtional piety, which, to our mind, if uttered at all, had been less objectionable in the retired closet of a diary, and in the sober raiment of prose. They do not clutch hold of the memory with the drowning pertinacity of Watts'; neither have they the interest of his occasional simple, lucky beauty. Burns, having fortunately been rescued by his humble station from the contaminating society of the "best models," wrote well and naturally from the first. Had he been unfortunate enough to have had an educated taste, we should have had a series of poems from which, as from his letters, we could sift here and there a kernel from the mass of chaff. Coleridge's youthful efforts give no promise whatever of that poetical genius which produced at once the wildest, tenderest, most original and most purely imaginative poems of modern times. Byron's *Hours of Idleness* would never find a reader except from an intrepid and indefatigable curiosity. In Wordsworth's first preludings there is but a dim foreboding of the creator of an era. From Southey's early poems, a safer augury might have been drawn. They show the patient investigator, the close student of history, and the unwearied explorer of the beauties of predecessors, but they give no assurances of a man who should add aught to [the] stock of household words, or to the rarer and more sacred delights of the fireside or the arbor. The earliest specimens of Shelley's poetic mind already, also, give tokens of that ethereal sublimation in which the spirit seems to soar above the region of words, but leaves its body, the verse, to be entombed, without hope of resurrection, in a mass of them. Cowley is generally instanced as a wonder of precocity. But his early insipidities show only a capacity for rhyming and for the metrical arrangement of certain conventional combinations of words, a capacity wholly dependent on a delicate physical organization, and an unhappy memory. An early poem is only remarkable when it displays an effort of *reason*, and the rudest verses in which we can trace some conception of the ends of poetry are worth all the miracles of smooth juvenile versification. A schoolboy, one would say, might acquire the regular seesaw of Pope merely by an association with the motion of the playground tilt.

Mr. Poe's early productions show that he could see through the verse to the spirit beneath, and that he already had a feeling that all the life and grace of the one must depend on and be modulated by the will of the other. We call them the most remarkable boyish poems that we have ever read. We know of none that can compare with them for maturity of purpose, and a nice understanding of the effects of language and meter. Such pieces are only valuable when they display what we can only express by the contradictory phrase of *innate experience*. We copy one of the shorter poems written when the author was only *fourteen!* There is a little dimness in the filling up, but the grace and symmetry of the outline are such as few poets ever attain. There is a smack of ambrosia about it.

TO HELEN

Helen, thy beauty is to me
  Like those Nicéan barks of yore,
That gently, o'er a perfumed sea,
    The weary, way-worn wanderer bore
    To his own native shore.

On desperate seas long wont to roam,
  Thy hyacinth hair, thy classic face,
Thy Naiad airs have brought me home
    To the glory that was Greece
    And the grandeur that was Rome.

> Lo! in yon brilliant window-niche
> How statue-like I see thee stand!
> The agate lamp within thy hand,
> Ah! Psyche, from the regions which
> Are Holy Land!

It is the *tendency* of the young poet that impresses us. Here is no "withering scorn," no heart "blighted" ere it has safely got into its teens, none of the drawing-room sansculottism which Byron had brought into vogue. All is limpid and serene, with a pleasant dash of the Greek Helicon in it. The melody of the whole, too, is remarkable. It is not of that kind which can be demonstrated arithmetically upon the tips of the fingers. It is of that finer sort which the inner ear alone can estimate. It seems simple, like a Greek column, because of its perfection. In a poem named *Ligeia,* under which title he intended to personify the music of nature, our boy-poet gives us the following exquisite picture:

> Ligeia! Ligeia!
>   My beautiful one,
> Whose harshest idea
>   Will to melody run,
> *Say, is it thy will*
>   *On the breezes to toss,*
> *Or, capriciously still,*
>   *Like the lone albatross,*
> *Incumbent on night,*
>   *As she on the air,*
> *To keep watch with delight*
>   *On the harmony there?*

John Neal, himself a man of genius, and whose lyre has been too long capriciously silent, appreciated the high merit of these and similar passages, and drew a proud horoscope for their author. The extracts which we shall presently make from Mr. Poe's later poems fully justify his predictions.

Mr. Poe has that indescribable something which men have agreed to call *genius*. No man could ever tell us precisely what it is, and yet there is none who is not inevitably aware of its presence and its power. Let talent writhe and contort itself as it may, it has no such magnetism. Larger of bone and sinew it may be, but the wings are wanting. Talent sticks fast to earth, and its most perfect works have still one foot of clay. Genius claims kindred with the very workings of Nature herself, so that a sunset shall seem like a quotation from Dante or Milton, and if Shakespeare be read in the very presence of the sea itself, his verses shall but seem nobler for the sublime criticism of ocean. Talent may make friends for itself, but only genius can give to its creations the divine power of winning love and veneration. Enthusiasm cannot cling to what itself is unenthusiastic, nor will he ever have disciples who has not himself impulsive zeal enough to be a disciple. Great wits are allied to madness only inasmuch as they are possessed and carried away by their demon, while talent keeps him, as Paracelsus did, securely prisoned in the pommel of its sword. To the eye of genius, the veil of the spiritual world is ever rent asunder, that it may perceive the ministers of good and evil who throng continually around it. No man of mere talent ever flung his inkstand at the devil.

When we say that Mr. Poe has genius, we do not mean to say that he has produced evidence of the highest. But to say that he possesses it at all is to say that he needs only zeal, industry, and a reverence for the trust reposed in him, to achieve the proudest triumphs and the greenest laurels. If we may believe the Longinuses and Aristotles of our newspapers, we have quite too many geniuses of the loftiest order to render a place among them at all desirable, whether for its hardness of attainment or its seclusion. The highest peak of our Parnassus is, according to these gentlemen, by far the most thickly settled portion of the country, a circumstance which must make it an uncomfortable residence for individuals of a poetical temperament, if love of solitude be, as immemorial tradition asserts, a necessary part of their idiosyncrasy. There is scarce a gentleman or lady of respectable moral character to whom these liberal dispensers of the laurel have not given a ticket to that once sacred privacy, where they may elbow Shakespeare and Milton at leisure. A transient visitor, such as a critic must necessarily be, sees these legitimate proprietors in common, parading their sacred enclosure as thick and buzzing as flies, each with "Entered according to act of Congress" labeled securely to his back. Formerly one Phœbus, a foreigner, we believe, had the monopoly of transporting all passengers thither, a service for which he provided no other conveyance than a vicious horse, named Pegasus, who could, of course, carry but one at a time, and even that but seldom, his back being a ticklish seat, and one fall proving generally enough to damp the ardor of the most zealous aspirant. The charges, however, were moderate, as the poet's pocket formerly occupied that position in regard to the rest of his outfit which is now more usually conceded to his head. But we must return from our little historical digression.

Mr. Poe has two of the prime qualities of genius, a faculty of vigorous yet minute analysis, and a wonderful fecundity of imagination. The first of these faculties is as needful to the artist in words, as a knowledge of anatomy is to the artist in colors or in stone. This enables him to conceive truly, to maintain a proper relation of parts, and to draw a correct outline, while the second groups, fills up, and colors. Both of these Mr. Poe has displayed with singular distinctness in his prose works, the last predominating in his earlier tales, and the first in his later ones. In judging of the merit of an author, and assigning him his niche among our household gods, we have a right to regard him from our own point of view, and to measure him by our own standard. But, in estimating his works, we must be governed by his own design, and, placing them by the side of his own ideal, find how much is wanting. We differ with Mr. Poe in his opinions of the objects of art. He esteems that object to be the creation of Beauty, and perhaps it is only in the definition of that word that we disagree with him. But in what we shall say of his writings we shall take his own standard as our guide. The temple of the god of song is equally accessible from every side, and there is room enough in it for all who bring offerings, or seek an oracle.

In his tales, Mr. Poe has chosen to exhibit his power chiefly in that dim region which stretches from the very utmost limits of the probable into the weird confines of superstition and unreality. He combines in a very remarkable manner two faculties which are seldom found united: a power of influencing the mind of the reader by the impalpable shadows of mystery, and a minuteness of detail which does not leave a pin or a button unnoticed. Both are, in truth, the natural results of the predominating quality of his mind, to which we have before alluded, analysis. It is this which distinguishes the artist. His mind at once reaches forward to the effect to be produced. Having resolved to bring about certain emotions in the reader, he makes all subordinate parts tend strictly to the common center. Even his mystery is mathematical to his own mind. To him x is a known quantity all along. In any picture that he paints, he understands the chemical properties of all his colors. However vague some of his figures may seem, however formless the shadows, to him the outline is as clear and distinct as that of a geometrical diagram. For this reason Mr. Poe has no sympathy with *Mysticism*. The Mystic dwells *in* the mystery, is enveloped with it; it colors all his thoughts; it affects his optic nerve especially, and the commonest things get a rainbow edging from it. Mr. Poe, on the other hand, is a spectator *ab extra*. He analyzes, he dissects, he watches.

> —with an eye serene,
> The very pulse of the machine,

for such it practically is to him, with wheels and cogs and piston rods all working to produce a certain end. It is this that makes him so good a critic. Nothing balks him, or throws him off the scent, *except now and then a prejudice*.

This analyzing tendency of his mind balances the poetical, and, by giving him the patience to be minute, enables him to throw a wonderful reality into his most unreal fancies. A monomania he paints with great power. He loves to dissect one of these cancers of the mind, and to trace all the subtle ramifications of its roots. In raising images of horror, also, he has a strange success; conveying to us sometimes by a dusky hint some terrible *doubt* which is the secret of all horror. He leaves to imagination the task of finishing the picture, a task to which only she is competent.

> For much imaginary work was there;
> Conceit deceitful, so compact, so kind,
> That for Achilles' image stood his spear
> Grasped in an armed hand; himself behind
> Was left unseen, save to the eye of mind.

We have hitherto spoken chiefly of Mr. Poe's *collected* tales, as by them he is more widely known than by those published since in various magazines, and which we hope soon to see collected. In these he has more strikingly displayed his analytic propensity.

Beside the merit of conception, Mr. Poe's writings have also that of form. His style is highly finished, graceful, and truly classical. It would be hard to find a living author who had displayed such varied powers. As an example of his style we would refer to one of his tales, *The House of Usher,* in the first volume of his *Tales of the Grotesque and Arabesque.* It has a singular charm for us, and we think that no one could read it without being strongly moved by its serene and somber beauty. Had its author written nothing else it would alone have been enough to stamp him as a man of genius, and the master of a classic style. In this tale occurs one of the most beautiful of his poems. It loses greatly by being taken out of its rich and appropriate setting, but we cannot deny ourselves the pleasure of copying it here. We know no modern poet who might not have been justly proud of it.

THE HAUNTED PALACE

In the greenest of our valleys,
   By good angels tenanted,
Once a fair and stately palace—
   Radiant palace—rear'd its head.
In the monarch Thought's dominion—
   It stood there!
Never seraph spread a pinion
   Over fabric half so fair!

Banners yellow, glorious, golden,
   On its roof did float and flow,
(This—all this—was in the olden
   Time, long ago,)
And every gentle air that dallied,
   In that sweet day,
Along the ramparts plumed and pallid,
   A winged odor went away.

Wanderers in that happy valley,
   Through two luminous windows, saw
Spirits moving musically,
   To a lute's well-tuned law,
Round about a throne where, sitting
   (Porphyrogene!)
In state his glory well befitting,
   The ruler of the realm was seen.

And all with pearl and ruby glowing
   Was the fair palace door,
Through which came flowing, flowing, flowing,
   And sparkling evermore,
A troop of Echoes, whose sweet duty
   Was but to sing,
In voices of surpassing beauty,
   The wit and wisdom of their king.

But evil things, in robes of sorrow,
    Assail'd the monarch's high estate.
(Ah, let us mourn!—for never morrow
    Shall dawn upon him desolate!)
And round about his home the glory
    That blush'd and bloom'd,
Is but a dim remember'd story
    Of the old time entomb'd.

And travelers, now, within that valley,
    Through the red-litten windows see
Vast forms, that move fantastically
    To a discordant melody,
While, like a ghasty rapid river,
    Through the pale door,
A hideous throng rush out forever,
    And laugh—but smile no more.

Was ever the wreck and desolation of a noble mind so musically sung?

A writer in the *London Foreign Quarterly Review,* who did some faint justice to Mr. Poe's poetical abilities, speaks of his resemblance to Tennyson. The resemblance, if there be any, is only in so sensitive an ear to melody as leads him sometimes into quaintness, and the germ of which may be traced in his earliest poems, published several years before the first of Tennyson's appeared.

We copy one more of Mr. Poe's poems, whose effect cannot fail of being universally appreciated.

LENORE

Ah, broken is the golden bowl!—the spirit flown forever!
Let the bell toll!—a saintly soul floats on the Stygian river.
And, Guy De Vere, hast *thou* no tear?—weep now or never more!
See, on yon drear and rigid bier, low lies thy love, Lenore!
Ah, let the burial rite be read—the funeral song be sung—

An anthem for the queenliest dead that ever died so young—
A dirge for her the doubly dead in that she died so young!

Wretches! ye loved her for her wealth and hated her for her
    pride,
And, when she fell in feeble health, ye blessed her—that she died.
How shall the ritual then be read?—the requiem how be sung
By you—by yours the evil eye—by yours the slanderous tongue,
That did to death the innocence that died and died so young?

Peccavimus; but rave not thus! and let a Sabbath song
Go up to God so solemnly the dead may feel no wrong.
The sweet Lenore hath "gone before," with Hope that flew be-
    side,
Leaving thee wild for the dear child that should have been thy
    bride—
For her the fair and *debonair* that now so lowly lies,
The life upon her yellow hair but not within her eyes—
The life still there, upon her hair—the death upon her eyes.

Avaunt!—tonight my heart is light; no dirge will I upraise,
But wait the angel on her flight with a pæan of old days!
Let *no* bell toll!—lest her sweet soul, amid its hallowed mirth,
Should catch the note as it doth float up from the damnéd earth.
To friends above, from fiends below, the indignant ghost is riven—
From Hell unto a high estate far up within the Heaven—
From moan and groan to a golden throne beside the King of
    Heaven.

How exquisite, too, is the rhythm!

    Beside his *Tales of the Grotesque and Arabesque*, and some
works unacknowledged, Mr. Poe is the author of *Arthur Gordon
Pym,* a romance, in two volumes, which has run through many
editions in London; of a system of Conchology, of a digest and
translation of Lemmonnier's *Natural History*, and has contributed
to several reviews in France, in England, and in this country. He
edited the *Southern Literary Messenger* during its novitiate, and
by his own contributions gained it most of its success and reputa-

tion. He was also, for some time, the editor of this magazine, and our readers will bear testimony to his ability in that capacity.

Mr. Poe is still in the prime of life, being about thirty-two years of age, and has probably as yet given but an earnest of his powers. As a critic, he has shown so superior an ability that we cannot but hope that he will collect his essays of this kind and give them a more durable form. They would be a very valuable contribution to our literature, and would fully justify all we have said in his praise. We could refer to many others of his poems than those we have quoted, to prove that he is the possessor of a pure and original vein. His tales and essays have equally shown him a master in prose. It is not for us to assign him his definite rank among contemporary authors, but we may be allowed to say that we know of *none* who has displayed more varied and striking abilities.

From A Fable for Critics

"There comes Emerson first, whose rich words, every one,
Are like gold nails in temples to hang trophies on,
Whose prose is grand verse, while his verse, the Lord knows,
Is some of it pr—No, 'tis not even prose;
I'm speaking of metres; some poems have welled
From those rare depths of soul that have ne'er been excelled;
They're not epics, but that doesn't matter a pin,
In creating, the only hard thing's to begin;
A grass-blade's no easier to make than an oak;
If you've once found the way, you've achieved the grand stroke;
In the worst of his poems are mines of rich matter,
But thrown in a heap with a crash and a clatter;
Now it is not one thing nor another alone
Makes a poem, but rather the general tone,
The something pervading, uniting the whole,
The before unconceived, unconceivable soul,
So that just in removing this trifle or that, you
Take away, as it were, a chief limb of the statue;

Roots, wood, bark, and leaves singly perfect may be,
But, clapt hodge-podge together, they don't make a tree.

  "But, to come bock to Emerson (whom, by the way,
I believe we left waiting),—his is, we may say,
A Greek head on right Yankee shoulders, whose range
Has Olympus for one pole, for t'other the Exchange;
He seems, to my thinking (although I'm afraid
The comparison must, long ere this, have been made),
A Plotinus-Montaigne, where the Egyptian's gold mist
And the Gascon's shrewd wit cheek-by-jowl coexist;
All admire, and yet scarcely six converts he's got
To I don't (nor they either) exactly know what;
For though he builds glorious temples, 'tis odd
He leaves never a doorway to get in a god.
'Tis refreshing to old-fashioned people like me
To meet such a primitive Pagan as he,
In whose mind all creation is duly respected
As parts of himself—just a little projected;
And who's willing to worship the stars and the sun,
A convert to—nothing but Emerson.
So perfect a balance there is in his head,
That he talks of things sometimes as if they were dead;
Life, nature, love, God, and affairs of that sort,
He looks at as merely ideas; in short,
As if they were fossils stuck round in a cabinet,
Of such vast extent that our earth's a mere dab in it;
Composed just as he is inclined to conjecture her,
Namely, one part pure earth, ninety-nine parts pure lecturer;
You are filled with delight at his clear demonstration,
Each figure, word, gesture, just fits the occasion,
With the quiet precision of science he'll sort 'em,
But you can't help suspecting the whole a *post mortem*.

● ● ●

  "There is Bryant, as quiet, as cool, and as dignified,
As a smooth, silent iceberg, that never is ignified,

Save when by reflection 'tis kindled o' nights
With a semblance of flame by the chill Northern Lights.
He may rank (Griswold says so) first bard of your nation
(There's no doubt that he stands in supreme iceolation),
Your topmost Parnassus he may set his heel on,
But no warm applauses come, peal following peal on,—
He's too smooth and too polished to hang any zeal on:
Unqualified merits, I'll grant, if you choose, he has 'em,
But he lacks the one merit of kindling enthusiasm;
If he stir you at all, it is just, on my soul,
Like being stirred up with the very North Pole.

• • •

"There is Whittier, whose swelling and vehement heart
Strains the strait-breasted drab of the Quaker apart,
And reveals the live Man, still supreme and erect,
Underneath the bemummying wrappers of sect;
There was ne'er a man born who had more of the swing
Of the true lyric bard and all that kind of thing;
And his failures arise (though he seem not to know it)
From the very same cause that has made him a poet,—
A fervor of mind which knows no separation
'Twixt simple excitement and pure inspiration,
As my Pythoness erst sometimes erred from not knowing
If 'twere I or mere wind through her tripod was blowing;
Let his mind once get head in its favorite direction
And the torrent of verse bursts the dams of reflection,
While, borne with the rush of the metre along,
The poet may chance to go right or go wrong,
Content with the whirl and delirium of song;
Then his grammar's not always correct, nor his rhymes,
And he's prone to repeat his own lyrics sometimes,
Not his best, though, for those are struck off at white-heats
When the heart in his breast like a trip-hammer beats,
And can ne'er be repeated again any more
Than they could have been carefully plotted before:

Like old what's-his-name there at the battle of Hastings
(Who, however, gave more than mere rhythmical bastings),
Our Quaker leads off metaphorical fights
For reform and whatever they call human rights,
Both singing and striking in front of the war,
And hitting his foes with the mallet of Thor;
Anne haec, one exclaims, on beholding his knocks,
Vestis filii tui, O leather-clad Fox?
Can that be thy son, in the battle's mid din,
Preaching brotherly love and then driving it in
To the brain of the tough old Goliath of sin,
With the smoothest of pebbles from Castaly's spring
Impressed on his hard moral sense with a sling?

● ● ●

"Here's Cooper, who's written six volumes to show
He's as good as a lord: well, let's grant that he's so;
If a person prefer that description of praise,
Why, a coronet's certainly cheaper than bays;
But he need take no pains to convince us he's not
(As his enemies say) the American Scott.
Choose any twelve men, and let C. read aloud
That one of his novels of which he's most proud,
And I'd lay any bet that, without ever quitting
Their box, they'd be all, to a man, for acquitting.
He has drawn you one character, though, that is new,
One wildflower he's plucked that is wet with the dew
Of this fresh Western world, and, the thing not to mince,
He has done naught but copy it ill ever since;
His Indians, with proper respect be it said,
Are just Natty Bumppo daubed over with red,
And his very Long Toms are the same useful Nat,
Rigged up in duck pants and a sou'-wester hat,
(Though once in a Coffin, a good chance was found
To have slipt the old fellow away underground).
All his other men-figures are clothes upon sticks,

The *dernière chemise* of a man in a fix,
(As a captain besieged, when his garrison's small,
Sets up caps upon poles to be seen o'er the wall);
And the women he draws from one model don't vary,
All sappy as maples and flat as a prairie.
When a character's wanted, he goes to the task
As a cooper would do in composing a cask;
He picks out the staves, of their qualities heedful,
Just hoops them together as tight as is needful,
And, if the best fortune should crown the attempt, he
Has made at the most something wooden and empty.

"Don't suppose I would underrate Cooper's abilities;
If I thought you'd do that, I should feel very ill at ease;
The men who have given to *one* character life
And objective existence are not very rife;
You may number them all, both prose-writers and singers,
Without overrunning the bounds of your fingers,
And Natty won't go to oblivion quicker
Than Adams the parson or Primrose the vicar.

"There is one thing in Cooper I like, too, and that is
That on manners he lectures his countrymen gratis,
Not precisely so either, because, for a rarity,
He is paid for his tickets in unpopularity.
Now he may overcharge his American pictures,
But you'll grant there's a good deal of truth in his strictures;
And I honor the man who is willing to sink
Half his present repute for the freedom to think,
And, when he has thought, be his cause strong or weak,
Will risk t'other half for the freedom to speak,
Caring naught for what vengeance the mob has in store,
Let that mob be the upper ten thousand or lower.

●　●　●

"There comes Poe, with his raven, like Barnaby Rudge,
Three-fifths of him genius and two-fifths sheer fudge,
Who talks like a book of iambs and pentameters,
In a way to make people of common sense damn metres,
Who has written some things quite the best of their kind,
But the heart somehow seems all squeezed out by the mind,
Who— But hey-day! What's this? Messieurs Mathews and Poe,
You mustn't fling mud-balls at Longfellow so,
Does it make a man worse that his character's such
As to make his friends love him (as you think) too much?
Why, there is not a bard at this moment alive
More willing than he that his fellows should thrive;
While you are abusing him thus, even now
He would help either one of you out of a slough;
You may say that he's smooth and all that till you're hoarse,
But remember that elegance also is force;
After polishing granite as much as you will,
The heart keeps its tough old persistency still;
Deduct all you can, *that* still keeps you at bay;
Why, he'll live till men weary of Collins and Gray.
I'm not over-fond of Greek metres in English,
To me rhyme's a gain, so it be not too jinglish,
And your modern hexameter verses are no more
Like Greek ones than sleek Mr. Pope is like Homer;
As the roar of the sea to the coo of a pigeon is,
So, compared to your moderns, sounds old Melesigenes;
I may be too partial, the reason, perhaps, o't is
That I've heard the old blind man recite his own rhapsodies,
And my ear with that music impregnate may be,
Like the poor exiled shell with the soul of the sea,
Or as one can't bear Strauss when his nature is cloven
To its deeps within deeps by the stroke of Beethoven;
But, set that aside, and 'tis truth that I speak,
Had Theocritus written in English, not Greek,
I believe that his exquisite sense would scarce change a line
In that rare, tender, virgin-like pastoral Evangeline.

That's not ancient nor modern, its place is apart
Where time has no sway, in the realm of pure Art,
'Tis a shrine of retreat from Earth's hubbub and strife
As quiet and chaste as the author's own life.

• • •

"There is Lowell, who's striving Parnassus to climb
With a whole bale of *isms* tied together with rhyme,
He might get on alone, spite of brambles and boulders,
But he can't with that bundle he has on his shoulders,
The top of the hill he will ne'er come nigh reaching
Till he learns the distinction 'twix singing and preaching;
His lyre has some chords that would ring pretty well,
But he'd rather by half make a drum of the shell,
And rattle away till he's old as Methusalem,
At the head of a march to the last new Jerusalem."

Walt Whitman

(1819–1892)

Walt Whitman is ranked as a towering figure in American literature for the intrinsic greatness of his best poetry and for his importance in changing the direction of American poetry and American thought.

Viewed in many quarters at first as "objectionable," "obscene," and "egocentric," Whitman eventually gained widespread acceptance as one of the foremost poets in the English-speaking world. His lofty position today is reflected in the praise of important critics and authorities on American literature and by the unreserved homage of other significant poets.

Whitman's historical significance is far-reaching. He widened the subject matter of poetry by treating material heretofore considered beyond polite discussion; he made blank verse the dominant medium in American poetry through his effective use of his particular patterns of expression; and he extended the vocabulary of poetry by using words formerly considered beyond the pale of consideration. His influence has been so great that he actually created a new school of poetry.

Whitman, like most other poets, attempted to explain in prose his philosophy of poetry, his thoughts on composition, and his critical theory in general. Although he worked diligently in this area, he did not produce anything of great import. His critical writings are interesting primarily for the reflection which they cast on his poety.

Whitman, who was born on Long Island, engaged in a rather wide variety of vocations before falling into the period of invalidism that eventually led to his death in Camden, New Jersey.

*He served as office boy, school teacher, printer, carpenter, news-
paper editor, government clerk, and volunteer hospital orderly.
Unmarried and with few family attachments, he was relatively
free to be a philosopher and "singer of America's praises." This he
accomplished, despite a lack of formal erudition, by capitalizing
on powers of observation, reflection, and mysticism such as few
men have ever possessed.*

*The passage below is taken from the preface to his great
volume* Leaves of Grass *(1855). The ideas expressed herein are
well worth a close examination as a record of the thoughts of a
great poet on the subject of poetry. They should also be seen as
an appealing revelation of the relationship of an unusual personality to the world wherein he "lived, and moved, and had his
being."*

From the Preface to *Leaves of Grass* [1855]

America does not repel the past or what it has produced under
its forms or amid other politics or the idea of castes or the old
religions . . . . accepts the lesson with calmness . . . is not so impatient as has been supposed that the slough still sticks to
opinions and manners and literature while the life which served
its requirements has passed into the new life of the new forms . . .
perceives that the corpse is slowly borne from the eating and
sleeping rooms of the house . . . perceives that it waits a little
while in the door . . . that it was fittest for its days . . . that its
action has descended to the stalwart and wellshaped heir who
approaches . . . and that he shall be fittest for his days.

The Americans of all nations at any time upon the earth have
probably the fullest poetical nature. The United States themselves are essentially the greatest poem. In the history of the earth
hitherto the largest and most stirring appear tame and orderly to
their ampler largeness and stir. Here at last is something in the
doings of man that corresponds with the broadcast doings of the
day and night. Here is not merely a nation but a teeming nation
of nations. Here is action untied from strings necessarily blind

to particulars and details magnificently moving in vast masses. Here is the hospitality which forever indicates heroes. . . . Here are the roughs and beards and space and ruggedness and non-chalance that the soul loves. Here the performance disdaining the trivial unapproached in the tremendous audacity of its crowds and groupings and the push of its perspective spreads with crampless and flowing breadth and showers its prolific and splendid extravagance. One sees it must indeed own the riches of the summer and winter, and need never be bankrupt while corn grows from the ground or the orchards drop apples or the bays contain fish or men beget children upon women.

Other states indicate themselves in their deputies . . . . but the genius of the United States is not best or most in its executives or legislatures, nor in its ambassadors or authors or colleges or churches or parlors, nor even in its newspapers or inventors . . . but always most in the common people. Their manners speech dress friendships—the freshness and candor of their physiognomy —the picturesque looseness of their carriage . . . their deathless attachment to freedom—their aversion to anything indecorous or soft or mean—the practical acknowledgment of the citizens of one state by the citizens of all other states—the fierceness of their roused resentment—their curiosity and welcome of novelty —their self-esteem and wonderful sympathy—their susceptibility to a slight—the air they have of persons who never knew how it felt to stand in the presence of superiors—the fluency of their speech—their delight in music, the sure symptom of manly tender-ness and native elegance of soul . . . their good temper and openhandedness—the terrible significance of their elections—the President's taking off his hat to them not they to him—these too are unrhymed poetry. It awaits the gigantic and generous treatment worthy of it.

●   ●   ●

Of all nations the United States with veins full of poetical stuff most need poets and will doubtless have the greatest and use them the greatest. Their Presidents shall not be their common referee so much as their poets shall. Of all mankind the great poet is the equable man. Not in him but off from him things are grotesque or eccentric or fail of their sanity. Nothing out of its place is good and nothing in its place is bad. He bestows on every object or quality its fit proportions neither more nor less. He is the arbiter of the diverse and he is the key. He is the equalizer of his age and land . . . . he supplies what wants supplying and checks what wants checking. If peace is the routine out of him speaks the spirit of peace, large, rich, thrifty, building vast and populous cities, encouraging agriculture and the arts and commerce—lighting the study of man, the soul, immortality—federal, state or municipal government, marriage, health, freetrade, intertravel by land and sea . . . . nothing too close, nothing too far off . . . the stars not too far off. In war he is the most deadly force of the war. Who recruits him recruits horse and foot . . . he fetches parks of artillery the best that engineer ever knew. If the time becomes slothful and heavy he knows how to arouse it . . . he can make every word he speaks draw blood. Whatever stagnates in the flat of custom or obedience or legislation he never stagnates. Obedience does not master him, he masters it. High up out of reach he stands turning a concentrated light . . . he turns the pivot with his finger . . . he baffles the swiftest runners as he stands and easily overtakes and envelops them. The time straying toward infidelity and confections and persiflage he withholds by his steady faith . . . he spreads out his dishes . . . he offers the sweet firmfibered meat that grows men and women. His brain is the ultimate brain. He is no arguer . . . he is judgment.

• • •

The known universe has one complete lover and that is the greatest poet. He consumes an eternal passion and is indifferent which chance happens and which possible contingency of fortune or misfortune and persuades daily and hourly his delicious pay. What balks or breaks others is fuel for his burning progress to contact and amorous joy. Other proportions of the reception of

pleasure dwindle to nothing to his proportions. All expected
from heaven or from the highest he is rapport with in the sight
of the daybreak or a scene of the winter woods or the presence of
children playing or with his arm round the neck of a man or
woman. His love above all love has leisure and expanse . . . . he
leaves room ahead of himself. He is no irresolute or suspicious
lover . . . he is sure . . . he scorns intervals. His experience and
the showers and thrills are not for nothing. Nothing can jar him
. . . . suffering and darkness cannot—death and fear cannot. To
him complaint and jealousy and envy are corpses buried and
rotten in the earth . . . . he saw them buried. The sea is not
surer of the shore or the shore of the sea than he is of the fruition
of his love and of all perfection and beauty.

The fruition of beauty is no chance of hit or miss . . . it is
inevitable as life . . . . it is exact and plumb as gravitation. From
the eyesight proceeds another eyesight and from the hearing proceeds another hearing and from the voice proceeds another voice
eternally curious of the harmony of things with man. To these
respond perfections not only in the committees that were supposed to stand for the rest but in the rest themselves just the
same. These understand the law of perfection in masses and
floods . . . that its finish is to each for itself and onward from
itself . . . that it is profuse and impartial . . . that there is not
a minute of the light or dark nor an acre of the earth or sea without it—nor any direction of the sky nor any trade or employment
nor any turn of events. This is the reason that about the proper
expression of beauty there is precision and balance . . . one part
does not need to be thrust above another. The best singer is not
the one who has the most lithe and powerful organ . . . the
pleasure of poems is not in them that take the handsomest
measure and similes and sound.

Without effort and without exposing in the least how it is done
the greatest poet brings the spirit of any or all events and passions and scenes and persons some more and some less to bear on
your individual character as you hear or read. To do this well is
to compete with the laws that pursue and follow time. What is

the purpose must surely be there and the clue of it must be there
. . . . and the faintest indication is the indication of the best and
then becomes the clearest indication. Past and present and future
are not disjoined but joined. The greatest poet forms the con-
sistence of what is to be from what has been and is. He drags
the dead out of their coffins and stands them again on their feet
. . . . he says to the past, Rise and walk before me that I may
realize you. He learns the lesson . . . . he places himself where
the future becomes present. The greatest poet does not only
dazzle his rays over character and scenes and passions . . . he
finally ascends and finishes all . . . he exhibits the pinnacles
that no man can tell what they are for or what is beyond . . . .
he glows a moment on the extremest verge. He is most wonderful
in his last half-hidden smile or frown . . . by that flash of the
moment of parting the one that sees it shall be encouraged or
terrified afterwards for many years. The greatest poet does not
moralize or make applications of morals . . . he knows the soul.
The soul has that measureless pride which consists in never ac-
knowledging any lessons but its own. But it has sympathy as
measureless as its pride and the one balances the other and
neither can stretch too far while it stretches in company with the
other. The inmost secrets of art sleep with the twain. The greatest
poet has lain close betwixt both and they are vital in his style and
thoughts.

The art of art, the glory of expression and the sunshine of the
light of letters is simplicity. Nothing is better than simplicity
. . . . nothing can make up for excess or for the lack of definite-
ness. To carry on the heave of impulse and pierce intellectual
depths and give all subjects their articulations are powers neither
common nor very uncommon. But to speak in literature with the
perfect rectitude and insouciance of the movements of animals
and the unimpeachableness of the sentiment of trees in the woods
and grass by the roadside is the flawless triumph of art. If you
have looked on him who has achieved it you have looked on one
of the masters of the artists of all nations and times. You shall
not contemplate the flight of the graygull over the bay or the

mettlesome action of the blood horse or the tall leaning of sun-
flowers on their stalk or the appearance of the sun journeying
through heaven or the appearance of the moon afterward with
any more satisfaction than you shall contemplate him. The
greatest poet has less a marked style and is more the channel of
thoughts and things without increase or diminution, and is the
free channel of himself. He swears to his art, I will not be meddle-
some, I will not have in my writing any elegance or effect or
originality to hang in the way between me and the rest like curtains. I will have nothing hang in the way, not the richest
curtains. What I tell I tell for precisely what it is. Let who may
exalt or startle or fascinate or sooth I will have purposes as health
or heat or snow has and be as regardless of observation. What I
experience or portray shall go from my composition without a
shred of my composition. You shall stand by my side and look in
the mirror with me.

● ● ●

The great poets are also to be known by the absence in them of
tricks and by the justification of perfect personal candor. Then
folks echo a new cheap joy and a divine voice leaping from their
brains: How beautiful is candor! All faults may be forgiven of
him who has perfect candor. Henceforth let no man of us lie, for
we have seen that openness wins the inner and outer world and
that there is no single exception, and that never since our earth
gathered itself in a mass have deceit or subterfuge or prevarica-
tion attracted its smallest particle or the faintest tinge of a shade—
and that through the enveloping wealth and rank of a state or the
whole republic of states a sneak or sly person shall be discovered
and despised . . . . and that the soul has never been once fooled
and never can be fooled . . . . and thrift without the loving nod of
the soul is only a foetid puff . . . . and there never grew up in any
of the continents of the globe nor upon any planet or satellite or
star, nor upon the asteroids, nor in any part of ethereal space, nor
in the midst of density, nor under the fluid wet of the sea, nor in
that condition which precedes the birth of babes, nor at any time

during the changes of life, nor in that condition that follows what we term death, nor in any stretch of abeyance or action afterward of vitality, nor in any process of formation or reformation anywhere, a being whose instinct hated the truth.

• • •

The poems distilled from other poems will probably pass away. The coward will surely pass away. The expectation of the vital and great can only be satisfied by the demeanor of the vital and great. The swarms of the polished deprecating and reflectors and the polite float off and leave no remembrance. America prepares with composure and goodwill for the visitors that have sent word. It is not intellect that is to be their warrant and welcome. The talented, the artist, the ingenious, the editor, the statesman, the erudite . . they are not unappreciated . . they fall in their place and do their work. The soul of the nation also does its work. No disguise can pass on it . . no disguise can conceal from it. It rejects none, it permits all. Only toward as good as itself and toward the like of itself will it advance half-way. An individual is as superb as a nation when he has the qualities which make a superb nation. The soul of the largest and wealthiest and proudest nation may well go half-way to meet that of its poets. The signs are effectual. There is no fear of mistake. If the one is true the other is true. The proof of a poet is that his country absorbs him as affectionately as he has absorbed it.

Edmund Clarence Stedman

(1833–1908)

Edmund Clarence Stedman belongs to that tradition of critics who, although neither brilliantly original nor unusually startling, nonetheless obtain the respect of a large segment of the discerning reading public. They are the critics who perform their tasks on a level clearly superior to that of most others but can lay only a small claim to any great stature.

Stedman relied on a wide reading, a carefully developed taste, and a judicious sense of appraisal to make his conclusions. Authoritatively knowledgeable in the important critical writings of the Western world, he leaned more toward Coleridge than toward any other figure. The Coleridgean influence is especially discernible in Stedman's endorsement of imagination as a dominant element in poetry. He also drew heavily, however, upon Classical critics, especially Aristotle and Horace, as is evident in his Aristotelian emphasis on form and his Horatian approval of the necessity of literature to "delight."

Though one can find little new in Stedman, he must still concede Stedman's demonstrated ability to identify the literary currents and trends of his time. His appraisals of contemporary and past personalities, such as Poe and Whitman, exhibit a deliberate thought and a thorough and careful evaluation. His Poets of America (1885) is historically important for its balanced and valid judgments on poets to his day.

Also of significance is Stedman's perceptiveness in discerning the true quality of American literature. Unlike most other critics of his time, he was able to see the greatness in the literature of his homeland. He was not a mere flag waver attempting to find quality where it did not exist. Rather, he was a competent evaluator who was able to rise above the prevailing prejudice against American literary achievement.

In his definitions, Stedman discloses lucidly the nature of his views. He defines poetry as "rhythmical, imaginative language, expressing the invention, taste, thought, passion, and insight of the human soul." Criticism he defines as "the art and practice of declaring in what degree any work, character or action conforms to the Right." Conversely, the office of criticism is, of course, to locate and identify that which is wrong—i.e., where and to what degree a work fails to "conform to the Right."

A poet of unusual talent, Stedman was born in Hartford, Connecticut. After study at Yale and a series of small positions, he served as war correspondent for the New York World *(1861–63), moving thereafter into the world of business as a stock broker and banker. Throughout all, he continued to study independently and to sharpen his critical abilities by publishing books and essays on other literary personages.*

The essay below is one of Stedman's most widely read works.

What Is Poetry? [1892]

These lectures, as I have intimated, are purposely direct of statement, and even elementary. From my point of view this does not of itself imply a lack of respect for the intelligence of the listener. The most advanced star-gazer holds to his mathematics; while, as to poetry, enthusiasts find it easier to build fine sentences than to make clear to others, if to themselves, the nature of that which affects them so inspiringly. I trust that you are willing, in place of the charm of style and the jest and epigram of discourses for entertainment, to accept a search for the very stuff whereof the Muse fashions her transubstantial garments—to discover what plant or moth supplies the sheeny fibre; in what heat, what light, the iridescent fabric is dyed and spun and woven.

It has occurred to me—I think it may not seem amiss to you—

that this eager modern time, when the world has turned critic, this curious evening of the century, when the hum of readers and the mists of thought go up from every village; when poetry is both read and written, whether well or ill, more generally than ever before; and when clubs are formed for its study and enjoyment, where commentators urban or provincial, masters and mistresses of analytics, devote nights to the elucidation of a single verse or phrase—it has occurred to me that this is an opportune time for the old questions, so often received as if it were a jet of cold water upon steam or the stroke of midnight at a masquerade—an apt time to ask ourselves, What, then, *is* poetry, after all? What are the elements beneath its emotion and intellectual delight? Let us have the primer itself. For, if such a primer be not constructible, if it be wholly missing or disdained, you may feel and enjoy a poem, but you will hardly be consistent in your discourse upon it, and this whether you concern yourself with Browning, or Meredith, or Ibsen,—as is now the mode,—or with the masterworks of any period.

Nevertheless, we too must begin our answer to the question, What is poetry? by declaring that the essential *spirit* of poetry is indefinable. It is something which is perceived and felt through a reciprocal faculty shared by human beings in various degrees. The range of these degrees is as wide as that between the boor and the sensitive adept—between the racial Celibans and Prosperos. The poetic spirit is absolute and primal, acknowledged but not reducible, and therefore we postulate it as an axiom of nature and sensation.

To state this otherwise: it is true that the poetic essence always has been a force, an energy, both subtile and compulsive; a primal force, like that energy the discovery of whose unities is the grand physical achievement of this century. The shapes which it informs are Protean, and have a seeming elusiveness. Still, even Proteus, as Vergil tells us, is capturable. Force, through its vehicle of light, becomes fixed within the substance of our planet; in the carbon of the fern, the tree, the lump of coal, the diamond. The poetic spirit becomes concrete through utterance, in that poetry which enters literature; that is, in the concrete utterances of age after age. Nothing of this is durably preserved but that which possesses the crystalline gift of receiving and giving out light indefinitely, yet losing naught from its reservoir. Poetry is the diamond of these concretions. It gives out light of its own, but anticipates also the light of after-times, and refracts it with sympathetic splendors.

With this uttered poetry, then, we are at present concerned. Whether sung, spoken, or written, it is still the most vital form of human expression. One who essays to analyze its constituents is an explorer undertaking a quest in which many have failed. Doubtless he too may fail, but he sets forth in the simplicity of a good knight who does not fear his fate too much, whether his desert be great or small.

In this mood seeking a definition of that poetic utterance which is or may become of record,—a definition both defensible and inclusive, yet compressed into a single phrase,—I have put together the following statement:

Poetry is rhythmical, imaginative language, expressing the invention, taste, thought, passion, and insight, of the human soul.

First of all, and as a corollary,—a resultant from the factors of imaginative invention and expression,—we infer that poetry is, in common with the other art products, a creation, of which the poet is the creator, the maker. *Expression* is the avowed function of all the arts, their excuse for being; out of the need for it, art in the rude and primitive forms has ever sprung. No work of art has real import, none endures, unless the maker has something to say—some thought which he must express imaginatively, whether to the eye in stone or on canvas, or to the ear in music or artistic speech; this thought, the imaginative conception moving him to utterance, being his creative idea—his art-ideal. This simple truth, persistently befogged by the rhetoric of those who do not "see clear and think straight" and who always underrate the strength and beauty of an elementary fact is the last to be realized by commonplace mechanicians. They go through the process of making pictures or verses without the slightest mis-

sion—really with nothing to say or reveal. They mistake the desire
to beget for the begetting power. Their mimes and puppets have
everything but souls. Now, the imaginative work of a true artist,
conveying his own ideal, is creative because it is the expression,
the new embodiment, of his particular nature, the materialization
of something which renders him a congener, even a part, of the
universal soul—that divinity whose eternal function it is to create.
The expressive artist is to this extent indeed fashioned after
his Maker. He can even declare, in the words of Beddoes, who
used them, however, to reveal his surprising glimpses of evolu-
tion:—

> "I have a bit of *Fiat* in my soul,
> And can myself create my little world."

At the same time, the quality of the poet's creation, be it lyrical,
narrative, or dramatic, is in a sense that of revelation. He cannot
invent forms and methods and symbols out of keeping with
what we term the nature of things; such inventions, if possible,
would be monstrous, baleful, not to be endured. But he utters,
reveals, and interprets what he sees with that inward vision, that
second sight, the prophetic gift of certain personages,—that which
I mean by "insight," and through which the poet is thought to be
inspired. This vision penetrates what Plato conceived to be the
quintessence of nature, what Wordsworth, in his very highest
mood, declares that we perceive only when

> "we are laid asleep
> In body, and become a living soul:
> While with an eye made quiet by the power
> Of harmony, and the deep power of joy,
> We see into the life of things."

The creative insight, according to its degree, is allied with, if
not the source of, the mysterious endowment named genius,
which humdrum intellects have sought to disallow, claiming that
it lies chiefly in one of its frequent attributes,—industry,—but
which the wisdom of generations has indubitably recognized.

The antique and idealistic notion of this gift is given in "Ion": "A poet . . . is unable to compose poetry until he becomes inspired and is out of his sober senses, and his imagination is no longer under his control; for he does not compose by art, but through a divine power." The modern and scientific rendering is that of the exact investigator, Hartmann, who traces this power of genius to its inmost cell, and classifies it as the spontaneous, involuntary force of the untrammelled soul,—in precise terms, "the activity and efflux of the Intellect freed from the domination of the Conscious Will." Whichever statement you accept,—and I see no reason why the two are not perfectly concordant,—here is the apparently superhuman gift which drew from Sophocles that cry of wonder, "Aeschylus does what is right without knowing it."

As an outcome of genius producing the semblance of what its insight discovers, poetry aims to convey beauty and truth in their absolute simplicity of kind, but limitless variety of guise and adaptation. The poet's vision of these is shared to some extent by all of us, else his appeal would not be universal. But to *his* inborn taste and wisdom is given the power of coadequate expression. Taste has been vilely mistaken for a sentiment, and disgust with its abuse may have incited the Wordsworthians and others to disqualify it. They limited their own range by so doing. The world forgives most sins more readily than those against beauty. There was something ridiculous, if heroic, in the supercilious attitude of our transcendentalists, not only putting themselves against the laity, but opposing the whole body of their fellow seers and artists, whose solace for all labors ever has been the favor of their beloved mistress Beauty,—the inspirer of creative taste.

The truth is that taste, however responsive to cultivation, is inborn,—as spontaneous as insight, and, indeed, with an insight of its own. Schlegel's alertness with respect to the aesthetic moved him to define even genius as "the almost unconscious choice of the highest degree of excellence, and, consequently," he added, "it is taste in its highest activity." Profound thinkers, lofty and unselfish natures, may flourish without taste: if so, they miss a sense, nor only one that is physical,—something else is lacking, if the body be the symbol of the soul. I would not go so far as to say of one born, for instance, without ear for melody, that there will be "no music in his soul" when that is disembodied. It is finer to believe that

> "whilst this muddy vesture of decay
>   Doth grossly close it in"

such a one cannot hear it; that

> "The soul, with nobler resolutions deck'd,
>   The body stooping, does herself erect."

But taste, whether in or out of the body, is a faculty for want of which many ambitious thinkers have in the end failed as poets. It is a sense, however, the functions of which are very readily assumed and mechanically imitated. At periods when what are called false and artificial standards have prevailed, as in French and English letters from 1675 to 1790, the word "taste" has been on every one's lips, and the true discernment of beauty has been supposed to be supreme, when in fact merely the crown and sceptre of taste have been set up and its mantle stuffed with straw. At this very time art is suffering everywhere from an immense variety of standards and models, and our taste, in spite of the diverse and soulless yet attractive productions of the studio and the closet, is that of an interregnum.

Assuming that the artist's conceptions are spontaneous and imaginative, their working out brings into play the conscious intellect. He gives us thought, building up masterpieces from the germinal hint or motive: his wisdom is of so pure a type that through it the poet and the philosopher, in their ultimate and possible development, seem united. It is the exclusive presentation of thought and truth that makes poetry didactical, and hence untrue in the artistic sense. For taste has been finely declared to be "the artistic ethics of the soul," and it is only through a just balance of all the elements in question that poetry rises above ordinary and universal human speech and becomes a veritable art.

Under the conditions of these reciprocal elements, the poet's nature, "all touch, all eye, all ear," exalted to a creative pitch, becomes *emotional*. Feeling is the excitant of genuine poetry. The Miltonic canon, requiring the sensuous beauty which taste alone insures, demands, last of all, as if laying stress upon its indispensability, that poetry should be passionate. It is the impassioned spirit that awakes the imagination, whose taste becomes alert, that hears whisperings which others do not hear,—which it does not itself hear in calmer periods,—that breaks into lyric fervor and melody, and that arouses kindred spirits with recital of its brave imaginings. Feeling of any kind is the touch upon the poet's electric keyboard; the *passio vera* of his more intense moods furnishes the impulse and the power for effective speech. His emotion instinctively acquires the tone and diction fitted to its best expression. Even the passion of a hateful nature is not without a certain distinction. Flame is magnificent, though it feed upon the homes of men.

Submitting these views with respect to a scientific definition of poetry, I ask your attention to a brief consideration of its bounds and liberties, as compared with those of music and the respective arts of design.

The specific province, by limitation, of Sculpture, the art consecrated to the antique precision of repose, is to express ideals of form *arrested as to movement and time*. Its beauteous or heroic attitudes are caught at the one fit moment, and forever transfixed in rigid stone or wood or metal. Painting has an additional limitation; it gives only the *similitude* of form in all its dimensions, and only from one point of a beholder's view. To offset this, the range of the painter is marvellously broadened by the truth of perspective, the magic and vital potency of color, the tremulous life of atmosphere, and the infinite gradations and contrasts of light and shade. The mystical warmth and force of the Christian humanities are radiant in this enrapturing art. Yet its office is to capture the one ideal moment, the lifelong desire of Faust, and to force it to obey the mandate:—

"Ah, still delay—thou art so fair!"

Such are the arts addressed to the eye alone, both of them lending their service to the earliest, the latest, the most various, of all material constructions—Architecture, whose pediments and roofs and walls originate in our bodily necessities, whose pinnacles typify our worship and aspiration, and which so soon becomes the beneficiary and the incasement of its decorative allies. None of the three can directly express time or movement, but there is practically no limit to their voiceless representation of space and multitude.

But movement in time is a special function of Music, that heavenly maid, never so young as now, and still the sovereign of the passions, reaching and rousing the soul through sound-vibrations perpetually changing as they flow. To this it adds the sympathetic force of harmonic counterpoint. Its range, then, is freer than that of the plastic and structural arts, by this element of progressive change. Under its spell, thrilling with the sensations which it can excite, and which really are immanent in our own nature, considering moreover the superb mathematics of its harmony, and again that it has been the last in development of all these arts, we question whether it is not only superior to them but even to that one to which these lectures are devoted. All feel, at least, the force of Poe's avowal that music and poetry at their highest must go together, because "in music the soul most nearly attains the great end for which it struggles,—supernal beauty." And so old John Davies, in praise of music,—

"The motion which the ninefold sacred quire
    Of angels make: the bliss of all the blest,
  Which (next the Highest) most fills the highest desire."

Schopenhauer thought that the musician, because there is no

sound in nature fit to give him more than a suggestion for a model, "approaches the original sources of existence more closely than all other artists, nay, even than Nature herself." Herbert Spencer has suggested that music may take rank as the highest of the fine arts, as the chief medium of sympathy, enabling us to partake the feeling which excites it, and "as an aid to the achievement of that higher happiness which it indistinctly shadows forth." And in truth, if the intercourse of a higher existence is to be effected through sound-vibrations rather than through the swifter light-waves, or by means of aught save the absolute celestial insight, one may fondly conceive music to be the language of the earth-freed, as of those imagined seraphim with whom feeling *is* "deeper than all thought."

Consider, on the other hand, how feeling governs the simple child, "that lightly draws its breath," while thought begins its office as the child grows in strength and knowledge, and it is a fair inference that thought is the higher attribute, and that the suggestion of emotion by music is a less vital art than that of intellectual speech. The dumb brutes partake far more of man's emotion than of his mental intelligence. Neither is music—despite our latter-day theorists who defy the argument of Lessing's[1] Laocoön and would make one art usurp the province of another, and despite its power as an indirect incentive to thought by rousing the emotions—a vehicle for the conveyance of precise and varied ideas. The clearer the idea, the more exact the language which utters and interprets it. This, then, is the obvious limitation of music: it can traverse a range of feeling that may govern the tone of the hearer's contemplations, it can "fill all the stops of life with tuneful breath" and prolong their harmonic intervals indefinitely, but the domain of absolute *thought*, while richer and more imperial for its excitation, is not mastered by it. Of that realm music can make no exact chart.

Thus far, we have no art without its special office, and none

[1] Gotthold Lessing (1729–1781), German dramatist and critic. The *Laocoön* was published in 1766.

that is not wanting in some capacity displayed by one or more of the rest. Each goes upon its appointed way. Now comes poetry,—rhythmical, creative language, compact of beauty, imagination, passion, truth,—in no wise related, like the plastic arts, to material substance; less able than its associate, music, to move the soul with those dying falls of sound that increase and lessen thought and the power to harbor it; almost a voiceless spirit of invention, working without hands, yet the more subtile, potent, inclusive, for this evasive ideality, and for creations that are impalpable except through the arbitrary and non-essential symbols by which it now addresses itself to the educated eye.

Permit me to select, almost at random, from Keats and Tennyson, ready illustrations of the bounds and capabilities of the various arts—passages necessarily familiar, since they *are* from Keats and Tennyson, but chosen from those masters because, of all English poets since Spenser, they are most given to picture-making, to the craft that is, as we say, artistic, picturesque. A stanza from the "Ode on a Grecian Urn" describes, and rivals in verse, the ravishing power of a bit of sculpture to perpetuate arrested form and attitude—yes, even the suggestion of arrested music:—

> "Heard melodies are sweet, but those unheard
>   Are sweeter; therefore, ye soft pipes, play on—
> Not to the sensual ear, but, more endear'd,
>   Pipe to the spirit ditties of no tone.
> Fair youth, beneath the trees, thou canst not leave
>   Thy song, nor ever can those trees be bare;
> Bold lover, never, never canst thou kiss,
>   Though winning near the goal; yet, do not grieve—
> She cannot fade, though thou hast not thy bliss;
>   Forever wilt thou love, and she be fair."

These undying lines not only define by words the power and limits of the sculptor, but are almost a matchless example of the farthest encroachment poetry can make upon sculpture's own province.[2] What it cannot do is to combine the details of the carving so as to produce them to the mind, as sculpture does to the eye, at a single instant of time. It lingers exquisitely upon each in succession. Progressive time is required for its inclusion of the effects of a Grecian frieze or scroll. Now, take from Tennyson's lovely but lighter poem, "The Day-Dream,"—a lyrical idyl at the acme of melodious and fanciful picture-making,—a stanza which seems to match with a certain roundness and color the transfixing effect of the painter's handiwork. It portrays a group entranced by the spell that has doomed to a hundred years of abeyance and motionlessness the life of the king's palace and the Sleeping Beauty. In the poems of Keats and Tennyson, as I say, artists find their sculptures and paintings already designed for them, so that these poets are the easiest of all to illustrate with some measure of adequacy. The theme of the following lines, rendered by a painter, would show the whole group and scene at a flash of the eye; poetry cannot do this, yet, aided by its moving panorama, the listener has painted all in his mind when the last word is uttered:—

> "More like a picture seemeth all
> Than those old portraits of old kings,
>   That watch the sleepers from the wall.
>
> "Here sits the butler with a flask
>   Between his knees, half-drain'd; and there
> The wrinkled steward at his task,
>   The maid-of-honor blooming fair;
> The page has caught her hand in his:
>   Her lips are sever'd as to speak:
> His own are pouted to a kiss:
>   The blush is fix'd upon her cheek."

[2] Since the first appearance of this lecture I have seen a finely penetrative essay by Mr. J. W. Comyns Carr (*The New Quarterly Magazine*, October, 1875), in which this same Ode is quoted to illustrate the ideal calm sought for by "The Artistic Spirit in Modern Poetry." As no better example can be found, in conveyance of the poetic and the plastic methods respectively, I do not hesitate to retain it. [Stedman's note]

It is to be noted, as we read, that Tennyson's personages, and those of Keats as well, are mostly conventional figures, as characterless as those on a piece of tapestry. The genius of neither poet is preferably dramatic: they do not get at individuality by dramatic insight like Shakespeare, nor by monodramatic soliloquy and analysis, like the strenuous Browning. Their dramas are for the most part masques containing *eidullia* (little pictures); though who can doubt that Keats, had he lived, would have developed the highest dramatic power? Remember what the less sensuous, more lyrical Shelley achieved in "The Cenci," when only four years beyond the age at which Keats imagined his "gold Hyperion, lovelorn Porphyro." But, to resume, see what poetry, in addition to the foregoing counterfeit of the painter's ocular presentment, can bring about in its own field through its faculty of *movement in time*—a power entirely wanting to the arts which it has just mimicked. Note how it breaks the spell of transfixed attitude, of breathless color and suspended action; how it lets loose the torrents of Life at the instant of the "fated fairy prince's" experimental kiss:—

> "A touch, a kiss! the charm was snapt.
>   There rose a noise of striking clocks,
> And feet that ran, and doors that clapt,
>   And barking dogs, and crowing cocks;
>
> A fuller light illumined all,
>   A breeze thro' all the garden swept,
> A sudden hubbub shook the hall,
>   And sixty feet the fountain leapt.
>
> • • •
>
> The maid and page renew'd their strife,
>   The palace bang'd, and buzz'd, and clackt,
> And all the long-pent stream of life
>   Dash'd downward in a cataract.

That is the stream which the painter has no art to undam. Only by a succession of pictures can he suggest its motion or follow the romance to its sequel; and that he can do even this with some fitness in the case of a Tennysonian ballad is because the laureate, as we see, counterfeits the painter's own method more artistically than other idyllists of rank in our time. If art is the fit and beautiful conformation of matter infused with the spirit of man, it must indeed have life. The most nimble, ardent, varied transfer of the vital spirit is by means of language, and of all language that of the poet is the most alive and expressive. Observe, again, that in what are called art circles—Arcadian groups of those devoted to art and letters—the imaginative writers are apt to interest themselves far more with respect to the plastic arts than the sculptors and painters with respect to poetry and romance; and well they may, since the poet enriches his work by using all artistic effects, while nothing is more dangerous to a painter, for example, than that he should give his picture a literary cast, as the phrase is, and make it too closely tell a story or rehearse a poem. This of itself tends to confirm Lessing's apothegm that "the poet is as far beyond the painter as life is better than a picture."

•   •   •

The conquests of poetry, in fine, are those of pure intelligence, and of emotion that is unfettered. Like the higher mathematics, it is not dependent on diagrams, for the mind to which it appeals is a responsive draughtsman of lines finer and more complex than any known to brush or graver. It creates no beauty of form beyond the accidental symbols grouped in script and print, none of light and color, while the ear is less touched by it than by the melodies or harmonies of music; for its melody is that of flexible speech, and it knows not counterpoint, but must resort to the value of successive strains. Yet we say that it has form and outline of its own, an architecture of its own, its own warmth and color, and, like music, life, and withal no little of music's vocal charm, in that through words it idealizes these "sweet influences," and is chartered to convey them all to the inward sight, the spiritual hearing, of the citadeled soul, with so apt suggestion that the poet's fellow-mortals, of like passions and perceptions with himself, see and hear and feel with much of his distinct individuality. Its vibrations excite the reflex action that creates in the mind of the receiver a vision corresponding to the imagination of the poet. Here is its specific eminence: it enables common mortals to think as the poet thinks, to use his wings, move through space and time, and out of space and time, untrammelled as the soul itself; it can feel, moan, weep, laugh, be eloquent, love, hate, aspire, for all—and with its maker; can reflect, and know, and ever seek for knowledge; can portray all times and seasons, and describe, express, interpret, the hiddenmost nature of man. Through poetry soul addresses soul without hindrance, by the direct medium of speech. Words are its atmosphere and very being: language, which raises man above the speechless intelligences; which, with resources of pitch, cadence, time, tone, and universal rhythm, is in a sense a more advanced and complex music than music itself—that idealized language which, as it ever has been the earliest form of emotional expression, appears almost a gift captured in man's infancy from some "imperial palace whence he came." To the true poet, then, we say, like the bard to Israfel:—

> "The ecstasies above
>   With thy burning measures suit—
> Thy grief, thy joy, thy hate, thy love,
>   With the fervor of thy lute—
>   Well may the stars be mute."

William Dean Howells

(1837–1920)

Few writers have been accorded the acclaim within their lifetime that befell William Dean Howells. Widely respected by his contemporaries as a major novelist and critic, he was also viewed as a guiding force in American letters—despite the fact that more gifted writers were on the scene. However, with the passing of time, his stature has decreased rather sharply. Now he is rarely classified as anything more than a second-rate novelist, and his critical pronouncements, once considered quite significant, are now respected, for the most part, only in their historical context.

Howells' eminence as a critic arose principally from his writings as a magazine editor and columnist. Between the years 1866 and 1881, he served successively as assistant editor and editor of The Atlantic Monthly. He then wrote book reviews and philosophical observations on literature as a columnist for Harper's Weekly Magazine, an undertaking that lasted from 1886 to 1892. All in all, he wrote over 400 critical pieces.

The most important aspect of Howells' criticism is his strong advocacy of realism. He believed so deeply in the "truthful treatment of material" that he constantly hammered away at this doctrine. Also, he advocated a distinctly liberal political philosophy. These two interests he combined and defended—often in the face of a rather concerted opposition.

Of further interest in Howells' criticism is his flat endorsement of "decency." Literature must not cater to the risqué or the immoral. Rather, it is to concern itself with the upright and the commendable. This idea naturally exposed Howells to the charge

*of prudishness, and his detractors, especially those of later gen-
erations, have been quick to disparage him on this count.*

*William Dean Howells, born on March 1, 1837, at Martin's
Ferry, Ohio, was associated throughout his life with printing and
writing. Son of a country printer and newspaper publisher,
Howells was helping to set type in his father's shop before the
age of ten. This first-hand contact with publishing and an un-
ceasing appetite for reading were the main sources of his education. However, Howell's program of self-education was apparently well conceived because his skill in writing, editing,
and criticizing—as well as his demonstrated knowledge of great
literature—evidences a broad and solid intellectual background.
Also, his ability to fill the editorial positions cited above further
proves the soundness of his background and ability.*

The passage below is from Howells' well-known Criticism and
Fiction.[1] *Herein one finds the essence of Howells' basic critical
tenets.*

From Criticism and Fiction [1891]

As I said, I hope the time is coming when not only the artist,
but the common, average man, who always "has the standard
of the arts in his power," will have also the courage to apply it,
and will reject the ideal grasshopper wherever he finds it, in
science, in literature, in art, because it is not "simple, natural, and
honest," because it is not like a real grasshopper. But I will own
that I think the time is yet far off, and that the people who have
been brought up on the ideal grasshopper, the heroic grasshopper,
the impassioned grasshopper, the self-devoted, adventureful,
good old romantic card-board grasshopper, must die out before
the simple, honest, and natural grasshopper can have a fair field. I
am in no haste to compass the end of these good people, whom I
find in the mean time very amusing. It is delightful to meet one
of them, either in print or out of it—some sweet elderly lady or
excellent gentleman whose youth was pastured on the literature

[1] Pp. 13, 17, 49.

of thirty or forty years ago—and to witness the confidence with which they preach their favorite authors as all the law and the prophets. They have commonly read little or nothing since, or, if they have, they have judged it by a standard taken from these authors, and never dreamed of judging it by nature; they are destitute of the documents in the case of the later writers; they suppose that Balzac was the beginning of realism, and that Zola is its wicked end; they are quite ignorant, but they are ready to talk you down, if you differ from them, with an assumption of knowledge sufficient for any occasion. The horror, the resentment, with which they receive any question of their literary saints is genuine; you descend at once very far in the moral and social scale, and anything short of offensive personality is too good for you; it is expressed to you that you are one to be avoided, and put down even a little lower than you have naturally fallen.

These worthy persons are not to blame; it is part of their intellectual mission to represent the petrifaction of taste, and to preserve an image of a smaller and cruder and emptier world than we now live in, a world which was feeling its way towards the simple, the natural, the honest, but was a good deal "amused and misled" by lights now no longer mistakable for heavenly luminaries. They belong to a time, just passing away, when certain authors were considered authorities in certain kinds, when they must be accepted entire and not questioned in any particular. Now we are beginning to see and to say that no author is an authority except in those moments when he held his ear close to Nature's lips and caught her very accent. These moments are not continuous with any authors in the past, and they are rare with all. Therefore I am not afraid to say now that the greatest classics are sometimes not at all great, and that we can profit by them only when we hold them, like our meanest contemporaries, to a strict accounting, and verify their work by the standard of the arts which we all have in our power, the simple, the natural, and the honest.

• • •

In the beginning of any art even the most gifted worker must be crude in his methods, and we ought to keep this fact always in mind when we turn, say, from the purblind worshippers of Scott to Scott himself, and recognize that he often wrote a style cumberous and diffuse; that he was tediously analytical where the modern novelist is dramatic, and evolved his characters by means of long-winded explanation and commentary; that, except in the case of his lower-class personages, he made them talk as seldom man and never woman talked; that he was tiresomely descriptive; that on the simplest occasions he went about half a mile to express a thought that could be uttered in ten paces across lots; and that he trusted his readers' intuitions so little that he was apt to rub in his appeals to them. He was probably right: the generation which he wrote for was duller than this; slower-witted, aesthetically untrained, and in maturity not so apprehensive of an artistic intention as the children of today. All this is not saying Scott was not a great man; he was a great man, and a very great novelist as compared with the novelists who went before him. He can still amuse young people, but they ought to be instructed how false and how mistaken he often is, with his mediaeval ideals, his blind Jacobitism, his intense devotion to aristocracy and royalty; his acquiescence in the division of men into noble and ignoble, patrician and plebeian, sovereign and subject, as if it were the law of God; for all which, indeed, he is not to blame as he would be if he were one of our contemporaries. Something of this is true of another master, greater than Scott in being less romantic, and inferior in being more German, namely, the great Goethe himself. He taught us, in novels otherwise now antiquated, and always full of German clumsiness, that it was false to good art—which is never anything but the reflection of life—to pursue and round the career of the persons introduced, whom he often allowed to appear and disappear in our knowledge as people in the actual world do. This is a lesson which the writers able to profit by it can never be too grateful for; and it is equally a benefaction to readers; but there is very little else in the conduct of the Goethean novels which is in advance of their time; this remains almost their sole contribution to the science of fiction. They are very primitive in certain characteristics, and unite with their calm, deep insight, an amusing helplessness in dramatization. "Wilhelm retired to his room, and indulged in the following reflections," is a mode of analysis which would not be practised nowadays; and all that fancifulness of nomenclature in Wilhelm Meister is very drolly sentimental and feeble. The adventures with robbers seem as if dreamed out of books of chivalry, and the tendency to allegorization affects one like an endeavor on the author's part to escape from the unrealities which he must have felt harassingly, German as he was. Mixed up with the shadows and illusions are honest, wholesome, every-day people, who have the air of wandering homelessly about among them, without definite direction; and the mists are full of a luminosity which, in spite of them, we know for common-sense and poetry. What is useful in any review of Goethe's methods is the recognition of the fact, which it must bring, that the greatest master cannot produce a masterpiece in a new kind. The novel was too recently invented in Goethe's day not to be, even in his hands, full of the faults of apprentice work.

• • •

More and more not only the criticism which prints its opinions, but the infinitely vaster and powerfuler criticism which thinks and feels them merely, will make this demand. I confess that I do not care to judge any work of the imagination without first of all applying this test to it. We must ask ourselves before we ask anything else, Is it true?—true to the motives, the impulses, the principles that shape the life of actual men and women? This truth, which necessarily includes the highest morality and the highest artistry—this truth given, the book cannot be wicked and cannot be weak; and without it all graces of style and feats of invention and cunning of construction are so many superfluities of naughtiness. It is well for the truth to have all these, and shine in them, but for falsehood they are merely meretricious, the bedizenment of the wanton; they atone for nothing, they count for nothing. But in fact they come naturally of truth, and grace it without solicitation; they are added unto it. In the whole range of fiction we know of no true picture of life—that is, of human nature—which is not also a masterpiece of literature, full of divine and natural beauty. It may have no touch or tint of this special civilization or of that; it had better have this local color well ascertained; but the truth is deeper and finer than aspects, and if the book is true to what men and women know of one another's souls it will be true enough, and it will be great and beautiful. It is the conception of literature as something apart from life superfinely aloof, which makes it really unimportant to the great mass of mankind, without a message or a meaning for them; and it is the notion that a novel may be false in its portrayal of causes and effects that makes literary art contemptible even to those whom it amuses, that forbids them to regard the novelist as a serious or right-minded person. If they do not in some moment of indignation cry out against all novels, as my correspondent does, they remain besotted in the fume of the delusions purveyed to them, with no higher feeling for the author than such maudlin affection as the habitué of an opium-joint perhaps knows for the attendant who fills his pipe with the drug.

Or, as in the case of another correspondent who writes that in his youth he "read a great many novels, but always regarded it as an amusement, like horse-racing and card-playing," for which he had no time when he entered upon the serious business of life, it renders them merely contemptuous. His view of the matter may be commended to the brotherhood and sisterhood of novelists as full of wholesome if bitter suggestion; and we urge them not to dismiss it with high literary scorn as that of some Bœotian dull to the beauty of art. Refuse it as we may, it is still the feeling of the vast majority of people for whom life is earnest, and who find only a distorted and misleading likeness of it in our books. We may fold ourselves in our scholars' gowns, and close the doors of our studies, and affect to despise this rude voice; but we cannot shut it out. It comes to us from wherever men are at work, from wherever they are truly living, and accuses us of unfaithfulness, of triviality, of mere stage-play; and none of us can escape conviction except he prove himself worthy of his time—a time in which the great masters have brought literature back to life, and filled its ebbing veins with the red tides of reality. We cannot all equal them; we need not copy them; but we can all go to the sources of their inspiration and their power; and to draw from these no one need go far—no one need really go out of himself.

Fifty years ago, Carlyle, in whom the truth was always alive, but in whom it was then unperverted by suffering, by celebrity, and by despair, wrote in his study of Diderot: "Were it not reasonable to prophesy that this exceeding great multitude of novel-writers and such like must, in a new generation, gradually do one of two things: either retire into the nurseries, and work for children, minors, and semi-fatuous persons of both sexes, or else, what were far better, sweep their novel-fabric into the dust-cart, and betake themselves with such faculty as they have to understand and record what is true, of which surely there is, and will forever be, a whole infinitude unknown to us of infinite importance to us? Poetry, it will more and more come to be understood, is nothing but higher knowledge; and the only genuine Romance (for grown persons), Reality."

If, after half a century, fiction still mainly works for "children, minors, and semi-fatuous persons of both sexes," it is nevertheless one of the hopefulest signs of the world's progress that it has begun to work for "grown persons," and if not exactly in the way that Carlyle might have solely intended in urging its writers to compile memoirs instead of building the "novel-fabric," still it has, in the highest and widest sense, already made Reality its Romance. I cannot judge it, I do not even care for it, except as it has done this; and I can hardly conceive of a literary self-respect in these days compatible with the old trade of make-believe, with the production of the kind of fiction which is too much honored by classification with card-playing and horse-racing. But let fiction cease to lie about life; let it portray men and women as they are, actuated by the motives and the passions in the measure we all know; let it leave off painting dolls and working them by springs and wires; let it show the different interests in their true proportions; let it forbear to preach pride and revenge, folly and insanity, egotism and prejudice, but frankly own these for what they are, in whatever figures and occasions they appear; let it not put on fine literary airs; let it speak the dialect, the language, that most Americans know—the language of unaffected people everywhere—and there can be no doubt of an unlimited future, not only of delightfulness but of usefulness, for it. . . .

Henry James

(1843–1916)

Few literary artists have taken their work more seriously than Henry James. Always deeply aware of the responsibility of the writer, James worked meticulously and exactingly in producing his many novels, short stories, and plays. He was also a careful and deliberate thinker as he wrote essays on a variety of subjects and a finely executed series of critical selections.

These critical writings are in the form of prefaces to novels, magazine articles, and letters. Throughout all, there is a recurring note of the writer's far-reaching responsibility and a detailed explanation of how the literary artist must think, write, and execute the other details of his work.

James is invariably classified as a realist. His friendship and basic agreement with William Dean Howells are constantly cited as proof of his endorsement of realism—as is his famous line, "The only reason for the existence of the novel is that it does attempt to represent life." However, one cannot classify James as a realist in the usual sense of the term because James endorses selectivity in creating fiction; that is, he argues that the literary artist must choose his details carefully. The novel is not to be a mere record or panoramic view. Instead, it must create an "illusion" that "makes it appear to us for the time that we have lived another life—that we have had a miraculous enlargement of experience." Hence it must be more than simple journalistic reporting.

In this viewpoint, James is stressing, of course, the idea of interpretation. He holds that the literary artist, like the painter, must be able to see and portray that which escapes others. Then, with the powers of portraiture which are peculiarly his, he must be able to present his vision to the beholder of his creation. Throughout all, he must be guided, of course, by the reality of the facts before him.

Henry James was a member of a distinguished family. His father was a well-known writer and lecturer in theology, and his brother, William, achieved wide renown as a psychologist and Harvard professor of philosophy. James—who never felt quite at home in the New York in which he was born or, indeed, anywhere in his native country—gravitated early toward Europe, living chiefly in London from 1869 until his death.

Below is a selection from James' widely read and respected essay "The Art of Fiction." This essay is actually a series of reflections which James assembled after a lecture delivered by Walter Besant under the same topic. Herein are the ideas which are most often associated with the critical thoughts of Henry James. These thoughts, therefore, are the essence of his critical theory.

From The Art of Fiction

I should not have affixed so comprehensive a title to these few remarks, necessarily wanting in any completeness upon a subject the full consideration of which would carry us far, did I not seem to discover a pretext for my temerity in the interesting pamphlet lately published under this name by Mr. Walter Besant. Mr. Besant's lecture at the Royal Institution—the original form of his pamphlet—appears to indicate that many persons are interested in the art of fiction, and are not indifferent to such remarks, as those who practice it may attempt to make about it. I am therefore anxious not to lose the benefit of this favorable association, and to edge in a few words under the cover of the attention which Mr. Besant is sure to have excited. There is something very encouraging in his having put into form certain of his ideas on the mystery of story-telling.

It is a proof of life and curiosity—curiosity on the part of the brotherhood of novelists as well as on the part of their readers.

Only a short time ago it might have been supposed that the English novel was not what the French call "discutable." It had no air of having a theory, a conviction, a consciousness of itself behind it—of being the expression of an artistic faith, the result of choice and comparison. I do not say it was necessarily the worse for that: it would take much more courage than I possess to intimate that the form of the novel as Dickens and Thackeray (for instance) saw it had any taint of incompleteness. It was, however, "naïf" (if I may help myself out with another French word); and evidently if it be destined to suffer in any way for having lost its "naïveté" it has now an idea of making sure of the corresponding advantages. During the period I have alluded to there was a comfortable, good-humored feeling abroad that a novel is a novel, as a pudding is a pudding, and that our only business with it could be to swallow it. But within a year or two, for some reason or other, there have been signs of returning animation—the era of discussion would appear to have been to a certain extent opened. Art lives upon discussion, upon experiment, upon curiosity, upon variety of attempt, upon the exchange of views and the comparison of standpoints; and there is a presumption that those times when no one has anything particular to say about it, and has no reason to give for practice or preference, though they may be times of honor, are not times of development—are times, possibly even, a little of dullness. The successful application of any art is a delightful spectacle, but the theory too is interesting; and though there is a great deal of the latter without the former I suspect there has never been a genuine success that has not had a latent core of conviction. Discussion, suggestion, formulation, these things are fertilizing when they are frank and sincere. Mr. Besant has set an excellent example in saying what he thinks, for his part, about the way in which fiction should be published; for his view of the "art," carried on into an appendix, covers that too. Other laborers in the same field will doubtless take up the argument, they will give it the light of their experience, and the effect will surely be to make our interest in the novel a little more what it had for some time threatened to fail to be—a serious, active, inquiring interest, under protection of which this delightful study may, in moments of confidence, venture to say a little more what it thinks of itself.

It must take itself seriously for the public to take it so. The old superstition about fiction being "wicked" has doubtless died out in England; but the spirit of it lingers in a certain oblique regard directed toward any story which does not more or less admit that it is only a joke. Even the most jocular novel feels in some degree the weight of the proscription that was formerly directed against literary levity: the jocularity does not always succeed in passing for orthodoxy. It is still expected, though perhaps people are ashamed to say it, that a production which is after all only a "make-believe" (for what else is a "story"?) shall be in some degree apologetic—shall renounce the pretension of attempting really to represent life. This, of course, any sensible, wide-awake story declines to do, for it quickly perceives that the tolerance granted to it on such a condition is only an attempt to stifle it disguised in the form of generosity. The old evangelical hostility to the novel, which was as explicit as it was narrow, and which regarded it as little less favorable to our immortal part than a stage play, was in reality far less insulting. The only reason for the existence of a novel is that it does attempt to represent life. When it relinquishes this attempt, the same attempt that we see on the canvas of the painter, it will have arrived at a very strange pass. It is not expected of the picture that it will make itself humble in order to be forgiven; and the analogy between the art of the painter and the art of the novelist is, so far as I am able to see, complete. Their inspiration is the same, their process (allowing for the different quality of the vehicle) is the same, their success is the same. They may learn from each other, they may explain and sustain each other. Their cause is the same, and the honor of one is the honor of another. The Mahometans think a picture an unholy thing, but it is a long time since any Christian did, and it is therefore the more odd that in the Christian mind the traces (dissimulated though they may be) of a suspicion of the sister art should linger to this day. The only effectual way to lay it to rest is to emphasize the analogy to which I just alluded—to insist on the fact that as the picture is reality, so the novel is history. That is the only general description (which does it justice) that we may give of the novel. But history also is allowed to represent life; it is not, any more than painting, expected to apologize. The subject matter of fiction is stored up likewise in documents and records, and if it will not give itself away, as they say in California, it must speak with assurance, with the tone of the historian. Certain accomplished novelists have a habit of giving themselves away which must often bring tears to the eyes of people who take their fiction seriously. I was lately struck, in reading over many pages of Anthony Trollope, with his want of discretion in this particular. In a digression, a parenthesis or an aside, he concedes to the reader that he and this trusting friend are only "making believe." He admits that the events he narrates have not really happened, and that he can give his narrative any turn the reader may like best. Such a betrayal of a sacred office seems to me, I confess, a terrible crime; it is what I mean by the attitude of apology, and it shocks me every whit as much in Trollope as it would have shocked me in Gibbon or Macaulay. It implies that the novelist is less occupied in looking for the truth (the truth, of course I mean, that he assumes, the premises that we must grant him, whatever they may be) than the historian, and in doing so it deprives him at a stroke of all his standing room. To represent and illustrate the past, the actions of men, is the task of either writer, and the only difference that I can see is, in proportion as he succeeds, to the honor of the novelist, consisting as it does in his having more difficulty in collecting his evidence, which is so far from being purely literary. It seems to me to give him a great character, the fact that he has at once so much in common with the philosopher and the painter; this double analogy is a magnificent heritage.

• • •

Nothing, of course, will ever take the place of the good old fashion of "liking" a work of art nor not liking it: the most improved criticism will not abolish that primitive, that ultimate test. I mention this to guard myself from the accusation of intimating that the idea, the subject, of a novel or a picture, does not matter. It matters, to my sense, in the highest degree, and if I might put up a prayer it would be that artists should select none but the richest. Some, as I have already hastened to admit, are much more remunerative than others, and it would be a world happily arranged in which persons intending to treat them should be exempt from confusions and mistakes. This fortunate condition will arrive only, I fear, on the fear, on the same day that critics become purged from error. Meanwhile, I repeat, we do not judge the artist with fairness unless we say to him, "Oh, I grant you your starting point, because if I did not I should seem to prescribe to you, and heaven forbid I should take that responsibility. If I pretend to tell you what you must not take, you will call upon me to tell you what you must take; in which case I shall be prettily caught. Moreover, it isn't till I have accepted your data that I can begin to measure you. I have the standard, the pitch; I have no right to tamper with your flute and then criticize your music. Of course I may not care for your idea at all; I may think it silly, or stale, or unclean; in which case I wash my hands of you altogether. I may content myself with believing that you will not have succeeded in being interesting, but I shall, of course, not attempt to demonstrate it, and you will be as indifferent to me as I am to you. I needn't remind you that there are all sorts of tastes: who can know it better? Some people, for excellent reasons, don't like to read about carpenters; others, for reasons even better, don't like to read about courtesans. Many object to Americans. Others (I believe they are mainly editors and publishers) won't look at Italians. Some readers don't like quiet subjects; others don't like bustling ones. Some enjoy a complete illusion, others the consciousness of large concessions. They choose their novels accordingly, and if they don't care about your idea they won't, "a fortiori," care about your treatment.

So that it comes back very quickly, as I have said, to the liking: in spite of M. Zola, who reasons less powerfully than he represents, and who will not reconcile himself to this absoluteness of taste, thinking that there are certain things that people ought to like, and that they can be made to like. I am quite at a loss to imagine anything (at any rate in this matter of fiction) that people *ought* to like or to dislike. Selection will be sure to take care of itself, for it has a constant motive behind it. That motive is simply experience. As people feel life, so they will feel the art that is most closely related to it. This closeness of relation is what we should never forget in talking of the effort of the novel. Many people speak of it as a factitious, artificial form, a product of ingenuity, the business of which is to alter and arrange the things that surround us, to translate them into conventional, traditional molds. This, however, is a view of the matter which carries us but a very short way, condemns the art to an eternal repetition of a few familiar *clichés*, cuts short its development, and leads us straight up to a dead wall. Catching the very note and trick, the strange irregular rhythm of life, that is the attempt whose strenuous force keeps Fiction upon her feet. In proportion as in what she offers us we see life *without* rearrangement so we feel that we are touching the truth; in proportion as we see it *with* rearrangement do we feel that we are being put off with a substitute, a compromise and convention. It is not uncommon to hear an extraordinary assurance of remark in regard to this matter of rearranging, which is often spoken of as if it were the last word of art. Mr. Besant seems to me in danger of falling into the great error with his rather unguarded talk about "selection." Art is essentially selection, but it is a selection whose main care is to be typical, to be inclusive. For many people art means rose-colored windowpanes, and selection means picking a bouquet for Mrs. Grundy. They will tell you glibly that artistic considerations have nothing to do with the disagreeable, with the ugly; they will rattle off shallow commonplaces about the province of art and the limits of art till you are moved to some wonder in return as to the province and the limits of ignorance. It appears to me that no one can ever have made a seriously artistic attempt without becoming conscious of an immense increase—a kind of revelation—of freedom. One perceives in that case—by the light of a heavenly ray—that the province of art is all life, all feeling, all observation, all vision. As Mr. Besant so justly intimates, it is all experience. That is a sufficient answer to those who maintain that it must not touch the sad things of life, who stick into its divine unconscious bosom little prohibitory inscriptions on the end of sticks, such as we see in public gardens—"It is forbidden to walk on the grass; it is forbidden to touch the flowers; it is not allowed to introduce dogs or to remain after dark; it is requested to keep to the right." The young aspirant in the line of fiction whom we continue to imagine will do nothing without taste, for in that case his freedom would be of little use to him; but the first advantage of his taste will be to reveal to him the absurdity of the little sticks and tickets. If he have taste, I must add, of course he will have ingenuity, and my disrespectful reference to that quality just now was not meant to imply that it is useless in fiction. But it is only a secondary aid; the first is a capacity for receiving straight impressions.

• • •

There is one point at which the moral sense and the artistic sense lie very near together; that is in the light of the very obvious truth that the deepest quality of a work of art will always be the quality of the mind of the producer. In proportion as that intelligence is fine will the novel, the picture, the statue partake of the substance of beauty and truth. To be constituted of such elements is, to my vision, to have purpose enough. No good novel will ever proceed from a superficial mind; that seems to me an axiom which, for the artist in fiction, will cover all needful moral ground: if the youthful aspirant take it to heart it will illuminate for him many of the mysteries of "purpose." There are many

other useful things that might be said to him, but I have come to
the end of my article, and can only touch them as I pass. The
critic in the Pall Mall *Gazette* . . . draws attention to the danger,
in speaking of the art of fiction, of generalizing. The danger that
he has in mind is rather, I imagine, that of particularizing, for
these are some comprehensive remarks which, in addition to those
embodied in Mr. Besant's suggestive lecture, might without fear
of misleading him be addressed to the ingenuous student. I
should remind him first of the magnificence of the form that is
open to him, which offers to sight so few restrictions and such
innumerable opportunities. The other arts, in comparison, appear confined and hampered; the various conditions under which
they are exercised are so rigid and definite. But the only condition that I can think of attaching to the composition of the
novel is, as I have already said, that it be sincere. This freedom
is a splendid privilege, and the first lesson of the young novelist
is to learn to be worthy of it. "Enjoy it as it deserves," I should
say to him; "take possession of it, explore it to its utmost extent,
publish it, rejoice in it. All life belongs to you, and do not listen
either to those who would shut you up into corners of it and
tell you that it is only here and there that art inhabits, or to
those who would persuade you that this heavenly messenger
wings her way outside of life altogether, breathing a superfine
air, and turning away her head from the truth of things. There
is no impression of life, no manner of seeing it and feeling it,
to which the plan of the novelist may not offer a place; you have
only to remember that talents so dissimilar as those of Alexandre
Dumas and Jane Austen, Charles Dickens and Gustave Flaubert
have worked in this field with equal glory. Do not think too much
about optimism and pessimism; try and catch the color of life
itself. In France today we see a prodigious effort (that of Emile
Zola, to whose solid and serious work no explorer of the capacity
of the novel can allude without respect), we see an extraordinary
effort vitiated by a spirit of pessimism on a narrow basis. M.
Zola is magnificent, but he strikes an English reader as ignorant;
he has an air of working in the dark; if he had as much light as

energy, his results would be of the highest value. As for the aberrations of a shallow optimism, the ground (of English fiction especially) is strewn with their brittle particles as with broken glass. If you must indulge in conclusions, let them have the taste of a wide knowledge. Remember that your first duty is to be as complete as possible—to make as perfect a work. Be generous and delicate and pursue the prize."

Mark Twain

(1835–1910)

The reader familiar with the broad history of American criticism may well wonder at the inclusion of Mark Twain in a book of readings in American criticism. He probably will recall immediately that Twain never wrote any extensive treatment of criticism or of critical theory; neither did he evaluate at length the work of any writer. Yet Twain does have a special kind of significance in American criticism.

It is a significance that arises from a great novelist's interesting pronouncements on literature in general and some writers in particular. Hence it is a significance that derives its appeal from the projection of Twain's personality into the area of criticism. Typical of Twain's pronouncements on individuals is his cryptically sarcastic statement on Henry James' The Bostonians—"I would rather be damned to John Bunyan's heaven than read that." Similarly representative are his acid remarks on Bret Harte, for whom he developed an almost pathological dislike.

Much more widely known, however, is his entertaining, if manifestly unfair, treatment of James Fenimore Cooper. In this work he relies on exaggeration, distortion, and misrepresentation to devastate Cooper; yet in the process, he causes the reader to laugh to the extent that he emerges victorious. This essay stands as clear proof that unusually appealing humor can take precedence over actual fact.

Especially worth noting in this work are the manner in which Twain presents his argument and the rhetorical devices which he employs. They are much more complex than a quick reading will indicate.

Mark Twain (Samuel Langhorne Clemens) was born in Florida, Missouri, and lived in many sections of the nation. He worked as river boat pilot, government office holder, journalist, editor, author, and lecturer. In each position, he seems to have found subject matter for his numerous writings—writings that include short stories, novels, vignettes, essays, plays, and travelogues—as well as material to fortify an especially appealing brand of humor. His great abilities reached their height, of course, in his master-piece, Huckleberry Finn *(1885).*

Fenimore Cooper's Literary Offenses

The Pathfinder *and* The Deerslayer *stand at the head of Cooper's novels as artistic creations. There are others of his works which contain parts as perfect as are to be found in these, and scenes even more thrilling. Not one can be compared with either of them as a finished whole.*

The defects in both of these tales are comparatively slight. They were pure works of art.   —Prof. Lounsbury

The five tales reveal an extraordinary fullness of invention . . . One of the very greatest characters in fiction, Natty Bumppo. . . .

The craft of the woodsman, the tricks of the trapper, all the delicate art of the forest, were familiar to Cooper from his youth up.
                         —Prof Brander Matthews.

Cooper is the greatest artist in the domain of romantic fiction yet produced by America.   —Wilkie Collins

It seems to me that it was far from right for the Professor of English Literature in Yale, the Professor of English Literature in Columbia, and Wilkie Collins to deliver opinions on Cooper's literature without having read some of it. It would have been much more decorous to keep silent and let persons talk who have read Cooper.

Cooper's art has some defects. In one place in *Deerslayer*, and in the restricted space of two-thirds of a page, Cooper has scored

114 offenses against literary art out of a possible 115. It breaks the record.

There are nineteen rules governing literary art in the domain of romantic fiction—some say twenty-two. In *Deerslayer* Cooper violated eighteen of them. These eighteen require:

1. That a tale shall accomplish something and arrive somewhere. But the *Deerslayer* tale accomplishes nothing and arrives in the air.

2. They require that the episodes of a tale shall be necessary parts of the tale and shall help to develop it. But as the *Deerslayer* tale is not a tale and accomplishes nothing and arrives nowhere, the episodes have no rightful place in the work, since there was nothing for them to develop.

3. They require that the personages in a tale shall be alive, except in the case of corpses, and that always the reader shall be able to tell the corpses from the others. But this detail has often been overlooked in the *Deerslayer* tale.

4. They require that the personages in a tale, both dead and alive, shall exhibit a sufficient excuse for being there. But this detail also has been overlooked in the *Deerslayer* tale.

5. They require that when the personages of a tale deal in conversation, the talk shall sound like human talk, and be talk such as human beings would be likely to talk in the given circumstances, and have a discoverable meaning, also a discoverable purpose and a show of relevancy, and remain in the neighborhood of the subject in hand, and be interesting to the reader, and help out the tale, and stop when the people cannot think of anything more to say. But this requirement has been ignored from the beginning of the *Deerslayer* tale to the end of it.

6. They require that when the author describes the character of a personage in his tale, the conduct and conversation of that personage shall justify said description. But this law gets little or no attention in the *Deerslayer* tale, as Natty Bumppo's case will amply prove.

7. They require that when a personage talks like an illustrated,

gilt-edged, tree-calf, hand-tooled, seven-dollar Friendship's Offering in the beginning of a paragraph, he shall not talk like a
Negro minstrel in the end of it. But this rule is flung down and
danced upon in the *Deerslayer* tale.

8. They require that crass stupidities shall not be played upon
the reader as "the craft of the woodsman, the delicate art of the
forest," by either the author or the people in the tale. But this
rule is persistently violated in the *Deerslayer* tale.

9. They require that the personages of a tale shall confine
themselves to possibilities and let miracles alone; or, if they
venture a miracle, the author must so plausibly set it forth as to
make it look possible and reasonable. But these rules are not
respected in the *Deerslayer* tale.

10. They require that the author shall make the reader feel a
deep interest in the personages of his tale and in their fate, and
that he shall make the reader love the good people in the tale
and hate the bad ones. But the reader of the *Deerslayer* tale dislikes the good people in it, is indifferent to the others, and wishes
they would all get drowned together.

11. They require that the characters in a tale shall be so clearly
defined that the reader can tell beforehand what each will do in
a given emergency. But in the *Deerslayer* tale this rule is
vacated.

In addition to these large rules there are some little ones. These
require that the author shall

12. *Say* what he is proposing to say, not merely come near it.

13. Use the right word, not its second cousin.

14. Eschew surplusage.

15. Not omit necessary details.

16. Avoid slovenliness of form.

17. Use good grammar.

18. Employ a simple and straightforward style.

Even these seven are coldly and persistently violated in the
Deerslayer tale.

Cooper's gift in the way of invention was not a rich endowment
but such as it was he liked to work it, he was pleased with the

effects, and indeed he did some quite sweet things with it. In his little box of stage-properties he kept six or eight cunning devices, tricks, artifices for his savages and woodsmen to deceive and circumvent each other with, and he was never so happy as when he was working these innocent things and seeing them go. A favorite one was to make a moccasined person tread in the tracks of the moccasined enemy, and thus hide his own trail. Cooper wore out barrels and barrels of moccasins in working that trick. Another stage-property that he pulled out of his box pretty frequently was his broken twig. He prized his broken twig above all the rest of his effects, and worked it the hardest. It is a restful chapter in any book of his when somebody doesn't step on a dry twig and alarm all the reds and whites for two hundred yards around. Every time a Cooper person is in peril and absolute silence is worth four dollars a minute, he is sure to step on a dry twig. There may be a hundred handier things to step on but that wouldn't satisfy Cooper. Cooper requires him to turn out and find a dry twig, and if he can't do it, go and borrow one. In fact, the Leatherstocking Series ought to have been called the Broken Twig Series.

I am sorry there is not room to put in a few dozen instances of the delicate art of the forest, as practised by Natty Bumppo and some of the other Cooperian experts. Perhaps we may venture two or three samples. Cooper was a sailor, a naval officer; yet he gravely tells us how a vessel, driving toward a lee shore in a gale, is steered for a particular spot by her skipper because he knows of an *undertow* there which will hold her back against the gale and save her. For just pure woodcraft, or sail or craft, or whatever it is, isn't that neat? For several years Cooper was daily in the society of artillery and he ought to have noticed that when a cannon-ball strikes the ground it either buries itself or skips a hundred feet or so, skips again a hundred feet or so, and so on till finally it gets tired and rolls. Now in one place he loses some "females"—as he always calls women—in the edge of a wood near a plain at night in a fog, on purpose to give Bumppo a chance to show off the delicate art of the forest before the reader. These mislaid people are hunting for a fort. They hear a cannon-blast, and a cannon-ball presently comes rolling into the wood and stops at their feet. To the females this suggests nothing. The case is very different with the admirable Bumppo. I wish I may never know peace again if he doesn't strike out promptly and *follow the track* of that cannon-ball across the plain through the dense fog and find the fort. Isn't it a daisy? If Cooper had any real knowledge of Nature's ways of doing things, he had a most delicate art in concealing the fact. For instance: one of his acute Indian experts, Chingachgook (pronounced Chicago, I think), has lost the trail of a person he is tracking through the forest. Apparently that trail is hopelessly lost. Neither you nor I could ever have guessed out the way to find it. It was very different with Chicago. Chicago was not stumped for long. He turned a running stream out of its course and there, in the slush in its old bed, were that person's moccasin tracks. The current did not wash them away, as it would have done in all other like cases—no, even the eternal laws of Nature have to vacate when Cooper wants to put up a delicate job of woodcraft on the reader.

We must be a little wary when Brander Matthews tells us that Cooper's books "reveal an extraordinary fullness of invention." As a rule, I am quite willing to accept Brander Matthews's literary judgments and applaud his lucid and graceful phrasing of them, but that particular statement needs to be taken with a few tons of salt. Bless your heart, Cooper hadn't any more invention than a horse, and I don't mean a high-class horse, either, I mean a clothes-horse. It would be very difficult to find a really clever "situation" in Cooper's books, and still more difficult to find one of any kind which he has failed to render absurd by his handling of it. Look at the episodes of "the caves"; and at the celebrated scuffle between Maqua and those others on the table-land a few days later; and at Hurry Harry's queer water-transit from the castle to the ark; and at Deerslayer's half-hour with his first corpse; and at the quarrel between Hurry Harry and Deerslayer later; and at— But choose for yourself, you can't go amiss.

If Cooper had been an observer his inventive faculty would

have worked better: not more interestingly but more rationally, more plausibly. Cooper's proudest creations in the way of "situations" suffer noticeably from the absence of the observer's protecting gift. Cooper's eye was splendidly inaccurate. Cooper seldom saw anything correctly. He saw nearly all things as through a glass eye, darkly. Of course a man who cannot see the commonest little every-day matters accurately is working at a disadvantage when he is constructing a "situation." In the *Deerslayer* tale Cooper has a stream which is fifty feet wide where it flows out of a lake; it presently narrows to twenty as it meanders along for no given reason, and yet when a stream acts like that it ought to be required to explain itself. Fourteen pages later the width of the brook's outlet from the lake has suddenly shrunk thirty feet and become "the narrowest part of the stream." This shrinkage is not accounted for. The stream has bends in it, a sure indication that it has alluvial banks and cuts them, yet these bends are only thirty and fifty feet long. If Cooper had been a nice and punctilious observer he would have noticed that the bends were oftener nine hundred feet long than short of it.

Cooper made the exit of that stream fifty feet wide in the first place for no particular reason; in the second place, he narrowed it to less than twenty to accommodate some Indians. He bends a "sapling" to the form of an arch over this narrow passage and conceals six Indians in its foliage. They are "laying" for a settler's scow or ark which is coming up the stream on its way to the lake; it is being hauled against the stiff current by a rope whose stationary end is anchored in the lake; its rate of progress cannot be more than a mile an hour. Cooper describes the ark, but pretty obscurely. In the matter of dimensions "it was little more than a modern canal-boat." Let us guess, then, that it was about one hundred and forty feet long. It was of "greater breadth than common." Let us guess, then, that it was about sixteen feet wide. This leviathan had been prowling down bends which were but a third as long as itself and scraping between banks where it had only two feet of space to spare on each side. We cannot too much admire this miracle. A low-roofed log dwelling occupies "two-

thirds of the ark's length"—a dwelling ninety feet long and sixteen
feet wide, let us say, a kind of vestibule train. The dwelling has
two rooms, each forty-five feet long and sixteen feet wide, let us
guess. One of them is the bedroom of the Hutter girls, Judith and
Hetty; the other is the parlor in the daytime, at night it is papa's
bed-chamber. The ark is arriving at the stream's exit now, whose
width has been reduced to less than twenty feet to accommodate
the Indians—say to eighteen. There is a foot to spare on each side
of the boat. Did the Indians notice that there was going to be
a tight squeeze there? Did they notice that they could make
money by climbing down out of that arched sapling and just
stepping aboard when the ark scraped by? No, other Indians
would have noticed these things but Cooper's Indians never
notice anything. Cooper thinks they are marvelous creatures for
noticing but he was almost always in error about his Indians.
There was seldom a sane one among them.

The ark is one hundred and forty feet long; the dwelling is
ninety feet long. The idea of the Indians is to drop softly and
secretly from the arched sapling to the dwelling as the ark creeps
along under it at the rate of a mile an hour, and butcher the
family. It will take the ark a minute and a half to pass under. It
will take the ninety-foot dwelling a minute to pass under. Now,
then, what did the six Indians do? It would take you thirty years to
guess and even then you would have to give up, I believe. Therefore, I will tell you what the Indians did. Their chief, a person of
quite extraordinary intellect for a Cooper Indian, warily watched
the canal-boat as it squeezed along under him and when he had
got his calculations fined down to exactly the right shade, as he
judged, he let go and dropped. And *missed the house!* That is
actually what he did. He missed the house and landed in the stern
of the scow. It was not much of a fall, yet it knocked him silly. He
lay there unconscious. If the house had been ninety-seven feet
long he would have made the trip. The fault was Cooper's, not
his. The error lay in the construction of the house. Cooper was
no architect.

There still remained in the roost five Indians. The boat has passed under and is now out of their reach. Let me explain what the five did—you would not be able to reason it out for yourself. No. 1 jumped for the boat but fell in the water astern of it. Then No. 2 jumped for the boat but fell in the water still farther astern of it. Then No. 3 jumped for the boat and fell a good way astern of it. Then No. 4 jumped for the boat and fell in the water *away* astern. Then even No. 5 made a jump for the boat—for he was a Cooper Indian. In the matter of intellect, the difference between a Cooper Indian and the Indian that stands in front of the cigar-shop is not spacious. The scow episode is really a sublime burst of invention but it does not thrill, because the inaccuracy of the details throws a sort of air of fictitiousness and general improbability over it. This comes of Cooper's inadequacy as an observer.

The reader will find some examples of Cooper's high talent for inaccurate observation in the account of the shooting-match in *The Pathfinder*.

A common wrought nail was driven lightly into the target, its head having been first touched with paint.

The color of the paint is not stated—an important omission, but Cooper deals freely in important omissions. No, after all, it was not an important omission, for this nail-head is *a hundred yards from* the marksmen and could not be seen by them at that distance, no matter what its color might be. How far can the best eyes see a common house-fly? A hundred yards? It is quite impossible. Very well, eyes that cannot see a house-fly that is a hundred yards away cannot see an ordinary nail-head at that distance, for the size of the two objects is the same. It takes a keen eye to see a fly or a nail-head at fifty yards—one hundred and fifty feet. Can the reader do it?

The nail was lightly driven, its head painted, and game called. Then the Cooper miracles began. The bullet of the first marksman chipped an edge of the nail-head; the next man's bullet drove the nail a little way into the target—and removed all the paint. Haven't the miracles gone far enough now? Not to suit Cooper, for the purpose of this whole scheme is to show off his prodigy, Deerslayer-Hawkeye-Long-Rifle-Leatherstocking-Pathfinder-Bumppo before the ladies.

"Be all ready to clench it, boys!" cried out Pathfinder, stepping into his friend's tracks the instant they were vacant. "Never mind a new nail; I can see that, though the paint is gone, and what I can see I can hit at a hundred yards, though it were only a mosquito's eye. Be ready to clench!"

The rifle cracked, the bullet sped its way, and the head of the nail was buried in the wood, covered by the piece of flattened lead.

There, you see, is a man who could hunt flies with a rifle, and command a ducal salary in a Wild West show today if we had him back with us.

The recorded feat is certainly surprising just as it stands, but it is not surprising enough for Cooper. Cooper adds a touch. He has made Pathfinder do this miracle with another man's rifle; and not only that, but Pathfinder did not have even the advantage of loading it himself. He had everything against him, and yet he made that impossible shot, and not only made it but did it with absolute confidence, saying, "Be ready to clench." Now a person like that would have undertaken the same feat with a brickbat, and with Cooper to help he would have achieved it, too.

Pathfinder showed off handsomely that day before the ladies. His very first feat was a thing which no Wild West show can touch. He was standing with the group of marksmen, observing— a hundred yards from the target, mind; one Jasper raised his rifle and drove the center of the bull's-eye. Then the Quartermaster fired. The target exhibited no result this time. There was a laugh. "It's a dead miss," said Major Lundie. Pathfinder waited an impressive moment or two, then said in that calm, indifferent, know-it-all way of his, "No, Major, he has covered Jasper's bullet, as will be seen if anyone will take the trouble to examine the target."

Wasn't it remarkable! How *could* he see that little pellet fly through the air and enter that distant bullethole? Yet that is what he did, for nothing is impossible to a Cooper person. Did any of those people have any deep-seated doubts about this thing? No; for that would imply sanity and these were all Cooper people.

The respect for Pathfinder's skill and for his *quickness and accuracy of sight* [the italics are mine] was so profound and general, that the instant he made this declaration the spectators began to distrust their own opinions, and a dozen rushed to the target in order to ascertain the fact. There, sure enough, it was found that the Quartermaster's bullet had gone through the hole made by Jasper's, and that, too, so accurately as to require a minute examination to be certain of the circumstance, which, however, was soon clearly established by discovering one bullet over the other in the stump against which the target was placed.

They made a "minute" examination; but never mind, how could they know that there were two bullets in that hole without digging the latest one out? for neither probe nor eyesight could prove the presence of any more than one bullet. Did they dig? No; as we shall see. It is the Pathfinder's turn now; he steps out before the ladies, takes aim, and fires.

But, alas! here is a disappointment, an incredible, an unimaginable disappointment—for the target's aspect is unchanged; there is nothing there but that same old bullet-hole!

"If one dared to hint at such a thing," cried Major Duncan, "I should say that the Pathfinder has also missed the target!"

As nobody had missed it yet, the "also" was not necessary, but never mind about that for the Pathfinder is going to speak.

"No, no, Major," said he, confidently, "that *would* be a risky declaration. I didn't load the piece, and can't say what was in it; but if it was lead, you will find the bullet driving down those of the Quartermaster and Jasper, else is not my name Pathfinder."

A shout from the target announced the truth of this assertion.

Is the miracle sufficient as it stands? Not for Cooper. The Pathfinder speaks again, as he "now slowly advances toward the stage occupied by the females":

"That's not all, boys, that's not all; if you find the target touched at all, I'll own to a miss. The Quartermaster cut the wood, but you'll find no wood cut by that last messenger."

The miracle is at last complete. He knew—doubtless *saw*—at the distance of a hundred yards—that his bullet had passed into the hole *without fraying the edges*. There were now three bullets in that one hole, three bullets embedded processionally in the body of the stump back of the target. Everybody knew this, somehow or other, and yet nobody had dug any of them out to make sure. Cooper is not a close observer but he is interesting. He is certainly always that, no matter what happens. And he is more interesting when he is not noticing what he is about than when he is. This is a considerable merit.

The conversations in the Cooper books have a curious sound in our modern ears. To believe that such talk really ever came out of people's mouths would be to believe that there was a time when time was of no value to a person who thought he had something to say, when it was the custom to spread a two-minute remark out to ten, when a man's mouth was a rolling-mill and busied itself all day long in turning four-foot pigs of thought into thirty-foot bars of conversational railroad iron by attenuation, when subjects were seldom faithfully stuck to but the talk wandered all around and arrived nowhere, when conversations consisted mainly of irrelevancies with here and there a relevancy, a relevancy with an embarrassed look, as not being able to explain how it got there.

Cooper was certainly not a master in the construction of dialogue. Inaccurate observation defeated him here as it defeated him in so many other enterprises of his. He even failed to notice that the man who talks corrupt English six days in the week must and will talk it on the seventh, and can't help himself. In the *Deerslayer* story he lets Deerslayer talk the showiest kind of book-talk sometimes, and at other times the basest of base dialects. For instance, when some one asks him if he has a sweetheart, and if so where she abides, this is his majestic answer:

"She's in the forest—hanging from the boughs of the trees, in a soft rain—in the dew on the open grass—the clouds that float about in the blue heavens—the birds that sing in the woods—the sweet springs where I slake my thirst—and in all the other glorious gifts that come from God's Providence!"

And he preceded that, a little before, with this:

"It consarns me as all things that touches a fri'nd consarns a fri'nd."

And this is another of his remarks:

"If I was Injin born, now, I might tell of this, or carry in the scalp and boast of the expl'ite afore the whole tribe; or if my inimy had only been a bear"—[and so on].

We cannot imagine such a thing as a veteran Scotch Commander-in-Chief comporting himself in the field like a windy melodramatic actor, but Cooper could. On one occasion Alice and Cora were being chased by the French through a fog in the neighborhood of their father's fort:

"*Point de quartier aux coquins!*" cried an eager pursuer, who seemed to direct the operations of the enemy.

"Stand firm and be ready, my gallant 60ths!" suddenly exclaimed a voice above them; "wait to see the enemy; fire low, and sweep the glacis."

"Father! father," exclaimed a piercing cry from out the mist; "it is I! Alice! thy own Elsie! spare, O! save your daughters!"

"Hold!" shouted the former speaker, in the awful tones of parental agony, the sound reaching even to the woods, and rolling back in solemn echo. " 'Tis she! God has restored me my children! Throw open the sallyport; to the field, 60ths, to the field! pull not a trigger, lest ye kill my lambs! Drive off these dogs of France with your steel!"

Cooper's word-sense was singularly dull. When a person has a poor ear for music he will flat and sharp right along without knowing it. He keeps near the tune, but it is *not* the tune. When a person has a poor ear for words, the result is a literary flatting and sharping; you perceive what he is intending to say but you also perceive that he doesn't *say* it. This is Cooper. He was not a word-musician. His ear was satisfied with the *approximate* word. I will furnish some circumstantial evidence in support of this charge. My instances are gathered from half a dozen pages of the tale called *Deerslayer*. He uses "verbal" for "oral"; "precision" for "facility"; "phenomena" for "marvels"; "necessary" for "predetermined"; "unsophisticated" for "primitive"; "preparation" for "expectancy"; "rebuked" for "subdued"; "dependent on" for "resulting from"; "fact" for "condition"; "fact" for "conjecture"; "precaution" for "caution"; "explain" for "determine"; "mortified" for "disappointed"; "meretricious" for "factitious"; "materially" for "considerably"; "decreasing" for "deepening"; "increasing" for "disappearing"; "embedded" for "inclosed"; "treacherous" for "hostile"; "stood" for "stooped"; "softened" for "replaced"; "rejoined" for "remarked"; "situation" for "condition"; "different" for "differing"; "insensible" for "unsentient"; "brevity" for "celerity"; "distrusted" for "suspicious"; "mental imbecility" for "imbecility"; "eyes" for "sight"; "counteracting" for "opposing"; "funeral obsequies" for "obsequies."

There have been daring people in the world who claimed that Cooper could write English but they are all dead now—all dead but Lounsbury. I don't remember that Lounsbury makes the claim in so many words, still he makes it for he says that *Deerslayer* is a "pure work of art." Pure, in that connection, means faultless—faultless in all details—and language is a detail. If Mr. Lounsbury had only compared Cooper's English with the English which he writes himself—but it is plain that he didn't, and so it is likely that he imagines until this day that Cooper's is as clean and compact as his own. Now I feel sure, deep down in my heart, that Cooper wrote about the poorest English that exists in our language and that the English of *Deerslayer* is the very worst that even Cooper ever wrote.

I may be mistaken, but it does seem to me that *Deerslayer* is not a work of art in any sense; it does seem to me that it is destitute of every detail that goes to the making of a work of art; in truth, it seems to me that *Deerslayer* is just simply a literary *delirium tremens*.

A work of art? It has no invention; it has no order, system, sequence, or result; it has no lifelikeness, no thrill, no stir, no seeming of reality; its characters are confusedly drawn and by their acts and words they prove that they are not the sort of people the author claims that they are; its humor is pathetic; its pathos is funny; its conversations are—oh! indescribable; its lovescenes odious; its English a crime against the language.

Counting these out, what is left is Art. I think we must all admit that.

George Edward Woodberry

(1855–1930)

The fame which George Edward Woodberry once enjoyed as a critic resulted primarily from the influence which he cast on a small group of men who eventually achieved prominence in the world of literature and the world of criticism. As a professor of comparative literature at Columbia, Woodberry worked mightily to inculcate into his students a love of literature and related subjects; and in the process, he convinced a large segment of the validity of his critical views. Because many of this group later gained important rostrums from which to pronounce critical judgments, Woodberry made a surprisingly strong impact on American critical thought.

Woodberry's theories, like those of many another critic, are actually a realigning of tenets from older schools. Primarily, he draws from Classicism. Literature, he argues, must always employ a clearly discernible form; that is, literature must always respect the "doctrine of order." Also, he endorses the Classical concept of literature as the product of a carefully disciplined and properly educated mind. Never can it be the careless, off-hand ramblings of a skittish or vague personality.

However, almost as a contradiction, Woodberry upholds the romanticist's emphasis on the subjective element by contending that literature reflects the personality of the author. Hence it must be granted the right to express feelings, emotions, and personal experiences.

This emphasis on the subjective, coupled with an insistence that literature be the product of a mature mind, then leads to Wood-

berry's interest in character depiction. The presentation of char-
acter in a novel, he maintains, is more important than the plot
or the action. For this reason, he praises Sir Walter Scott as
an important novelist while he relegates other highly respected
writers to a secondary position.

In the realm of poetry, Woodberry attaches considerable im-
portance to artistic purpose and moral precept. He feels that
poetry must respect ethics and moral purpose as fundamental
aims—although he does not demand a didactic element. He fur-
ther avers that the critic can rightfully test the soundness of the
poet's statements in the light of their truth or falsity.

Viewed from today's perspective, Woodberry's lofty position
in his time remains difficult to comprehend. One can easily
demonstrate that Woodberry evidenced nothing really new, that
he never fully comprehended the flow of American literature, and
that he fell victim to an overestimate of the past. Nonetheless, he
does evince a certain freshness of tone and atmosphere in his
writings; and his personality reflects an appealing quality. These
attributes are especially noticeable in Two Phases of Criticism,
Historical and Aesthetic *(1914), his most significant and widely*
read work.

Woodberry, born in Beverly, Massachusetts, on May 12, 1885,
held one earned degree (A.B., Harvard, 1877) and honorary
degrees from Harvard, Western Reserve, and Amherst. For the
most part, it seems, he preferred to study independently, even
when an undergraduate. Woodberry taught for two brief periods
(1877–78, 1880–82) at the University of Nebraska and for a thir-
teen-year stay (1891–1904) at Columbia University. During the
other years, he devoted himself full time to his numerous books
and critical writings. The philosophy by which he lived is es-
pecially clear in his The Torch *(1905), a series of lectures, and*
The North Shore Watch *(1890),* Ideal Passion *(1917), and* The
Roamer *(1920), each of which is a volume of poetry.*

Below are three passages from his America in Literature

(1903).[1] *These excerpts afford an interesting comparison between Woodberry's judgments and those which are prevalent at the moment.*

From America in Literature

Emerson was intellectually cultured, . . . but his power of expression in poetry was lacking in fluidity, roundness, and ease; his poetry, artistically, is Byzantine in its crudity, like his very figure, so stiff, so serious, so formal in its formlessness; but that is the accident of the body; the insight, the imagination, the flash of originality from within or of beauty caught from without, make the inwardness of the verse, and judged by the great qualities of the spirit, and especially by that greatest one of an absolute unconscious simplicity, Emerson's poetry pierces heaven at the highest altitude of all our bards. His prose essays, liberating as they are to the mind and stimulating to the spiritual life, are on a lower level; his patriotic sayings, his great American lines—and no poet has so many, bright as the lightnings of Zeus—are in his verse; but his essays are the flower of transcendentalism, which stood in American life for religious revolt sympathetic with the movement of enlightenment on the Continent, and they are the result of that internal conflict consequent on a change in ideals in the spiritual sphere which has so often been the motive power of great works in literature, but was here attended by none of that dark stress which is shown in the Revolutionary poets of all Europe, and even in the life, though not the works, of Cardinal Newman.

The whole transcendental movement, in its literary record, is a striking instance of that absence of turbulence, of desperate battle, and deep desire, in our literature, which has been emphasized as characteristic in our men of letters. In Hawthorne only is there found the sense of spiritual peril, and he presents it objectively and historically as a primary experience in the moral life of the founders of New England, most significantly in *The*

[1] Pp. 195–200, 202–04, 240–43.

Scarlet Letter, and again less dramatically and more speculatively in Donatello; but in none of his work is it a religious struggle,—it is a moral catastrophe that he illuminates. Hawthorne is, for this reason, the most profound and vitally spiritual in his expression of human experience, the deepest prober of the breast, of all our authors, whether poets or prose-writers; and he comes to this overmastering interest in sin, rather than crime, and in the operations of conscience and the recovery of the soul through suffering and its entrance on a greater life thereby, because of his American inheritance and environment, his American genius.

Bryant is a fading and almost Ossianic figure, a wintry ghost, to most of us; Emerson and Hawthorne, a figure of light and a figure of darkness, are the companion spirits, American through and through, who now seem the greatest American writers of the last century. Longfellow and Lowell, associated together in fame as in life, may find, the one a wider acceptance, the other an academic vogue. Longfellow's poetry is less valued now by the critical class, but it is not likely that his hold on the homes of his countrymen has lessened; the critical class has lost in the sense of refinement, and is dull to the quality of Longfellow; but his trust, his humanity, his hospitality to the joys and sorrows of domestic life, his tenderness, his consolation, his noble nature, his just taste in what to say and what to leave unsaid about the crises of lives, not tragic, but touched with human things that "have been and may be again," his companionableness for souls not overstrenuous, but full of all the pieties of life endearing life—these things give him long lease of fame; and within his emphatic range he has an unsuspected variety, and thereby expresses without weariness, except to the life-jaded, an American nature of such sweetness, refinement, and purity that it has become almost exemplary of an ideal of the literary life on this soil. Lowell has not touched his people to the same degree; he is over-intellectual for some and has defects of taste which repulse others, and great unevenness; he remains our only critic of the first rank, but in other respects his fame seems a doubtful matter. To these names, with full right, that of Poe is added because of his originality in lyric tone and motive, and its power, now long demonstrated, in this country and abroad; and also because of the peculiar horror of his tales.

• • •

In the fields of endeavor that neighbor literature, in history, oratory, state papers, and the like, distinction has been won as high in those provinces of expression as any in the pure literary art. But to examine our literature in this comprehensive way in order to exhibit our true performance would be as vain a task as to endeavor to show our inventive genius by a catalogue of the patent-office instead of by those supreme examples which have been gifts to all the world. The national life, it is true, has found expression in many authors besides those of genius, and in many men of literary faculty approaching genius—its moral experience in Whittier, its democratic crudity in Whitman, its later culture in the elder poets still living, its abolished Southern civilization in *Uncle Tom's Cabin,* its border and mining-camp romance in Bret Harte; but the writers in these cases belong in a secondary class in comparison with Bryant, Irving, Cooper, Emerson, Hawthorne, Longfellow, Lowell, and Poe. These last are the authors whom the nation as a whole regards as its great writers in pure literature, and none besides. They are themselves in a second class in comparison with the English or French authors of the century; and, in fact, they fall, in almost a solid group, just below the greatest names in English literature, and above all others who are reckoned as second in England, and Emerson, Hawthorne, and Poe are unique each in his kind. The work they and those associated with them have done has been distinguished by artistic conscientiousness, to a degree rarely paralleled, and also by purity; no nation has so pure, few so painstaking, a literature; it fails of the highest rank only because it lacks inspiration, passion, that deep stirring of the spirit of man which, with all its cost, is the cause of his highest reach in imagination, intellect, and desire.

• • •

Walt Whitman, to take the typical case, is an idealist—all live Americans are idealists—and he exemplifies in literature, in a highly developed form, that variety of the American idealist who is a believer in ideas, usually in one idea which he seizes, and is thereupon possessed, and often transported even to living in a fanatical world. Walt Whitman was one of these. The appealing thing in him is the pure primitiveness of the ideas he seized; the arresting thing—to neglect what is merely grotesque in his work— is the boldness of outline and a certain uncramped strength with which he presented these ideas of nature, fraternity, and toil. The ideas themselves are as fundamental in the social world as are the ideas of the Declaration of Independence. In their acceptance abroad as a peculiarly American expression there was an element of preconception; such primitiveness, so loud an emphasis, such a careless defiance of conventions of art and speech, belonged to a democracy—it was as Shakespeare might have portrayed it; but to the minds who accepted Whitman, the democrat was still a cousin to Caliban. Whitman had natural poetic force without art; when he forgot his camerado role as the democrat vagabond under whose sombrero was all America, he wrote a few fine lyrics; but to foreigners, who find in him the nationality they miss in the old group, the result must be disappointingly small as the type and outcome of three centuries of slowly culminating English toil in a great land; and to us at home, gazing half humorously on, when we take time to think of it with a moment's passing seriousness, it seems only the caricature that deforms truth. So Doré might have drawn us, so Rabelais have humorized us; extravagance of line and laughter could go no further. To become what Whitman was, Americans, who, more than Englishmen, are the heirs of all Europe, must first denude themselves of that larger civilization with which they are integral, and be an Ishmael among nations. A poet in whom a whole nation declines to find its likeness cannot be regarded as representative, though he may smack strongly of some raw earth in the great domain. It is more reasonable to find the national literary genius, as a fellow of universal art with its peers, in the appropriation of our best by foreign nations in those authors that are now classical with us, the group in whom we find, as a nation, our past, our ideals, and our daily life of home and heaven.

Irving Babbitt

(1865–1933)

Any study of criticism in America in the early decades of the current century must focus attention on the New Humanism, a movement which occasioned an endless and a spirited controversy. Expressed in simple terms, the New Humanism called for an endorsement of lofty values from the past, a carefully exercised check on undisciplined thinking, and a heavy emphasis on learning—particularly on a group of selected writers who lived before the nineteenth century. The New Humanism had little use for democratic approaches either in government or in making important decisions within society. It was an approach that demanded an intellectual élite to make judgments and to handle affairs for those less gifted.

The central figure in the movement was Irving Babbitt, who was supported vigorously and capably by Paul Elmer More. However, More eventually took issue with Babbitt's judgments— as did T. S. Eliot and others who at one time were devotees of the New Humanism—thus leaving Babbitt to carry the battle without aid from any prestigious individual. Babbitt fought on, despite the fury of the opposition, and held his viewpoint throughout the embitterment of his declining years.

Babbitt places an unusually high premium on reason. He believes that man, if sufficiently endowed with intelligence, can eventually find a higher law that yields an understanding of problems now considered unanswerable. From this understanding, man then proceeds to obtain truth. Any other approach Babbitt regards as simple-minded or foolish. This opinion Babbitt often propounds with a bombast that borders on the insulting.

In Babbitt's critical theory, one can easily detect the impact of the literature and the criticism of Classical antiquity. One can also discern the influence of Continental literature, a literature which Babbitt taught as professor of French and comparative literature at Harvard. Even more, however, one can see Babbitt's own strong mind and his rebellion against the lessening of decorum and restraint in his day.

As a result of his strong convictions, Babbitt is prone to overstatement, excessively inflexible categorizing, and vituperative judgment of opponents. These weaknesses his adversaries naturally seized upon, often reducing Babbitt to ridicule.

Still, Babbitt is not to be regarded lightly. Because of the inherent strength of some of his ideas, the influence he cast on a generation of students, and the location of his rostrum, he was a genuine power in American critical thought until the depression years of the 1930's made social criticism the dominant approach.

Irving Babbitt was born in Dayton, Ohio, on August 2, 1865. After receiving the A.B. degree from Harvard in 1889 and the A.M. from the same institution in 1893, he taught for one year at Williams College before joining the Harvard faculty in 1894. Thereafter, he focused his attention on teaching, writing, and independent study. Occasionally, he left the Harvard campus to lecture at other institutions or to accept brief tenures as a visiting professor; but his professional life and work were bound inextricably with his Alma Mater. Among the collegiate institutions where he taught were Kenyon, Yale, Stanford, and the Sorbonne.

Below is an essay which contains the essence of Babbitt's critical theories.

Standards in Criticism

We are told that Louis XIV once submitted a sonnet he had written to the judgment of Boileau, who said, after reading it: "Sire, nothing is impossible for your Majesty. You set out to write some bad verses, and you have succeeded." The point of this story, for the modern reader, lies not so much in the courage of the critic as in the meekness of the king. With the progress of democracy one man's opinion in literature has come to be as good as another's—a deal better, too, the Irishman would add—and such words as deference and humility are in a fair way to become obsolete. We can scarcely conceive to what an extent men once allowed their personal impressions to be overawed and held in check by a body of outer prescriptions. Only a century ago an Edinburgh reviewer could write: "Poetry has thus much at least in common with religion, that its standards were fixed long ago by certain inspired writers whose authority it is no longer lawful to question." Racine tells us that the audience was afraid, at the first performance of his comedy *Les Plaideurs*, that "it had not laughed according to the rules."

The revolt came at last from this tyranny of the "rules," and the romantic critics opposed to the neoclassic narrowness their plea for wider knowledge and wider sympathy; they would see before they began to oversee, and be historical rather than dogmatic; they would neither exclude nor conclude, but explain; above all, they would be appreciative, and substitute the fruitful criticism of beauties for the barren criticism of faults. The weakness of the whole school has been its proneness to forget that knowledge and sympathy are after all only the feminine virtues of the critic. Hence the absence of the masculine note in so much modern criticism; hence the tendency of judgment to be swallowed up completely in sympathy and comprehension— *tout comprendre, c'est tout pardonner.* Renan, one of the most perfect embodiments of the ideal of wider knowledge and wider sympathy, says that when anyone was presented to him he tried to enter into this person's point of view and serve up to him his own ideas in advance. One thinks almost involuntarily of Dr. Johnson and how, when people disagreed with him, he "roared them down"; how men like Reynolds and Gibbon and Burke ventured to present their protest to him only in the form of a round robin, so that the awful Aristarch might not know on whom first to visit his wrath. It is of course well, and indeed indispensable, that the critic should cultivate the feminine virtues, but on condition, as Tennyson has put it, that he be man-woman and not woman-man. Through neglect of this truth criticism has tended in its development during the past century to become first a form of history, and then a form of biography, and finally a form of gossip. History and biography remind us in their gradual encroachments upon critical judgment of those mayors of the palace in Merovingian times who insinuated themselves under cover of the services they rendered and at last thrust themselves into their masters' place. It is true that judgment would not have been thus dispossessed if it had not first shown itself a *roi fainé-ant*.

Sainte-Beuve himself, as we saw, labored during the latter part of his life to correct, or one might more fairly say to complete, his earlier method and to assert once more the supremacy of judgment. It is curious to trace the transformation of the militant romanticist of 1830 into the conservative who finally extols as the true type of the critic Malherbe and Boileau and Dr. Johnson. He follows these men in founding his own judgments for the most part on the traditional standards of the classicist; yet no one knew better than Sainte-Beuve that these standards were doomed. "Let us be the last of our kind," he exclaims, "before the great confusion."

The "great confusion" that Sainte-Beuve foresaw is now upon us. I pointed out that he himself has been correctly defined in his influence on his successors, not as a defender of standards and judgment, but as a great doctor of relativity. Now nearly all recent criticism, so far as it is anything more than a form of gossip and small talk, may be roughly classified as either impressionistic or scientific; and it is in this doctrine of relativity that both impressionistic and scientific critics unite. The impressionist is interested in a book only as it relates itself to his sensibility, and his manner of praising anything that makes this appeal to him is to say that it is "suggestive." The scientific critic for his part is interested solely in the way a book is related as a phenomenon to other phenomena, and when it is the culminating point or the point of departure of a large number of these relationships, he says that it is "significant" (the favorite word of Goethe). If the impressionist is asked to rise above his sensibility and judge by a more impersonal standard, he answers that there is no such impersonal element in art, but only "suggestiveness," and is almost ready to define art with a recent French writer as an "attenuated hypnosis." If the scientific critic in turn is urged to get behind the phenomena and rate a book with reference to a scale of absolute values, he absconds into his theory of the "unknowable."

We may illustrate by a familiar passage from Taine, who is easily the most eminent of those who have attempted to make criticism scientific. "What do we see," he says in his *English Literature*, "under the fair glazed pages of a modern poem? A modern poet who has studied and traveled, a man like Alfred de Musset, Victor Hugo, Lamartine, or Heine, in a black coat and gloves, welcomed by the ladies, and making every evening his fifty bows and his score of *bons mots* in society; reading the papers in the morning, lodging as a rule on a second floor; not overgay, because he has nerves, and especially because, in this dense democracy where we stifle one another, the discredit of official dignities has exaggerated his pretensions, while increasing his importance, and because the keenness of his feelings in general rather disposes him to think himself a god."

Now in the first place the results of this attempt to infer from a poem the life and personality of the poet are strangely uncertain. We read in the recently published letters of John Richard Green that when Taine was in England getting information for the last volume of his *English Literature,* he began talking about Tennyson with Palgrave, a great friend of the laureate.

"Wasn't he in early youth rich, luxurious, fond of pleasure, self-indulgent?" Taine asked. "I see it all in his early poems—his riot, his adoration of physical beauty, his delight in jewels, in the abandonment of all to pleasure, in wine, and . . ."

"Stop! stop!" said Palgrave, out of all patience. "As a young man Tennyson was poor—he had little more than one hundred pounds a year, his habits were, as they still are, simple and reserved, he cared then as he cares now for little more than a chat and a pipe; he has never known luxury in your sense."

Taine thanked Palgrave for his information—and when the book came out Tennyson was found still painted as the young voluptuary of the critic's fancy.

Even assuming that Taine's inferences could be drawn correctly, he would have us fix our attention on precisely those features of a poem that are least poetical. The very prosaic facts he is looking for would be at least as visible in the writing of some mediocrity as in a work of the first order. It is, indeed, when Taine starts out to deal in this fashion with a poet of genius like Milton, to reduce *Paradise Lost* to a mere "sign," that the whole method is seen to be grotesquely inadequate. "Adam," says Taine in his critique of Milton, "is your true paterfamilias with a vote, an M.P., an old Oxford man," etc. He listens to the conversation of Adam and Eve, the first pair, only to hear "an English household, two reasoners of the period—Colonel Hutchinson and his wife. Good heavens! dress them at once"; and he continues in this vein for pages.

But, says M. Bourget, speaking for the impressionists, there is another way of approaching the volume of verse that Taine would treat solely from the point of view of its "significance"; and in rendering the "suggestiveness" of the volume to the impressionist sensibility, M. Bourget proceeds to employ a luxuriance of epithet that lack of space forbids our quoting. He asks us to imagine a young woman alone in her boudoir on an overcast winter afternoon. A vague melancholy steals upon her as she reclines at ease in her long chair; all aquiver with ineffable longing, she turns to her favorite poet. She does not surmise behind the delicately tinted pages of the beloved book the prosaic facts of environment, the obscure animal origins of talent that are so visible to Taine. What she does perceive is the dream of the poet— "the inexpressible and mysterious beyond that he has succeeded in throwing like a halo round his verses." For Taine the stanzas are a result; for the young woman "who intoxicates her heart with them so deliciously," they are a cause. "She does not care for the alembic in which the magic philter has been distilled, provided only this magic is operative, provided her reading culminates in an exquisite and trembling exaltation" and "suggests to her dreams either sweet or sad, but always productive of ecstasy." Who does not see, concludes M. Bourget, that entirely different theories of art are applied in the two ways of approaching the volume of verse?

The two theories are different, indeed; yet they are alike in this, that neither the "significance" of the volume to Taine nor its "suggestiveness" to M. Bourget affords any real means of escape from the quicksands of relativity to some firm ground of judgment. We may be sure that a third-rate bit of contemporary sentimentality will "suggest" more ineffable dreams to the young woman in the long chair than a play of Sophocles. To state the case more generally, how many books there are that were once infinitely suggestive and are still of the highest significance in literary history which yet intrinsically are now seen to be of very inferior value! This is eminently true of certain writings of Rousseau, to whom much of the peculiar exaggeration of the *sense propre* or individual sense that one finds in the impressionists can ultimately be traced. If the special modes of sensibility that impressionism exhibits go back to Rousseau, its philosophical theory may best be considered as a reappearance in modern thought of the ancient maxim that man is the measure of all things. This celebrated dictum became current at a decisive moment in Greek life and would indeed seem to sum up almost necessarily the point of view of any age that has cast off traditional standards. The all-important question is whether one interprets the maxim in the spirit of the sophists or in that of Socrates. The resemblance between the impressionistic and the sophistical understanding of the maxim is unmistakable; not only the individual man, but his present sensations and impressions are to be made the measure of all things. "All of us," says M. Anatole France, "judge everything by our own measure. How could we do otherwise, since to judge is to compare, and we have only one measure, which is ourselves; and this measure is constantly changing? We are all of us the sport and playthings of mobile appearances." Perhaps no recent writer has shown more of the Socratic spirit in his use of the maxim than Emerson. "A true man," he says, "belongs to no other time and place, but is the center of things. Where he is, there is nature. He measures you and all men and all events." Though Emerson thus asserts the maxim, he has not therefore succumbed, like M. France, to the doctrine of relativity and the feeling of universal illusion that accompanies it; on the contrary, he has attained to a new sense of the unity of human nature—a unity founded not on tradition but on insight. He says somewhere that he finds such an identity both of thought and sentiment in the best books of the world, that they seem to him to be the work of "one all-seeing, all-hearing gentleman." Now it is evidently this one all-seeing, all-hearing gentleman who is for Emerson the measure of all things. The individual man is the measure of all things only in so far as he has realized in himself this essential human nature. To be sure, the line is often hard to draw in practice between the two types of individualist. There were persons in ancient Athens—for example, Aristophanes in *The Clouds*—who treated Socrates as an ordinary sophist. In the same way, there are persons today who fail to see the difference between Emerson and an ordinary impressionist. "The source of Emerson's power," says Professor Santayana, "lay not in his doctrine but in his temperament."

Emerson's language is often indistinguishable from that of the impressionist. "I would write on the lintels of my doorpost, *whim*." "Dream delivers us to dream, and there is no end to illusion." "Life is a flux of moods." But he is careful to add that "there is that in us which changes not and which ranks all sensations and states of mind." The impressionist denies this element of absolute judgment and so feels free to indulge his temperament with epicurean indolence; at the same time he has the contemptuous indulgence for others that befits beings who are the "sport and playthings of mobile appearances." M. France says that he "despises men tenderly." We would reply in the words of Burke that the "species of benevolence which arises from contempt is no true charity." Impressionism has led to a strange increase in the number of dilettantes and *jouisseurs littéraires,* who to the precept *de gustibus non*[1] have given developments that would certainly have surprised its author. The Horatian plea for an honest liberty of taste has its necessary corrective in the truth that is very bluntly stated in a Spanish proverb: "There are tastes that deserve the cudgel." We are told that Sainte-Beuve was once so offended by an outrageous offense to good taste in a remark of Nicolardot's that, yielding to an irresistible impulse, he kicked him out of the room. Dante, in replying to a certain opponent, says with the instinct of a true Italian, that he would like to answer such "bestiality not with words but with a knife." We must remember that "good taste" as formerly understood was made up of two distinct elements: first, one's individual sensibility, and secondly, a code of outer rules by which this sensibility was disciplined and held in check. The observance of these rules became for the community of well-bred people a sort of *noblesse oblige,* and taste in this sense has been rightly defined by Rivarol as a man's literary honor. Now that the outer code has been abrogated, taste is not therefore delivered over to the caprices of a vagrant sensibility; taste is attained only when this sensibility is rectified with reference to standards inwardly apprehended, and in this sense may be defined as a man's literary conscience; it is, in short, only one aspect of the struggle between our lower and higher selves. Some, indeed, would maintain that taste is not a thing thus to be won by an effort of the will, but is rather an inborn and incommunicable tact, a sort of mysterious election, a free gift of the muses to a predestined few; that in literature many are called and few are chosen. In the article "Goût" of the *Philosophical Dictionary,* Voltaire discourses on the small number of the elect in matters of taste, and in almost the next article ("Grâce") turns all his powers of mockery on those who assert

[1] [This is part of the Latin proverb, "De Gustibus Non Est Disputandum," which means "There is no disputing tastes."]

the same doctrine in religion. Not only individuals but whole nations were once held to be under the reprobation of the muses. As Voltaire says sadly, *presque tout l'univers est barbare.* Perhaps even today persons might be found who would regard as legitimate the famous query of Father Bouhours whether a German can have wit. There are only too many examples in Germany and elsewhere of how far infinite industry and good intentions are from sufficing for the attainment of taste. However it may be in theology, it remains true in literature, as Gautier remarks, that works without grace are of no avail.

But one may recognize an element of predestination in the problem of taste and not therefore acquiesce in the impressionist's preaching of the fatality and finality of temperament. Everyone, to be sure, has an initial or temperamental taste, but it is hard to say how far this taste may be transformed by subordinating it to the higher claims of our nature. Dr. Johnson says that if he had no duties and no reference to futurity he should spend his life in driving briskly in a post chaise with a pretty woman. Here then is the temperamental taste of Dr. Johnson, and if he had been a disciple of M. France, he might have accepted it as final. Boswell reports an outburst of Johnson on this very subject: "Do not, sir, accustom yourself to trust to *impressions.* By trusting to impressions, a man may gradually come to yield to them, and at length be subject to them, so as not to be a free agent, or what is the same thing in effect, to *suppose* that he is not a free agent. A man who is in that state should not be suffered to live; . . . there can be no confidence in him, no more than in a tiger."

Johnson would evidently have agreed with the Buddhists in looking on the indolent settling down of a man in his own temperament as the chief of all the deadly sins. A fulmination like the foregoing is good to clear the air after the debilitating sophistries of M. France. Yet we feel that Johnson's point of view implies an undue denial of the individual's right to his own impressions and that therefore it has become in some measure obsolete. It is well for us, after all, to have fresh and vivid and personal impressions; it is well for us, in short, to awaken our senses;

but we should "awaken our senses that we may the better judge" —and not simply that we may the better enjoy. For instance, Walter Pater continually dwells on the need of awakening our senses, but when he speaks of "living in the full stream of refined sensation," when he urges us to gather ourselves together "into one desperate effort to see and touch," there is a hedonistic flavor in these utterances that can escape no one. On the other hand, there should be no ascetic denial of the value of the impression in itself. Brunetière is reported to have said to another critic, whom he suspected of intellectual epicureanism: "*You* always praise what pleases you; *I* never do." This is an asceticism of taste worthy of the spectator of Racine's comedy who wished to laugh according to the rules. And so Brunetière was led naturally into his reactionary attitude; seeing only the evil possibilities of individualism, he would have the modern man forego his claim to be the measure of all things and submit once more to outer authority. A certain type of seventeenth-century critic attempted to establish a standard that was entirely outside the individual. The impressionist has gone to the opposite extreme and set up a standard that is entirely within the individual. The problem is to find some middle ground between Procrustes and Proteus; and this right mean would seem to lie in a standard that is in the individual and yet is felt by him to transcend his personal self and lay hold of that part of his nature that he possesses in common with other men.

The impressionist not only refuses the individual man any such principle of judgment to which he may appeal from his fleeting impressions; he goes further and refuses men collectively any avenue of escape from universal illusion and relativity; he denies, in short, the doctrine embodied in the old church maxim, "*Securus judicat orbis terrarum,*" a doctrine so fundamental, we may note in passing, that in the form attributed to Lincoln it has become the cornerstone of democracy: "You cannot fool all the people all the time." M. Anatole France is fond of insisting, like Sainte-Beuve before him, that there inheres in mankind as a whole no such power of righting itself and triumphing over its own errors and illusions. A whole chapter might be made up of passages from Sainte-Beuve on the vanity of fame. "Posterity has allowed three fourths of the works of antiquity to perish," says M. France in turn; "it has allowed the rest to be frightfully corrupted . . . In the little that it has kept there are detestable books which are none the less immortal. Varius, we are told, was the equal of Virgil. He has perished. Aelian was an ass, and he survives. There is posterity for you," etc. Here again the contrast between the two types of individualist is absolute. "There is no luck in literary reputation," says Emerson. "They who make up the final verdict for every book are not the partial and noisy public of the hour, but a court as of angels; a public not to be bribed, not to be entreated, and not to be overawed decides upon every man's title to fame. Only those books come down which deserve to last. Blackmore, Kotzebue, or Pollock may endure for a night, but Moses and Homer stand forever. The permanence of all books is fixed by no effort friendly or hostile, but by their own specific gravity or the intrinsic importance of their contents to the constant mind of man."

We should add, then, in order to define our critical standard completely, that the judgment of the keen-sighted few in the present needs to be ratified by the verdict of posterity.

Frank Norris

(1870-1902)

The name of Frank Norris (Benjamin Franklin Norris) is inevitably associated with the naturalism that made its strongest appearance in the literature of the years immediately before and after the opening of the present century. Stated in simple terms, naturalism sees man as the victim of a determinism that exists within himself and his immediate environment. It is a belief that man is essentially a creation of nature and, like the animals, is controlled largely by inborn drives and stresses and the environmental conditions of his world.

Norris wrote six novels, of which the best known are McTeague *(1899),* The Octopus *(1901), and* The Pit *(1903). In these works, he employs the naturalistic approach which he espoused throughout his brief career. In each, he makes his central characters victims of their basic natures or the forces in their world. In each, the strong strokes of the young, firmly convinced believer in naturalism are all too apparent.*

Norris made an impact in the world of criticism as a reviewer and editor for newspapers and magazines and as the author of a volume of criticism. Of all his critical writings, the most widely known is his The Responsibilities of the Novelist *(1903), a work which actually incorporates much of his earliest ideas and writings.*

Examined from today's perspective, the shortcomings of this work are conspicuous. Norris oversimplifies; he treats his subject superficially; and he makes several rather questionable conclusions. Yet the work is important for its author's attempt to defend naturalism and its definition of naturalism as opposed to romanticism and realism. The book had, it seems, a heavy impact because of a surprisingly wide readership.

Norris, born in Chicago, was enrolled first at the University of California and then Harvard before leaving for Paris where he studied art for two years, 1887–89. His brief life, however, was not to be spent as a painter. Upon returning to the United States, he turned to writing and editing, serving as war correspondent for the San Francisco Chronicle *(1895–96) during the African insurrection and again for McClure's* Magazine *during the battles in Cuba in 1898. Although he was editor of the San Francisco* Wave *(1896–97), his most famous editorial work occurred with the signing of Theodore Dreiser to a Doubleday contract for* Sister Carrie *(1900). This act—one of the most significant in the history of freedom of expression in the novel—is indicative of Norris' forthrightness and courage.*

Zola as a Romantic Writer[1]

It is curious to notice how persistently M. Zola is misunderstood. How strangely he is misinterpreted even by those who conscientiously admire the novels of the "man of the iron pen." For most people Naturalism has a vague meaning. It is a sort of inner circle of realism—a kind of romanticism, a theory of fiction wherein things are represented "as they really are," inexorable, with the truthfulness of a camera. This idea can be shown to be far from right, that Naturalism, as understood by Zola, is but a form of romanticism after all.

Observe the methods employed by the novelists who profess and call themselves "realists"—Mr. Howells, for instance. Howells' characters live across the street from us, they are "on our block." We know all about them, about their affairs, and the story of their lives. One can go even further. We ourselves are Mr. Howells' characters, so long as we are well behaved and ordinary and bourgeois, so long as we are not adventurous or not rich or not

[1] Published as an article in *Wave*, XV (June 27, 1896).

unconventional. If we are otherwise, if things commence to happen to us, if we kill a man or two, or get mixed up in a tragic affair, or do something on a large scale, such as the amassing of enormous wealth or power or fame, Mr. Howells cuts our acquaintance at once. He will none of us if we are out of the usual.

This is the real Realism. It is the smaller details of every-day life, things that are likely to happen between lunch and supper, small passions, restricted emotions, dramas of the reception-room, tragedies of an afternoon call, crises involving cups of tea. Every one will admit there is no romance here. The novel is interesting— which is after all the main point—but it is the commonplace tale of commonplace people made into a novel of far more than commonplace charm. Mr. Howells is not uninteresting; he is simply not romantic. But that Zola should be quoted as a realist, and as a realist is a strange perversion.

Reflect a moment upon his choice of subject and character and episode. The Rougon-Macquart live in a world of their own; they are not of our lives any more than are the Don Juans, the Jean Valjeans, the Gil Blases, the Marmions, or the Ivanhoes. We, the bourgeois, the commonplace, the ordinary, have no part nor lot in the *Rougon-Macquart*, in *Lourdes*, or in *Rome;* it is not our world, not because our social position is different, but because we are *ordinary*. To be noted of M. Zola we must leave the rank and the file, either run to the forefront of the marching world, or fall by the roadway; we must separate ourselves; we must become individual, unique. The naturalist takes no note of common people, common in so far as their interests, their lives, and the things that occur in them are common, are ordinary. Terrible things must happen to the characters of the naturalistic tale. They must be twisted from the ordinary, wrenched out from the quiet, uneventful round of every-day life, and flung into the throes of a vast and terrible drama that works itself out in unleashed passions, in blood, and in sudden death. The world of M. Zola is a world of big things; the enormous, the formidable, the terrible, is what counts; no teacup tragedies here. Here Nana holds her

monstrous orgies, and dies horribly, her face distorted to a frightful mask; Etienne Lantier, carried away by the strike of coal
miners of *Le Voreux* (the strike that is almost war), is involved
in the vast and fearful catastrophe that comes as a climax of the
great drama; Claude Lantier, disappointed, disillusioned, ac-
knowledging the futility of his art after a life of effort, hangs
himself to his huge easel; Jacques Lantier, haunted by an
hereditary insanity, all his natural desires hideously distorted,
cuts the throat of the girl he loves, and is ground to pieces under
the wheels of his own locomotive; Jean Macquart, soldier and
tiller of the fields, is drawn into the war of 1870, passes through
the terrible scenes of Sedan and the Siege of Paris only to bayonet
to death his truest friend and sworn brother-at-arms in the streets
of the burning capital.

Everything is extraordinary, imaginative, grotesque even, with
a vague note of terror quivering throughout like the vibration
of an ominous and low-pitched diapason. It is all romantic, at
times unmistakably so, as in *Le Rêve* or *Rome,* closely resembling
the work of the greatest of all modern romanticists, Hugo. We
have the same huge dramas, the same enormous scenic effects, the
same love of the extraordinary, the vast, the monstrous, and the
tragic.

Naturalism is a form of romanticism, not an inner circle of
realism. Where is the realism in the *Rougon-Macquart?* Are such
things likely to happen between lunch and supper? That Zola's
work is not purely romantic as was Hugo's, lies chiefly in the
choice of Milieu. These great, terrible dramas no longer happen
among the personnel of a feudal and Renaissance nobility, those
who are in the fore-front of the marching world, but among the
lower—almost the lowest—classes; those who have been thrust or
wrenched from the ranks, who are falling by the roadway. This
is not romanticism—this drama of the people, working itself out
in blood and ordure. It is not realism. It is a school by itself,
unique, somber, powerful beyond words. It is naturalism.

A Plea for Romantic Fiction[2]

Let us at the start make a distinction. Observe that one speaks of Romanticism and not of sentimentalism. One claims that the latter is as distinct from the former as is that other form of art which is called Realism. Romance has been often put upon and overburdened by being forced to bear the onus of abuse that by right should fall to sentiment; but the two should be kept very distinct, for a very high and illustrious place will be claimed for Romance, while sentiment will be handed down the scullery stairs.

Many people today are composing mere sentimentalism, and calling it and causing it to be called Romance, so with those who are too busy to think much upon these subjects, but who none the less love honest literature, Romance too has fallen into disrepute. Consider now the cut-and-thrust stories. They are all labelled Romances, and it is very easy to get the impression that Romance must be an affair of cloaks and daggers, or moonlight and golden hair. But this is not so at all. The true Romance is a more serious business than this. It is not merely a conjurer's trick box, full of flimsy quackeries, tinsel and clap traps, meant only to amuse, and relying upon deception to do even that. Is it not something better than this? Can we not see in it an instrument, keen, finely tempered, flawless—an instrument with which we may go straight through the clothes and tissues and wrappings of flesh down deep into the red, living heart of things?

Is all this too subtle, too merely speculative and intrinsic, too *precieuse* and nice and "literary"? Devoutly one hopes the contrary. So much is made of so-called Romanticism in present day fiction, that the subject seems worthy of discussion, and a protest against the misuse of a really noble and honest formula of literature appears to be timely—misuse, that is, in the sense of limited use. Let us suppose for the moment that a Romance can be made out of the cut-and-thrust business. Good Heavens, are there no

[2] *Boston Evening Transcript,* December 18, 1901, p. 14.

other things that are romantic, even in this—falsely, falsely called
—humdrum world of today? Why should it be that so soon as the
novelist addresses himself—seriously—to the consideration of
contemporary life he must abandon Romance and take up that
harsh, loveless, colorless, blunt tool called Realism?

Now, let us understand at once what is meant by Romance and
what by Realism. Romance—I take it—is the kind of fiction that
takes cognizance of variations from the type of normal life.
Realism is the kind of fiction that confines itself to the type of
normal life. According to this definition, then, Romance may
even treat of the sordid, the unlovely—as for instance, the novels
of M. Zola. (Zola has been dubbed a realist, but he is, on the
contrary, the very head of the Romanticists.) Also, Realism, used
as it sometimes is as a term of reproach, need not be in the remotest sense or degree offensive, but on the other hand respectable as a church and proper as a deacon—as, for instance, the
novels of Mr. Howells.

The reason why one claims so much for Romance, and quarrels
so pointedly with Realism, is that Realism stultifies itself. It notes
only the surface of things. For it Beauty is not even skin-deep, but
only a geometrical plane, without dimensions of depth, a mere
outside. Realism is very excellent so far as it goes, but it goes no
farther than the Realist himself can actually see, or actually hear.
Realism is minute, it is the drama of a broken teacup, the tragedy
of a walk down the block, the excitement of an afternoon call, the
adventure of an invitation to dinner. It is the visit to my neighbor's house, a formal visit, from which I may draw no conclusions. I see my neighbor and his friends—very, oh, such very!
probable people—and that is all. Realism bows upon the doormat
and goes away and says to me, as we link arms on the sidewalk:
"That is life." And I say it is not. It is not, as you would very well
see if you took Romance with you to call upon your neighbor.

Lately you have been taking Romance a weary journey across
the water—ages and the flood of years—and haling her into the
fubsy, musty, worm-eaten, moth-riddled, rust-corroded "Grandes
Salles" of the Middle Ages and the Renaissance, and she has

found the drama of a bygone age for you there. But would you take her across the street to your neighbor's front parlor (with the bisque fisher boy on the mantel and the photograph of Niagara Falls on glass hanging in the front window); would you introduce her there? Not you. Would you take a walk with her on Fifth avenue, or Beacon street, or Michigan avenue? No indeed. Would you choose her for a companion of a morning spent in Wall Street, or an afternoon in the Waldorf-Astoria? You just guess you would not.

She would be out of place, you say, inappropriate. She might be awkward in my neighbor's front parlor, and knock over the little bisque fisher boy. Well, she might. If she did, you might find underneath the base of the statuette, hidden away, tucked away—what? God knows. But something which would be a complete revelation of my neighbor's secretest life.

So you think Romance would stop in the front parlor and discuss medicated flannels and mineral waters with the ladies? Not for more than five minutes. She would be off upstairs with you, prying, peeping, peering into the closets of the bedroom, into the nursery, into the sitting-room; yes, and into that little iron box screwed to the lower shelf of the closet in the library; and into those compartments and pigeon-holes of the *secretaire* in the study. She would find a heartache (may-be) between the pillows of the mistress's bed, and a memory carefully secreted in the master's deedbox. She would come upon a great hope amid the books and papers of the study table of the young man's room, and—perhaps—who knows—an affair, or, great heavens, an intrigue, in the scented ribbons and gloves and hairpins of the young lady's bureau. And she would pick here a little and there, making up a bag of hopes and fears, and a package of joys and sorrows—great ones, mind you—and then come down to the front door, and stepping out into the street, hand you the bags and package, and say to you—"That is Life!"

Romance does very well in the castles of the Middle Ages and the Renaissance chateaux, and she has the entrée there and is very well received. That is all well and good. But let us protest against limiting her to such places and such times. You will find her, I grant you, in the chatelaine's chamber and the dungeon of the man-at-arms; but, if you choose to look for her, you will find her equally at home in the brownstone house on the corner and in the office building downtown. And this very day, in this very hour, she is sitting among the rags and wretchedness, the dirt and despair of the tenements of the East Side of New York.

"What?" I hear you say, "look for Romance—the lady of the silken robes and golden crown, our beautiful, chaste maiden of soft voice and gentle eyes—look for her among the vicious ruffians, male and female, of Allen street and Mulberry Bend?" I tell you she is there, and to your shame be it said you will not know her in those surroundings. You, the aristocrats, who demand the fine linen and the purple in your fiction; you, the sensitive, the delicate, who will associate with your Romance only so long as she wears a silken gown. You will not follow her to the slums, for you believe that Romance should only amuse and entertain you, singing you sweet songs and touching the harp of silver strings with rosy-tipped fingers. If haply she should call to you from the squalor of a dive, or the awful degradation of a disorderly house, crying: "Look! listen! This, too, is life. These, too, are my children, look at them, know them and, knowing, help!" Should she call thus, you would stop your ears; you would avert your eyes, and you would answer, "Come from there, Romance. Your place is not there!" And you would make of her a harlequin, a tumbler, a sword dancer, when, as a matter of fact, she should be by right divine a teacher sent from God.

She will not always wear the robe of silk, the gold crown, the jeweled shoon, will not always sweep the silver harp. An iron note is hers if so she choose, and coarse garments, and stained hands; and, meeting her thus, it is for you to know her as she passes—know her for the same young queen of the blue mantle and lilies. She can teach you, if you will be humble to learn. Teach you by showing. God help you, if at last you take from Romance her mission of teaching, if you do not believe that she has a purpose, a nobler purpose and a mightier than mere amusement, mere entertainment. Let Realism do the entertaining with its meticulous presentation of teacups, rag carpets, wall paper and haircloth sofas, stopping with these, going no deeper than it sees, choosing the ordinary, the untroubled, the commonplace.

But to Romance belongs the wide world for range, and the unplumbed depths of the human heart, and the mystery of sex, and the problems of life, and the black, unsearched penetralia of the soul of man. You, the indolent, must not always be amused. What matter the silken clothes, what matter the prince's houses? Romance, too, is a teacher, and if—throwing aside the purple— she wears the camel's hair and feeds upon the locusts, it is to cry aloud unto the people, "Prepare ye the way of the Lord; make straight his path."

Ezra Pound

(b. 1885)

Ezra Pound's position in American criticism is often obscured by the ringing support of his admirers and the equally loud disparagement of his detractors. He has always been, in short, one who engenders spirited support and challenge.

Pound developed early a deep interest in learning—especially in the fields of language and comparative literature—and his writings radiate this facet of his personality. Widely read in Greek, Latin, French, Italian, and Oriental literature, he draws heavily on this knowledge to express both his simplest and his most involved thoughts. Consequently, his poetry, essays, and critical writings are replete with subtle and unfamiliar references, thereby demanding of his reader an extraordinary background and effort.

In his day-to-day life, Pound has also been a controversial figure. He supported the Fascism of Benito Mussolini; he has extolled the benefits of several totalitarian governments; and he constantly propounds a socialist philosophy. Throughout all, he has moved with a characteristically strong hand, alternately contemptuous and unmindful of the opposition. Naturally, this behavior has done little to earn either the respect or the sympathy of the general public.

Pound's greatest critical impact was centered in the Imagist movement of the early part of this century. Working in association with such figures as Amy Lowell, "H. D.," and William Carlos Williams, Pound upheld and practiced the Imagist philosophy. In its essence, this philosophy endorses objectivity, freedom of form, and distinct economy of language in the writing of poetry.

In addition to promoting the tenets of the Imagists, Pound has

been influential in stressing the value of science, especially
psychology, in providing techniques for the study of literature.
He has also been a strong critical force as an editor and critic
for the magazine Poetry, as a central personality in several poet-
author-critic circles, and as a direct influence on T. S. Eliot and
several lesser figures.

Pound, born in Hailey, Idaho, on October 30, 1885, pursued
his undergraduate education at the University of Pennsylvania
and Hamilton College (A.B., 1905). He then returned to the
University of Pennsylvania for graduate work leading to the
Master of Arts degree (1906) in romance languages, followed by
an additional year of study in Renaissance literature. His formal
education now completed, he went abroad, never to return to
the United States for any extended period. In fact, after World
War I, he considered himself an expatriate.

At present, Pound lives in Italy. He returned there upon being released by the United States government which had imprisoned him on a charge of treason immediately following the
Italian campaign of World War II. (Pound had been broadcasting
Axis propaganda to American troops during the war.) Actually,
Pound never stood trial on the charge because he was declared
insane, committed to a mental institution, and eventually set
free. In 1958, the treason charges were dismissed.

In the essay which follows, Pound explains Imagism and other
basic tenets of his critical theory.

Vorticism

"It is no more ridiculous that a person should receive or convey
an emotion by means of an arrangement of shapes, or planes,
or colours, than that they should receive or convey such emotion
by an arrangement of musical notes."

I suppose this proposition is self-evident. Whistler said as
much, some years ago, and Pater proclaimed that "All arts approach the condition of music."

Whenever I say this I am greeted with a storm of "Yes, but

. . . ." "But why isn't this art futurism?" "Why isn't" "Why don't?" and above all: "What, in Heaven's name, has it got to do with your Imagiste poetry?"

Let me explain at leisure, and in nice, orderly, old-fashioned prose.

We are all futurists to the extent of believing with Guillaume Apollinaire that "On ne peut pas porter *partout* avec soi le cadavre de son père." But "futurism," when it gets into art, is, for the most part, a descendant of impressionism. It is a sort of accelerated impressionism.

There is another artistic descent *via* Picasso and Kandinsky; *via* cubism and expressionism. One does not complain of neo-impressionism or of accelerated impressionism and "simultaneity," but one is not wholly satisfied by them. One has perhaps other needs.

It is very difficult to make generalities about three arts at once. I shall be, perhaps, more lucid if I give, briefly, the history of the vorticist art with which I am most intimately connected, that is to say, vorticist poetry. Vorticism has been announced as including such and such painting and sculpture and "Imagisme" in verse. I shall explain "Imagisme," and then proceed to show its inner relation to certain modern paintings and sculpture.

Imagisme, in so far as it has been known at all, has been known chiefly as a stylistic movement, as a movement of criticism rather than of creation. This is natural, for, despite all possible celerity of publication, the public is always, and of necessity, some years behind the artists' actual thought. Nearly anyone is ready to accept "Imagisme" as a department of poetry, just as one accepts "lyricism" as a department of poetry.

There is a sort of poetry where music, sheer melody, seems as if it were just bursting into speech.

There is another sort of poetry where painting or sculpture seems as if it were "just coming over into speech."

The first sort of poetry has long been called "lyric." One is accustomed to distinguish easily between "lyric" and "epic" and "didactic." One is capable of finding the "lyric" passages in a drama or in a long poem not otherwise "lyric." This division is in the grammars and school books, and one has been brought up to it.

The other sort of poetry is as old as the lyric and as honourable, but, until recently, no one had named it. Ibycus and Liu Ch'e presented the "Image." Dante is a great poet by reason of this faculty, and Milton is a wind-bag because of his lack of it. The "image" is the furthest possible remove from rhetoric. Rhetoric is the art of dressing up some unimportant matter so as to fool the audience for the time being. So much for the general category. Even Aristotle distinguishes between rhetoric, "which is persuasion," and the analytical examination of truth. As a "critical" movement, the "Imagisme" of 1912 to '14 set out "to bring poetry up to the level of prose." No one is so quixotic as to believe that contemporary poetry holds any such position. . . . Stendhal formulated the need in his *De L'Amour:*—

"La poésie avec ses comparaisons obligées, sa mythologie que ne croit pas le poète, sa dignité de style à la Louis XIV et tout l'attirail de ses ornements appelés poétique, est bien au dessous de la prose dès qu'il s'agit de donner une idée claire et précise des mouvements de coeur, or dans ce genre on n'émeut que par la clarté."

Flaubert and De Maupassant lifted prose to the rank of a finer art, and one has no patience with contemporary poets who escape from all the difficulties of the infinitely difficult art of good prose by pouring themselves into loose verses.

The tenets of the Imagiste faith were published in March, 1913, as follows:—

I. Direct treatment of the "thing," whether subjective or objective.

II. To use absolutely no word that does not contribute to the presentation.

III. As regarding rhythm: to compose in sequence of the musical phrase, not in sequence of the metronome.

There followed a series of about forty cautions to beginners, which need not concern us here.

The arts have indeed "some sort of common bond, some inter-recognition." Yet certain emotions or subjects find their most appropriate expression in some one particular art. The work of art which is most "worth while" is the work which would need a hundred works of any other kind of art to explain it. A fine statue is the core of a hundred poems. A fine poem is a score of symphonies. There is music which would need a hundred paintings to express it. There is no synonym for the *Victory of Samothrace* or for Mr. Epstein's flenites. There is no painting of Villon's *Frères Humains*. Such works are what we call works of the "first intensity."

A given subject or emotion belongs to that artist, or to that sort of artist who must know it most intimately and most intensely before he can render it adequately in his art. A painter must know much more about a sunset than a writer, if he is to put it on canvas. But when the poet speaks of "Dawn in russet mantle clad," he presents something which the painter cannot present.

I said in the preface to my *Guido Cavalcanti* that I believed in an absolute rhythm. I believe that every emotion and every phase of emotion has some toneless phrase, some rhythm-phrase to express it.

(This belief leads to *vers libre* and to experiments in quantitative verse.)

To hold a like belief in a sort of permanent metaphor is, as I understand it, "symbolism" in its profounder sense. It is not necessarily a belief in a permanent world, but it is a belief in that direction.

Imagisme is not symbolism. The symbolists dealt in "association," that is, in a sort of allusion, almost of allegory. They degraded the symbol to the status of a word. They made it a form of metonomy. One can be grossly "symbolic," for example, by using the term "cross" to mean "trial." The symbolist's *symbols* have a fixed value, like numbers in arithmetic, like 1, 2, and 7. The imagiste's images have a variable significance, like the signs *a, b,* and *x* in algebra.

Moreover, one does not want to be called a symbolist, because symbolism has usually been associated with mushy technique.

On the other hand, Imagisme is not Impressionism, though one borrows, or could borrow, much from the impressionist method of presentation. But this is only negative definition. If I am to give a psychological or philosophical definition "from the inside," I can only do so autobiographically. The precise statement of such a matter must be based on one's own experience.

In the "search for oneself," in the search for "sincere self-expression," one gropes, one finds some seeming verity. One says "I am" this, that, or the other, and with the words scarcely uttered one ceases to be that thing.

I began this search for the real in a book called *Personæ*, casting off, as it were, complete masks of the self in each poem. I continued in long series of translations, which were but more elaborate masks.

Secondly, I made poems like "The Return," which is an objective reality and has a complicated sort of significance, like Mr. Epstein's "Sun God," or Mr. Brzeska's "Boy with a Coney." Thirdly, I have written "Heather," which represents a state of consciousness, or "implies," or "implicates" it.

A Russian correspondent, after having called it a symbolist poem, and having been convinced that it was not symbolism, said slowly: "I see, you wish to give people new eyes, not to make them see some new particular thing."

These two latter sorts of poems are impersonal, and that fact brings us back to what I said about absolute metaphor. They are Imagisme, and in so far as they are Imagisme, they fall in with the new pictures and the new sculpture.

Whistler said somewhere in the *Gentle Art:* "The picture is interesting not because it is Trotty Veg, but because it is an arrangement in colour." The minute you have admitted that, you let in the jungle, you let in nature and truth and abundance and cubism and Kandinsky, and the lot of us. Whistler and Kandinsky and some cubists were set to getting extraneous matter out

of their art; they were ousting literary values. The Flaubertians
talk a good deal about "constatation." "The 'nineties" saw a
movement against rhetoric. I think all these things move together, though they do not, of course, move in step.

The painters realise that what matters is form and colour.
Musicians long ago learned that programme music was not the
ultimate music. Almost anyone can realize that to use a symbol
with an ascribed or intended meaning is, usually, to produce very
bad art. We all remember crowns, and crosses, and rainbows, and
what not in atrociously mumbled colour.

The Image is the poet's pigment.[1] The painter should use his
colour because he sees it or feels it. I don't much care whether
he is representative or non-representative. He should *depend,* of
course, on the creative, not upon the mimetic or representational
part in his work. It is the same in writing poems, the author must
use his *image* because he sees it or feels it, *not* because he thinks
he can use it to back up some creed or some system of ethics or
economics.

An *image,* in our sense, is real because we know it directly. If it
have an age-old traditional meaning this may serve as proof to
the professional student of symbology that we have stood in the
deathless light, or that we have walked in some particular
arbour of his traditional paradiso, but that is not our affair. It is
our affair to render the *image* as we have perceived or conceived
it.

Browning's "Sordello" is one of the finest *masks* ever presented.
Dante's "Paradiso" is the most wonderful *image.* By that I
do not mean that it is a perseveringly imagistic performance.
The permanent part is Imagisme, the rest, the discourses with
the calendar of saints and the discussions about the nature of the
moon, are philology. The form of sphere above sphere, the
varying reaches of light, the minutiæ of pearls upon foreheads, all
these are parts of the Image. The image is the poet's pigment;
with that in mind you can go ahead and apply Kandinsky, you

---

[1] The image has been defined as "that which presents an intellectual and
emotional complex in an instant of time." AUTHOR'S NOTE.

can transpose his chapter on the language of form and colour and apply it to the writing of verse. As I cannot rely on your having read Kandinsky's *Ueber das Geistige in der Kunst,* I must go on with my autobiography.

Three years ago in Paris I got out of a "metro" train at La Concorde, and saw suddenly a beautiful face, and then another and another, and then a beautiful child's face, and then another beautiful woman, and I tried all that day to find words for what this had meant to me, and I could not find any words that seemed to me worthy, or as lovely as that sudden emotion. And that evening, as I went home along the Rue Raynouard, I was still trying and I found, suddenly, the expression. I do not mean that I found words, but there came an equation . . . not in speech, but in little splotches of colour. It was just that—a "pattern," or hardly a pattern, if by "pattern" you mean something with a "repeat" in it. But it was a word, the beginning, for me, of a language in colour. I do not mean that I was unfamiliar with the kindergarten stories about colours being like tones in music. I think that sort of thing is nonsense. If you try to make notes permanently correspond with particular colours, it is like tying narrow meanings to symbols.

That evening, in the Rue Raynouard, I realized quite vividly that if I were a painter, or if I had, often, *that kind* of emotion, or even if I had the energy to get paints and brushes and keep at it, I might found a new school of painting, of "non-representative" painting, a painting that would speak only by arrangements in colour.

And so, when I came to read Kandinsky's chapter on the language of form and colour, I found little that was new to me. I only felt that some one else understood what I understood, and had written it out very clearly. It seems quite natural to me that an artist should have just as much pleasure in an arrangement of planes or in a pattern of figures, as in painting portraits of fine ladies, or in portraying the Mother of God as the symbolists bid us.

When I find people ridiculing the new arts, or making fun

of the clumsy odd terms that we use in trying to talk of them amongst ourselves; when they laugh at our talking about the "ice-block quality" in Picasso, I think it is only because they do not know what thought is like, and that they are familiar only with argument and gibe and opinion. That is to say, they can only enjoy what they have been brought up to consider enjoyable, or what some essayist has talked about in mellifluous phrases. They think only "the shells of thought," as De Gourmont calls them; the thoughts that have been already thought out by others.

Any mind that is worth calling a mind must have needs beyond the existing categories of language, just as a painter must have pigments or shades more numerous than the existing names of the colours.

Perhaps this is enough to explain the words in my "Vortex":—

"Every concept, every emotion, presents itself to the vivid consciousness in some primary form. It belongs to the art of this form."

That is to say, my experience in Paris should have gone into paint. If instead of colour I had perceived sound or planes in relation, I should have expressed it in music or in sculpture. Colour was, in that instance, the "primary pigment"; I mean that it was the first adequate equation that came into consciousness. The Vorticist uses the "primary pigment." Vorticism is art before it has spread itself into flaccidity, into elaboration and secondary applications.

What I have said of one vorticist art can be transposed for another vorticist art. But let me go on then with my own branch of vorticism, about which I can probably speak with greater clarity. All poetic language is the language of exploration. Since the beginning of bad writing, writers have used images as ornaments. The point of Imagisme is that it does not use images *as ornaments*. The image is itself the speech. The image is the word beyond formulated language.

I once saw a small child go to an electric light switch and say,

"Mamma, can I *open* the light?" She was using the age-old language of exploration, the language of art. It was a sort of
metaphor, but she was not using it as ornamentation.

One is tired of ornamentations, they are all a trick, and any
sharp person can learn them.

The Japanese have had the sense of exploration. They have
understood the beauty of this sort of knowing. A Chinaman said
long ago that if a man can't say what he has to say in twelve
lines he had better keep quiet. The Japanese have evolved the
still shorter form of the *hokku*.

> The fallen blossom flies back to its branch:
> A butterfly.

That is the substance of a very well-known *hokku*. Victor Plarr
tells me that once, when he was walking over snow with a
Japanese naval officer, they came to a place where a cat had
crossed the path, and the officer said, "Stop, I am making a
poem." Which poem was, roughly, as follows:—

> The footsteps of the cat upon the snow:
> (are like) plum-blossoms.

The words "are like" would not occur in the original, but I add
them for clarity.

The "one image poem" is a form of super-position, that is to
say, it is one idea set on top of another. I found it useful in getting
out of the impasse in which I had been left by my metro emotion.
I wrote a thirty-line poem, and destroyed it because it was what
we call work "of second intensity." Six months later I made a
poem half that length; a year later I made the following
hokku-like sentence:—

> The apparition of these faces in the crowd:
> Petals, on a wet, black bough.

I dare say it is meaningless unless one has drifted into a certain vein of thought.[2] In a poem of this sort one is trying to record the precise instant when a thing outward and objective transforms itself, or darts into a thing inward and subjective.

This particular sort of consciousness has not been identified with impressionist art. I think it is worthy of attention.

The logical end of impressionist art is the cinematograph. The state of mind of the impressionist tends to become cinematographical. Or, to put it another way, the cinematograph does away with the need of a lot of impressionist art.

There are two opposed ways of thinking of a man: firstly, you may think of him as that toward which perception moves, as the toy of circumstance, as the plastic substance *receiving* impressions; secondly, you may think of him as directing a certain fluid force against circumstance, as *conceiving* instead of merely reflecting and observing. One does not claim that one way is better than the other, one notes a diversity of the temperament. The two camps always exist. In the 'eighties there were symbolists opposed to impressionists, now you have vorticism, which is, roughly speaking, expressionism, neo-cubism, and imagism gathered together in one camp and futurism in the other. Futurism is descended from impressionism. It is, in so far as it is an art movement, a kind of accelerated impressionism. It is a spreading, or surface art, as opposed to vorticism, which is intensive.

The vorticist has not this curious tic for destroying past glories. I have no doubt that Italy needed Mr. Marinetti, but he did not set on the egg that hatched me, and as I am wholly opposed to his aesthetic principles I see no reason why I, and various men who agree with me, should be expected to call ourselves futurists. We do not desire to evade comparison with the past. We prefer that the comparison be made by some intelligent person

---

[2] Mr. Flint and Mr. Rodker have made longer poems depending on a similar presentation of matter. So also have Richard Aldington, in his *In Via Sestina,* and "H. D." in her *Oread,* which latter poems express much stronger emotions than that in my lines here given. Mr. Hueffer gives an interesting account of a similar adventure of his own in his review of the Imagiste anthology.

whose idea of "the tradition" is not limited by the conventional taste of four or five centuries and one continent.

Vorticism is an intensive art. I mean by this, that one is concerned with the relative intensity, or relative significance of different sorts of expression. One desires the most intense, for certain forms of expression *are* "more intense" than others. They are more dynamic. I do not mean they are more emphatic, or that they are yelled louder. I can explain my meaning best by mathematics.

There are four different intensities of mathematical expression known to the ordinarily intelligent undergraduate, namely: the arithmetical, the algebraic, the geometrical, and that of analytical geometry.

For instance, you can write

$$3 \times 3 + 4 \times 4 = 5 \times 5,$$
$$\text{or, differently, } 3^2 + 4^2 = 5^2.$$

That is merely conversation or "ordinary common sense." It is a simple statement of one fact and does not implicate any other.

Secondly, it is true that

$$3^2 + 4^2 = 5^2, 6^2 + 8^2 = 10^2, 9^2 + 12^2 = 15^2, 39^2 + 52^2 = 65^2.$$

These are all separate facts, one may wish to mention their underlying similarity; it is a bore to speak about each one in turn. One expresses their "algebraic relation" as

$$a^2 + b^2 = c^2.$$

That is the language of philosophy. It MAKES NO PICTURE. This kind of statement applies to a lot of facts, but it does not grip hold of Heaven.

Thirdly, when one studies Euclid one finds that the relation of $a^2 + b^2 = c^2$ applies to the ratio between the squares on the two sides of a right-angled triangle and the square on the hypotenuse. One still writes it $a^2 + b^2 = c^2$, but one has begun to talk about form. Another property or quality of life has crept into one's matter. Until then one had dealt only with numbers.

But even this statement does not *create* form. The picture is given you in the proposition about the square on the hypotenuse of the right-angled triangle being equal to the sum of the squares on the two other sides. Statements in plane and descriptive geometry are like talk about art. They are a criticism of the form. The form is not created by them.

Fourthly, we come to Descartian or "analytical geometry." Space is conceived as separated by two or by three axes (depending on whether one is treating form in one or more planes). One refers points to these axes by a series of co-ordinates. Given the idiom, one is able *actually to create.*

Thus, we learn that the equation $(x - a)^2 + (y - b)^2 = r^2$ governs the circle. It is the circle. It is not a particular circle, it is any circle and all circles. It is nothing that is not a circle. It is the circle free of space and time limits. It is the universal, existing in perfection, in freedom from space and time. Mathematics is dull ditchwater until one reaches analytics. But in analytics we come upon a new way of dealing with form. It is in this way that art handles life. The difference between art and analytical geometry is the difference of subject-matter only. Art is more interesting in proportion as life and the human consciousness are more complex and more interesting than forms and numbers.

This statement does not interfere in the least with "spontaneity" and "intuition," or with their function in art. I passed my last *exam.* in mathematics on sheer intuition. I saw where the line *had* to go, as clearly as I ever saw an image, or felt *caelestem intus vigorem.*

The statements of "analytics" are "lords" over fact. They are the thrones and dominations that rule over form and recurrence. And in like manner are great works of art lords over fact, over race-long recurrent moods, and over to-morrow.

Great works of art contain this fourth sort of equation. They cause form to come into being. By the "image" I mean such an equation; not an equation of mathematics, not something about *a, b,* and *c,* having something to do with form, but about *sea, cliffs, night,* having something to do with mood.

The image is not an idea. It is a radiant node or cluster; it is what I can, and must perforce, call a VORTEX, from which, and through which, and into which, ideas are constantly rushing. In decency one can only call it a VORTEX. And from this necessity came the name "vorticism." *Nomina sunt consequentia rerum,* and never was that statement of Aquinas more true than in the case of the vorticist movement. . . .

NOTE

I am often asked whether there can be a long imagiste or vorticist poem. The Japanese, who evolved the *hokku,* evolved also the Noh plays. In the best "Noh" the whole play may consist of one image. I mean it is gathered about one image. Its unity consists in one image, enforced by movement and music. I see nothing against a long vorticist poem.

On the other hand, no artist can possibly get a vortex into every poem or picture he does. One would like to do so, but it is beyond one. Certain things seem to demand metrical expression, or expression in a rhythm more agitated than the rhythms acceptable to prose, and these subjects, though they do not contain a vortex, may have some interest, an interest as "criticism of life" or of art. It is natural to express these things, and a vorticist or imagiste writer may be justified in presenting a certain amount of work which is not vorticism or imagisme, just as he might be justified in printing a purely didactic prose article. Unfinished sketches and drawings have a similar interest; they are trials and attempts toward a vortex.

H. L. Mencken

(1880–1956)

If one were to seek the most fiery, outspoken, and iconoclastic personality ever to appear on the American critical scene, he would have to give extensive consideration to Henry Louis Mencken.

Born in Baltimore, Maryland, Mencken never left his home town for more than a short period. He was of that city, and he observed life from that base. These observations he fortified with a rather wide, if selective, reading—especially in the works of the philosopher Friedrich Nietzsche—and early in his career he formulated a philosophy of extremes which he held, almost unchanged, to the end.

Mencken was distinctly a believer in the concept of the gifted as opposed to the limited man—or the superman as opposed to the mere man. He also believed that the affairs of the world must be handled by those most capable. Hence he rejected any really democratic form of government. Further, he was violently opposed to the Christian morality which he saw at the foundation of the society about him.

From these beliefs, he then developed a yardstick by which he measured an extensive range of subjects. Where he found something which pleased him, he praised it highly. Where he encountered something which displeased him, he resorted to a scorching invective. He was not, in short, a man to strike a midway or compromising position. Thus his criticism of life, books, people, institutions, or whatever else he adjudged was invariably a criticism of extremes.

Mencken's critical views are important for the impact which

they made upon the general citizenry—especially between 1915
and 1930—when he was quoted in many quarters with the
respect commonly reserved for the literary dictator. In fact, he
was probably the most widely read critical force of that period.
With the rising of the new generation of the depression years of
the thirties, however, he seemed to lose his grasp on the American
consciousness.

The critical thrust which Mencken possessed was demonstrated
when his essay on Theodore Dreiser (1917) vaulted Dreiser to a
front-ranking position with the reading public. Mencken's stature
is also evident in the numerous critical passages appearing in
the columns of the Baltimore Sun papers, the publications with
which his name is invariably associated. Then, too, one should
note his Prejudices (1919) and The American Language (1919),
two of the most widely read books of their kind in all Americana.

Mencken centered his whole life about writing. Graduated
from the Baltimore Polytechnic Institute at 16, he studied independently for three years—rather than attend a college—and then
began his long association with newspapers, magazines, and publishing houses. While working full time on the Baltimore Sun
newspapers, he also wrote for and edited magazines and served
as a consultant to publisher Alfred A. Knopf—meanwhile producing his several books.

Mencken's closing years were sad and disillusioning. The
ravages of ill health and the neglect of a once-admiring public
made life a difficult trial for the mind once afire with startling
ideas in many fields.

The essay below is taken from Prejudices: Third Series (1922).

Footnote on Criticism

Nearly all the discussions of criticism that I am acquainted with
start off with a false assumption, to wit, that the primary motive
of the critic, the impulse which makes a critic of him instead of,
say, a politician, or a stockbroker, is pedagogical—that he writes
because he is possessed by a passion to advance the enlighten-

ment, to put down error and wrong, to disseminate some specific
doctrine: psychological, epistemological, historical, or aesthetic.
This is true, it seems to me, only of bad critics, and its degree of
truth increases in direct ratio to their badness. The motive of
the critic who is really worth reading—the only critic of whom,
indeed, it may be said truthfully that it is at all possible to read
him, save as an act of mental discipline—is something quite
different. That motive is not the motive of the pedagogue, but
the motive of the artist. It is no more and no less than the simple
desire to function freely and beautifully, to give outward and
objective form to ideas that bubble inwardly and have a fascinat-
ing lure in them, to get rid of them dramatically and make an
articulate noise in the world. It was for this reason that Plato
wrote the "Republic," and for this reason that Beethoven wrote
the Ninth Symphony, and it is for this reason, to drop a million
miles, that I am writing the present essay. Everything else is
afterthought, mock-modesty, messianic delusion—in brief, af-
fectation and folly. Is the contrary conception of criticism widely
cherished? Is it almost universally held that the thing is a brother
to jurisprudence, advertising, laparotomy, chautauqua lecturing
and the art of the schoolmarm? Then certainly the fact that it is
so held should be sufficient to set up an overwhelming probability
of its lack of truth and sense. If I speak with some heat, it is as one
who has suffered. When, years ago, I devoted myself diligently
to critical pieces upon the writings of Theodore Dreiser, I found
that practically every one who took any notice of my proceedings
at all fell into either one of two assumptions about my underlying
purpose: (a) that I had a fanatical devotion for Mr. Dreiser's
ideas and desired to propagate them, or (b) that I was an ardent
patriot, and yearned to lift up American literature. Both assumptions were false. I had then, and I have now, very little interest in many of Mr. Dreiser's main ideas; when we meet, in fact,
we usually quarrel about them. And I am wholly devoid of public
spirit, and haven't the least lust to improve American literature; if
it ever came to what I regard as perfection my job would be gone.
What, then, was my motive in writing about Mr. Dreiser so

copiously? My motive, well known to Mr. Dreiser himself and to every one else who knew me as intimately as he did, was simply and solely to sort out and give coherence to the ideas of Mr. Mencken, and to put them into suave and ingratiating terms, and to discharge them with a flourish, and maybe with a phrase of pretty song, into the dense fog that blanketed the Republic.

The critic's choice of criticism rather than of what is called creative writing is chiefly a matter of temperament—perhaps, more accurately of hormones—with accidents of education and environment to help. The feelings that happen to be dominant in him at the moment the scribbling frenzy seizes him are feelings inspired, not directly by life itself, but by books, pictures, music, sculpture, architecture, religion, philosophy—in brief, by some other man's feelings about life. They are thus, in a sense, second-hand, and it is no wonder that creative artists so easily fall into the theory that they are also second-rate. Perhaps they usually are. If, indeed, the critic continues on this plane—if he lacks the intellectual agility and enterprise needed to make the leap from the work of art to the vast and mysterious complex of phenomena behind it—then they *always* are, and he remains no more than a fugleman or policeman to his betters. But if a genuine artist is concealed within him—if his feelings are in any sense profound and original, and his capacity for self-expression is above the average of educated men—then he moves inevitably from the work of art to life itself, and begins to take on a dignity that he formerly lacked. It is impossible to think of a man of any actual force and originality, universally recognized as having those qualities, who spent his whole life appraising and describing the work of other men. Did Goethe, or Carlyle, or Matthew Arnold, or Sainte-Beuve, or Macaulay, or even, to come down a few pegs, Lewes, or Lowell, or Hazlitt? Certainly not. The thing that becomes most obvious about the writings of all such men, once they are examined carefully, is that the critic is always being swallowed up by the creative artist—that what starts out as the review of a book, or a play, or other work of art, usually develops very quickly into an independent essay upon the theme of that work of art, or upon some theme that it suggests—in a word, that it becomes a fresh work of art, and only indirectly related to the one that suggested it. This fact, indeed, is so plain that it scarcely needs statement. What the pedagogues always object to in, for example, the *Quarterly* reviewers is that they forgot the books they were supposed to review, and wrote long papers—often, in fact, small books—expounding ideas suggested (or not suggested) by the books under review. Every critic who is worth reading falls inevitably into the same habit. He cannot stick to his task: what is before him is always infinitely less interesting to him than what is within him. If he is genuinely first-rate—if what is within him stands the test of type, and wins an audience, and produces the reactions that every artist craves—then he usually ends by abandoning the criticism of specific works of art altogether, and setting up shop as a general merchant in general ideas, *i.e.*, as an artist working in the materials of life itself.

Mere reviewing, however conscientiously and competently it is done, is plainly a much inferior business. Like writing poetry, it is chiefly a function of intellectual immaturity. The young literatus just out of the university, having as yet no capacity for grappling with the fundamental mysteries of existence, is put to writing reviews of books, or plays, or music, or painting. Very often he does it extremely well; it is, in fact, not hard to do well, for even decayed pedagogues often do it, as such graves of the intellect as the New York *Times* bear witness. But if he continues to do it, whether well or ill, it is a sign to all the world that his growth ceased when they made him *Artium Baccalaureus*. Gradually he becomes, whether in or out of the academic grove, a professor, which is to say, a man devoted to diluting and retailing the ideas of his superiors—not an artist, not even a bad artist, but almost the antithesis of an artist. He is learned, he is sober, he is painstaking and accurate—but he is as hollow as a jug. Nothing is in him save the ghostly echoes of other men's thoughts and feelings. If he were a genuine artist he would have thoughts and feelings of his own, and the impulse to give them objective form would be irresistible. An artist can no more withstand that impulse than a politician can withstand the temptations of a job. There are no mute, inglorious Miltons, save in the hallucinations of poets. The one sound test of a Milton is that he functions as a Milton. His difference from other men lies precisely in the superior vigor of his impulse to self-expression, not in the superior beauty and loftiness of his ideas. Other men, in point of fact, often have the same ideas, or perhaps even loftier ones, but they are able to suppress them, usually on grounds of decorum, and so they escape being artists, and are respected by right-thinking persons, and die with money in the bank, and are forgotten in two weeks.

Obviously, the critic whose performance we are commonly called upon to investigate is a man standing somewhere along the path leading from the beginning that I have described to the goal. He has got beyond being a mere cataloguer and valuer of other men's ideas, but he has not yet become an autonomous artist—he is not yet ready to challenge attention with his own ideas alone. But it is plain that his motion, in so far as he is moving at all, must be in the direction of that autonomy—that is, unless one imagines him sliding backward into senile infantilism: a spectacle not unknown to literary pathology, but too pathetic to be discussed here. Bear this motion in mind, and the true nature of his aims and purposes becomes clear; more, the incurable falsity of the aims and purposes usually credited to him becomes equally clear. He is not actually trying to perform an impossible act of arctic justice upon the artist whose work gives him a text. He is not trying with mathematical passion to find out exactly what was in that artist's mind at the moment of creation, and to display it precisely and in an ecstasy of appreciation. He is not trying to bring the work discussed into accord with some transient theory of aesthetics, or ethics, or truth, or to determine its degree of departure from that theory. He is not trying to lift up the fine arts, or to defend democracy against sense, or to promote happiness at the domestic hearth, or to convert sophomores into right-thinkers, or to serve God. He is not trying to fit a group of novel phenomena into the orderly process of history. He is not even trying to discharge the catalytic office that I myself, in a romantic moment, once sought to force upon him. He is, first and last, simply trying to express himself. He is trying to arrest and challenge a sufficient body of readers, to make them pay attention to him, to impress them with the charm and novelty of his ideas, to provoke them into an agreeable (or shocked) awareness of him, and he is trying to achieve thereby for his own inner ego the grateful feeling of a function performed, a tension relieved, a *katharsis* attained which Wagner achieved when he wrote "Die Walküre," and a hen achieves every time she lays an egg.

Joseph Conrad is moved by that necessity to write romances; Bach was moved to write music; poets are moved to write poetry; critics are moved to write criticism. The form is nothing; the only important thing is the motive power, and it is the same in all cases. It is the pressing yearning of every man who has ideas in him to empty them upon the world, to hammer them into plausible and ingratiating shapes, to compel the attention and respect of his equals, to lord it over his inferiors. So seen, the critic becomes a far more transparent and agreeable fellow than ever he was in the discourses of the psychologists who sought to make him a mere appraiser in an intellectual customs house, a gauger in a distillery of the spirit, a just and infallible judge upon the cosmic bench. Such offices, in point of fact, never fit him. He always bulges over their confines. So labeled and estimated, it inevitably turns out that the specific critic under examination is a very bad one, or no critic at all. But when he is thought of, not as pedagogue, but as artist, then he begins to take on reality, and, what is more, dignity. Carlyle was surely no just and infallible judge; on the contrary, he was full of prejudices, biles, naïvetés, humors. Yet he is read, consulted, attended to. Macaulay was unfair, inaccurate, fanciful, lyrical—yet his essays live. Arnold had his faults too, and so did Sainte-Beuve, and so did Goethe, and so did many another of that line—and yet they are remembered today, and all the learned and conscientious critics of their time, laboriously concerned with the precise intent of the artists under review, and passionately determined to set it forth with god-like care and to relate it exactly to this or that great stream of ideas—all these pedants are forgotten. What saved Carlyle, Macaulay and company is as plain as day. They were first-rate artists. They could make the thing charming, and that is always a million times more important than making it true.

Truth, indeed, is something that is believed in completely only by persons who have never tried personally to pursue it to its fastnesses and grab it by the tail. It is the adoration of second-rate men—men who always receive it at second-hand. Pedagogues believe in immutable truths and spend their lives trying to determine them and propagate them; the intellectual progress of man consists largely of a concerted effort to block and destroy their enterprise. Nine times out of ten, in the arts as in life, there is actually no truth to be discovered; there is only error to be exposed. In whole departments of human inquiry it seems to me quite unlikely that the truth ever *will* be discovered. Nevertheless, the rubber-stamp thinking of the world always makes the assumption that the exposure of an error is identical with the discovery of the truth—that error and truth are simple opposites. They are nothing of the sort. What the world turns to, when it has been cured of one error, is usually simply another error, and maybe one worse than the first one. This is the whole history of the intellect in brief. The average man of today does not believe in precisely the same imbecilities that the Greek of the fourth century before Christ believed in, but the things that he *does* believe in are often quite as idiotic. Perhaps this statement is a bit too sweeping. There is, year by year, a gradual accumulation of what may be called, provisionally, truths—there is a slow accretion of ideas that somehow manage to meet all practicable human tests, and so survive. But even so, it is risky to call them absolute truths. All that one may safely say of them is that no one, as yet, has demonstrated that they are errors. Soon or late, if experience teaches us anything, they are likely to succumb too.

The profoundest truths of the Middle Ages are now laughed at by schoolboys. The profoundest truths of democracy will be laughed at, a few centuries hence, even by schoolteachers.

In the department of aesthetics, wherein critics mainly disport themselves, it is almost impossible to think of a so-called truth that shows any sign of being permanently true. The most profound of principles begins to fade and quiver almost as soon as it is stated. But the work of art, as opposed to the theory behind it, has a longer life, particularly if that theory be obscure and questionable, and so cannot be determined accurately. "Hamlet," the Mona Lisa, "Faust," "Dixie," "Parsifal," "Mother Goose," "Annabel Lee," "Huckleberry Finn"—these things, so baffling to pedagogy, so contumacious to the categories, so mysterious in purpose and utility—these things live. And why? Because there is in them the flavor of salient, novel and attractive personality, because the quality that shines from them is not that of correct demeanor but that of creative passion, because they pulse and breathe and speak, because they are genuine works of art. So with criticism. Let us forget all the heavy effort to make a science of it; it is a fine art, or nothing. If the critic, retiring to his cell to concoct his treatise upon a book or play or what-not, produces a piece of writing that shows sound structure, and brilliant color, and the flash of new and persuasive ideas, and civilized manners, and the charm of an uncommon personality in free function, then he has given something to the world that is worth having, and sufficiently justified his existence. Is Carlyle's "Frederick" true? Who cares? As well ask if the Parthenon is true, or the C minor Symphony, or "Wiener Blut." Let the critic who is an artist leave such necropsies to professors of aesthetics, who can no more determine the truth than he can, and will infallibly make it unpleasant and a bore.

It is, of course, not easy to practice this abstention. Two forces, one within and one without, tend to bring even a Hazlitt or a Huneker under the campus pump. One is the almost universal human susceptibility to messianic delusions—the irresistible tendency of practically every man, once he finds a crowd in front of him, to strut and roll his eyes. The other is the public demand, born of such long familiarity with pedagogical criticism that no other kind is readily conceivable, that the critic teach something as well as say something—in the popular phrase, that he be constructive. Both operate powerfully against his free functioning, and especially the former. He finds it hard to resist the flattery of his customers, however little he may actually esteem it. If he knows anything at all, he knows that his following, like that of every other artist in ideas, is chiefly made up of the congenitally subaltern type of man and woman—natural converts, lodge joiners, me-toos, stragglers after circus parades. It is precious seldom that he ever gets a positive idea out of them; what he usually gets is mere unintelligent ratification. But this troop, despite its obvious failings, corrupts him in various ways. For one thing, it enormously reenforces his belief in his own ideas, and so tends to make him stiff and dogmatic—in brief, precisely everything that he ought not to be. And for another thing, it tends to make him (by a curious contradiction) a bit pliant and politic: he begins to estimate new ideas, not in proportion as they are amusing or beautiful, but in proportion as they are likely to please. So beset, front and rear, he sometimes sinks supinely to the level of a professor, and his subsequent proceedings are interesting no more. The true aim of a critic is certainly not to make converts. He must know that very few of the persons who are susceptible to conversion are worth converting. Their minds are intrinsically flabby and parasitical, and it is certainly not sound sport to agitate minds of that sort. Moreover, the critic must always harbor a grave doubt about most of the ideas that they lap up so greedily—it must occur to him not infrequently, in the silent watches of the night, that much that he writes is sheer buncombe. As I have said, I can't imagine any idea—that is, in the domain of aesthetics—that is palpably and incontrovertibly sound. All that I am familiar with, and in particular all that I announce most vociferously, seem to me to contain a core of quite obvious nonsense. I thus try to avoid cherishing them too lovingly, and it always gives me a shiver to see any one else

gobble them at one gulp. Criticism, at bottom, is indistinguishable
from skepticism. Both launch themselves, the one by aesthetic
presentations and the other by logical presentations, at the common human tendency to accept whatever is approved, to take in
ideas ready-made, to be responsive to mere rhetoric and gesticu-
lation. A critic who believes in anything absolutely is bound to
that something quite as helplessly as a Christian is bound to the
Freudian garbage in the Book of Revelation. To that extent, at
all events, he is unfree and unintelligent, and hence a bad critic.

The demand for "constructive" criticism is based upon the same
false assumption that immutable truths exist in the arts, and that
the artist will be improved by being made aware of them. This
notion, whatever the form it takes, is always absurd—as much
so, indeed, as its brother delusion that the critic, to be competent,
must be a practitioner of the specific art he ventures to deal with,
i.e., that a doctor, to cure a belly-ache, must have a belly-ache.
As practically encountered, it is disingenuous as well as absurd,
for it comes chiefly from bad artists who tire of serving as performing monkeys, and crave the greater ease and safety of
sophomores in class. They demand to be taught in order to avoid
being knocked about. In their demand is the theory that instruction, if they could get it, would profit them—that they are capable
of doing better work than they do. As a practical matter, I doubt
that this is ever true. Bad poets never actually grow any better;
they invariably grow worse and worse. In all history there has
never been, to my knowledge, a single practitioner of any art who,
as a result of "constructive" criticism, improved his work. The
curse of all the arts, indeed, is the fact that they are constantly
invaded by persons who are not artists at all—persons whose
yearning to express their ideas and feelings is unaccompanied by
the slightest capacity for charming expression—in belief, persons
with absolutely nothing to say. This is particularly true of the art
of letters, which interposes very few technical obstacles to the
vanity and garrulity of such invaders. Any effort to teach them to
write better is an effort wasted, as every editor discovers for himself; they are as incapable of it as they are of jumping over the

moon. The only sort of criticism that can deal with them to any profit is the sort that employs them frankly as laboratory animals. It cannot cure them, but it can at least make an amusing and perhaps edifying show of them. It is idle to argue that the good in them is thus destroyed with the bad. The simple answer is that there *is* no good in them. Suppose Poe had wasted his time trying to dredge good work out of Rufus Dawes, author of "Geraldine." He would have failed miserably—and spoiled a capital essay, still diverting after three-quarters of a century. Suppose Beethoven, dealing with Gottfried Weber, had tried laboriously to make an intelligent music critic of him. How much more apt, useful and durable the simple note: "Arch-ass! Double-barreled ass!" Here was absolutely sound criticism. Here was a judgment wholly beyond challenge. Moreover, here was a small but perfect work of art.

Upon the low practical value of so-called constructive criticism I can offer testimony out of my own experience. My books are commonly reviewed at great length, and many critics devote themselves to pointing out what they conceive to be my errors, both of fact and of taste. Well, I cannot recall a case in which any suggestion offered by a constructive critic has helped me in the slightest, or even actively interested me. Every such wet-nurse of letters has sought fatuously to make me write in a way differing from that in which the Lord God Almighty, in His infinite wisdom, impels me to write—that is, to make me write stuff which, coming from me, would be as false as an appearance of decency in a Congressman. All the benefits I have ever got from the critics of my work have come from the destructive variety. A hearty slating always does me good, particularly if it be well written. It begins by enlisting my professional respect; it ends by making me examine my ideas coldly in the privacy of my chamber. Not, of course, that I usually revise them, but I at least examine them. If I decide to hold fast to them, they are all the dearer to me thereafter, and I expound them with a new passion and plausibility. If, on the contrary, I discern holes in them, I shelve them in a *pianissimo* manner, and set about hatching new ones to take their place. But constructive criticism irritates me. I do not object to being denounced, but I can't abide being schoolmastered, especially by men I regard as imbeciles.

I find, as a practicing critic, that very few men who write books are even as tolerant as I am—that most of them, soon or late, show signs of extreme discomfort under criticism, however polite its terms. Perhaps this is why enduring friendships between authors and critics are so rare. All artists, of course, dislike one another more or less, but that dislike seldom rises to implacable enmity, save between opera singer and opera singer, and creative author and critic. Even when the latter two keep up an outward show of good will, there is always bitter antagonism under the surface. Part of it, I daresay, arises out of the impossible demands of the critic, particularly if he be tinged with the constructive madness. Having favored an author with his good opinion, he expects the poor fellow to live up to that good opinion without the slightest compromise or faltering, and this is commonly beyond human power. He feels that any letdown compromises *him* —that his hero is stabbing him in the back, and making him ridiculous—and this feeling rasps his vanity. The most bitter of all literary quarrels are those between critics and creative artists, and most of them arise in just this way. As for the creative artist, he on his part naturally resents the critic's air of pedagogical superiority and he resents it especially when he has an uneasy feeling that he has fallen short of his best work, and that the discontent of the critic is thus justified. Injustice is relatively easy to bear; what stings is justice. Under it all, of course, lurks the fact that I began with: the fact that the critic is himself an artist, and that his creative impulse, soon or late, is bound to make him neglect the punctilio. When he sits down to compose his criticism, his artist ceases to be a friend, and becomes mere raw material for his work of art. It is my experience that artists invariably resent this cavalier use of them. They are pleased so long as the critic confines himself to the modest business of interpreting them— preferably in terms of their own estimate of themselves—but the moment he proceeds to adorn their theme with variations of his own, the moment he brings new ideas to the enterprise and begins contrasting them with their ideas, that moment they grow restive. It is precisely at this point, of course, that criticism becomes genuine criticism; before that it was mere reviewing. When a critic passes it he loses his friends. By becoming an artist, he becomes the foe of all other artists.

But the transformation, I believe, has good effects upon him: it makes him a better critic. Too much *Gemütlichkeit* is as fatal to criticism as it would be to surgery or politics. When it rages unimpeded it leads inevitably either to a dull professorial sticking on of meaningless labels or to log-rolling, and often it leads to both. One of the most hopeful symptoms of the new *Aufklärung* in the Republic is the revival of acrimony in criticism—the renaissance of the doctrine that aesthetic matters are important, and that it is worth the while of a healthy male to take them seriously, as he takes business, sport and amour. In the days when American literature was showing its first vigorous growth, the native criticism was extraordinarily violent and even vicious; in the days when American literature swooned upon the tomb of the Puritan *Kultur* it became flaccid and childish. The typical critic of the first era was Poe, as the typical critic of the second was Howells. Poe carried on his critical jehads with such ferocity that he often got into law suits, and sometimes ran no little risk of having his head cracked. He regarded literary questions as exigent and momentous. The lofty aloofness of the don was simply not in him. When he encountered a book that seemed to him to be bad, he attacked it almost as sharply as a Chamber of Commerce would attack a fanatic preaching free speech, or the corporation of Trinity Church would attack Christ. His opponents replied in the same berserker manner. Much of Poe's surviving ill-fame, as a drunkard and dead-beat, is due to their inordinate denunciations of him. They were not content to refute him; they constantly tried to dispose of him altogether. The very ferocity of that ancient row shows that the native literature, in those days, was in a healthy state. Books of genuine value were produced. Literature always thrives best, in fact, in an atmosphere of hearty strife. Poe, surrounded by admiring professors, never challenged, never aroused to the emotions of revolt, would probably have written poetry indistinguishable from the hollow stuff of, say, Prof. Dr. George E. Woodberry. It took the persistent (and often grossly unfair and dishonorable) opposition of Griswold *et al.* to stimulate him to his highest endeavors. He needed friends, true enough, but he also needed enemies.

Today, for the first time in years, there is strife in American criticism, and the Paul Elmer Mores and Hamilton Wright Mabies are no longer able to purr in peace. The instant they fall into stiff professorial attitudes they are challenged, and often with anything but urbanity. The *ex cathedra* manner thus passes out, and free discussion comes in. Heretics lay on boldly, and the professors are forced to make some defense. Often, going further, they attempt counter-attacks. Ears are bitten on. Noses are bloodied. There are wallops both above and below the belt. I am, I need not say, no believer in any magical merit in debate, no matter how free it may be. It certainly does not necessarily establish the truth; both sides, in fact, may be wrong, and they often are. But it at least accomplishes two important effects. On the one hand, it exposes all the cruder fallacies to hostile examination, and so disposes of many of them. And on the other hand, it melodramatizes the business of the critic, and so convinces thousands of bystanders, otherwise quite inert, that criticism is an amusing and instructive art, and that the problems it deals with are important. What men will fight for seems to be worth looking into.

Van Wyck Brooks

(1886–1963)

*Among all American critics, few have created the contro-
versies occasioned by literary historian and critic Van Wyck
Brooks. A man of strong convictions, Brooks laid down his theses
and his ideas with the assurance of the seasoned performer; and
when his pronouncements drew fire, he came briskly and loudly
to their defense. As a result, he was, like most such critics, an
uneven and sometimes an inadequate performer.*

*In the early part of his career, Brooks leaned sharply toward
the kind of psychological criticism inspired by Freudian psychoanalysis. His* The Ordeal of Mark Twain *(1920; revised,
1933), for instance, attempts to explain Twain in terms of a
"miscarriage in his creative life, a balked personality, an arrested
development of which he was himself almost wholly unaware,
but which for him destroyed the meaning of life." To substantiate
this thesis, Brooks explains the frustration which he detects in
Twain as a result of his early home life, the influence of his
mother, and the values inculcated into him against his basic nature. The vastness and the finality of this judgment are typical
of much of Brooks' writing; and the scorn and the lofty disdain
of Bernard De Voto's answer to Brooks in* Mark Twain's America
*(1932) are typical of the treatment which has been accorded this
controversial figure.*

*In all Brooks' criticism, a certain common denominator is
discernible. He believes in the actual existence of truth, and he
holds that the critic must search for that truth. Further, he believes strongly in a usable past; that is, he sees an extensive value
in analyzing the past with a view to retaining that which is sound*

while discarding that which is unsound. Even more pronounced, however, is his oft-challenged tenet that standards do exist and that a properly equipped, inquiring mind can discern those standards.

In Brooks, no critical theory is to be found. The reason is that he eschews all attempts at theory. He believes firmly in literature as the product of a fine mind, giving vent to its finest thoughts. Consequently he has little use for schools of criticism and currently employed critical terms. Similarly, he dismisses any attempt to reduce criticism to a set of procedures such as those employed by the new critics in general and critics like Cleanth Brooks and John Crowe Ransom in particular. For Brooks, any critic who may disagree is simply badly off target.

Despite the low esteem in which Brooks is held by professional critics, however, he has enjoyed a wide and often devoted following among the general public. He has been read, quoted, and respected in many quarters; and therefore, he is to be ranked as an important figure in the realm of criticism.

Van Wyck Brooks, born in Plainfield, New Jersey, on February 16, 1886, spent almost his entire working life in the field of writing. After receiving the A.B. degree from Harvard in 1908, he studied independently before teaching briefly (1911–13) as Instructor in English at Stanford. Then he launched into his long career of editor, free lance writer, and author—a career that earned him a wide popular success and nine honorary doctorates from leading colleges and universities.

Typical of Brooks' ideas is the passage below, taken from an address which he delivered at Hunter College, New York, on October 10, 1940, and published under the title of the address itself.

From On Literature Today

I have been asked to speak on the state of our literature today. We live in a very unhappy world at present, a time of great confusion, and the public has a right to expect from its poets and thinkers some light on the causes of our problems and the way to a better future. Few writers, I think, at present, are living up to these expectations. But still the belief in literature persists, because so many writers in the past have performed their true public function. "In literature alone," said Leopardi, "the regeneration of our country can have a substantial beginning." This may seem a large claim, and yet there is some truth in it, for, as Ibsen said, "Except as afterwards invented"—invented, that is, by thinking minds—"the conscious guiding principle is never present in the general sentiment of the people." The world can only be changed by desires, but we are always desiring things, and only ideas can make desires effective; and so the minds that invent and express have a powerful influence over us. What then is literature doing for us in these perplexing times? And if it is not doing more and better, what are the reasons for this?

Literature at all times is a very complex phenomenon. When you see it in perspective, historically, it seems simple enough. We know what we call the Victorian age. As it appears in the histories, it is like the map of a country, all one colour, with novelists, poets, and essayists of various sizes, corresponding to towns and cities, dotted over the surface, united by currents of thought as clearly represented as rivers and railroads. But if one had lived in that age, it would all have seemed very different. An age is a chaos while one is living in it, and the past would be a chaos also if it were not interpreted for us. Besides, it is difficult to understand living writers because they are involved in our problems, which we cannot solve for ourselves. To generalize about the present is therefore a hazardous undertaking, although we are compelled to undertake it. All manner of writers are living in the world, and if, confining oneself to America, one thinks of talent, and even genius, the present seems to me beyond all question one of the brilliant epochs. In literary capacity, in vigour of style, in the number of our novelists, poets and critics, we are obviously in the midst of a revival; and I am only quoting foreign writers, English, Irish, French, Scandinavian, Russian, when I say that never before, outside this country, wherever books are read, have

American writers been so influential. But, aside from this question of talent, there is another question, implied in my quotations from Leopardi and Ibsen. Among these brilliant writers, where does one find the "conscious guiding principle"? How far do they contribute to "regenerate the country"? Let the Russian writer Chekhov reply to these questions. "Lift the robe of our muse and you will find within an empty void." Chekhov said this fifty years ago, and perhaps it expresses your feeling about our current literature. You may agree with a further observation which I have found in Chekhov's Letters: "Let me remind you that the writers who, we say, are for all time, or are simple good, and who intoxicate us, have one common and very important characteristic. They are going towards something and are summoning you towards it, too, and you feel, not with your mind, but with your whole being, that they have some object. . . . The best of them are realists and paint life as it is, but, through every line's being soaked in the consciousness of an object, you feel, besides life as it is, the life which ought to be, and that captivates you. And we? We paint life as it is, but beyond that—nothing at all. We have neither immediate nor remote aims, and in our soul there is a great empty space."

I quote this long passage because it suggests the dominant note of our epoch. We have, to be sure, many writers who do not convey this impression, writers who make us feel what ought to be and for whom life is noble and important. In Robert Frost, in Lewis Mumford, to mention two of these, one feels a joyous confidence in human nature, an abounding faith in the will, a sense of the heroic in the human adventure, good will, the leaven of existence. All good things seem possible as one reads these writers. I remember a remark of John Butler Yeats, the father of the Irish poet. Thirty years ago, in New York, I used to see him every day, and one day he spoke of an old friend of his in Dublin, a judge who had retired from the bench. When someone asked this judge what remained in his mind, what had most deeply impressed him, during his fifty years in the criminal courts, his answer was, "The goodness of human nature." The grand old

Yeats, who also loved his species, quoted this with a smile of agreement, for although he did not take an easy view of life, he felt that a seasoned magistrate knew whereof he spoke. I have never forgotten this remark, and I have always felt that literature, if it is to carry out its function, must contain this germ of faith, and that the greatest literature has always done so. The writers who retain this faith are what we call idealists. Robert Frost and Lewis Mumford—let me repeat their names, and there are many others—stand in our time for this position. In them one feels the power of the healthy will. Whenever I think of them, I remember Whitman's line, "Allons, the road is before us."

This mood of health, will, courage, faith in human nature, is the dominant mood in the history of literature. It was the mood of Homer, and writers will always return to it, as water always rises to the level of its source. It is the warp of literature—the rest is the woof. But this is not the mood of the last two decades, and it seems as if these writers had lost the day, as if the poet Yeats were right in saying (although perhaps in quite a different sense),—

> The best lack all conviction, while the worst
> Are full of passionate intensity.

A mood of desperate unhappiness reigns in the world, and this is marked especially in most of the writers. Have you thought how strange it is that so much of the world swallowed Spengler whole? —and I do not deny that Spengler was a very great genius, I do not deny the reality of his intuitions. The temperamental cards of our time are stacked in favour of despair, and a somewhat sterile despair. One error that an optimist makes destroys his whole case, while a pessimist can get away with murder. It seems as if our writers passively wallowed in misery, calling it fate; as if the most powerful writers, from James Joyce to Hemingway, from Eliot of *The Waste Land* to Eugene O'Neill and Theodore Dreiser, were bent on proving that life is a dark little pocket. Influence in literature goes with intensity. The intense minds, good or evil, are those that wield the power; and the genius that has moulded the mind of the present is almost wholly destructive; and even where, as in many cases, these writers are fighting for social justice, they still picture life as hardly worth the trouble of fighting for it. Their tone is cynical, bleak, hard-boiled, hard-bitten, and life for them is vain, dark and empty, the plaything, in Theodore Dreiser's phrase, of "idle rocking forces" or currents of material interest. What did Joyce's *Ulysses* say if not that life is a bad joke? What do our novelists say if not that nothing good exists, that only the ugly is real, the perverted, the distorted? You know the picture of life you find in the novels of William Faulkner, Dos Passos, James T. Farrell and so many others, who carry the day with their readers because they are writers of great power. They seem to delight in kicking their world to pieces, as if civilization were all a pretense and everything noble a humbug. There are teachers and psychologists who back them up. Only the other day I was reading a well-known psychologist who made two statements that he took for granted; 1, Men have always known that the romantic picture of love is false; 2, That which portrays the neurotic and defeated in human nature is closer to truth than that which pictures the aspirations of men. Love is a lie, in short, and the only realities are defeat and failure. This mood of incredulity and despair has penetrated millions of minds, and one finds it in the most unexpected places. There are people, educated people, who really think that Plutarch's heroes were humbugs, that Plutarch was pulling the wool over his readers' eyes when he pretended that heroes had ever existed. For these people, and they are many, all the closets are full of skeletons; for them even Diogenes was optimistic. What a gullible fellow Diogenes was— imagine wasting one's time, going about with a lantern, looking for an honest man, as if such a thing were to be conceived of! Not long ago I was talking with a distinguished professor about Eugene O'Neill's play *Mourning Becomes Electra.* He said that O'Neill had given the only truthful picture of New England, the New England not only of the present but of the past—that Cambridge and Concord a hundred years ago were just like this village in the play, whited sepulchres, full of dead men's bones.

As for the old New England writers, who presented a different picture, they were all hypocrites and liars. So far has this iron of incredulity entered into the modern soul.

What this all means is seldom discussed in the critical writing of the present. Most of our critical writing deals with technical questions, and technical novelty, as it seems to me, is almost the only virtue it demands or praises. Not whether a writer contributes to life, but whether he excels in some trick, is the question that is usually asked. It is their formal originality that has given prestige to writers like Joyce, Eliot and Gertrude Stein; and perhaps this is natural in an age of technics. But how can we ignore the larger questions involved in this drift of the modern mind? It seems to me it represents the "death-drive," as certain psychologists call it, the will to die that is said to exist side by side in our minds with the will to live. Defeat and unhappiness can reach a point where we accept them and embrace them and rejoice in our enervation and disintegration. And whether we rejoice in it or not, this literature is disintegrating. "All that is ugly," Nietzsche said, "weakens and afflicts man. It reminds him of deterioration, of danger and of impotence. He actually suffers loss of power by it. The effect of ugliness," Nietzsche continues, "can be measured by the dynamometer. Whenever man is depressed, he has a sense of the proximity of something ugly. His sense of power, his will to power, his courage, his pride—they decrease with the ugly, they increase with the beautiful." That is what I mean by suggesting that all these writers represent the death-drive. And if, with their technical virtues, they destroy our faith, our will to make the world worth living in, we cannot let their influence go unchallenged.

• • •

But, to return to their cynicism, does it really deny ideals? Is it not properly seen, rather, a desperate affirmation of them? The depth of the despair of the present is the measure of its defeated expectation. It demands, it presupposes, the things it denies. Our writers like to say that "free will" is played out. They think they are determinists, but they always turn out to be fatalists, and that is quite a different matter. William James marked the distinction. "The fatalistic argument" he said, "is really no argument for simple determinism. There runs through it the sense of a force which might make things otherwise from one moment to another, if it were only strong enough to breast the tide. A person who feels the impotence of free effort in this way has the acutest notion of what is meant by it, and of its possible independent power. How else could he be so conscious of its absence and of that of its effects? But genuine determinism occupies a totally different ground: not the *impotence*, but the *unthinkability* of free will is what it affirms." There is the Asiatic attitude, and one could never imagine an Asiatic writing as Faulkner writes, or Dos Passos, or Dreiser, or Hemingway or any of our writers. It takes long generations of disappointment, hundreds and thousands of years of disillusion, to produce the deterministic frame of mind. The determinist is one who has never had any expectations, but our American fatalism presupposes hope. It does not argue that free will does not exist; it merely affirms that the will is not effective. It pays the highest tribute to the will, for it says that life is meaningless and empty precisely because of this negation. The only unthinkable thing, for American minds, is that the will should not exist; and that is the reason why, when it is not effective, its impotence seems to Americans so overwhelming.

So it appears that the mood of these writers is a kind of inverted idealism. Their harsh incredulity is the measure of their potential faith; and when I think of the loose talk about "high ideals" that governed the general mind when I was a boy, and that went hand in hand with so many abuses, it seems to me that this turn of thought should prove in the end beneficial, creative of all that it misses. The ideal has often been maintained by those who have denied it in their youth; and, while there are no Saint Augustines in my generation, or any John Bunyans that I know of, I think the mind of the country, as a whole, has had its adolescence in our time—old as the sections were, the South, New England. It has gone through terrible growing pains, but the nation will be, in consequence, more mature. It is a good thing, surely, that young people now are so exacting, so wary of hypocrisy and humbug. And is there not a visible reaction against the defeatist mind, and against these parasites and air-plants, who have thriven in a discouraged world, as Spanish moss thrives on decaying trees? I see on all sides a hunger for affirmations, for a world without confusion, waste or groping, a world that is full of order and purpose, and for ourselves, in America, a chance to build it. When Europe too had its chance, and Americans were hankering for Europe, William James wrote, "Europe has been made what it is by men staying in their homes and fighting stubbornly, generation after generation, for all the beauty, comfort and order they have got. We must abide and do the same." Europe still has its chance, no doubt; but Europe is reaping whirlwinds far worse than ours and has lost the charm for us that it once possessed. It has thrown us back upon ourselves, and America has risen immensely in its power to charm us. Thousands of novels, biographies and histories, published in recent years, have shown us what multifarious strivings and failures and what multifarious victories lie behind us; and young writers now are settling in the remotest regions, determined to find them interesting or make them so. You never hear now of Greenwich Village, which used to be a haven for the exiles from Alabama and Kansas, the West and the South; and the reason you never hear of it is that the exiles have gone back to Alabama and to Kansas. They are founding schools in Iowa City and writing novels about Montana, and some are poet-farmers in Vermont. They are cultivating their roots where the seeds were sown, and where they are sure to yield their flowers and fruit.

T. S. Eliot

(1888-1965)

One can begin to understand the importance of T. S. Eliot by realizing that some anthologists and literary historians have begun to refer to the period from 1920 to mid-century as the "Age of Eliot."

Although Eliot cast a far-reaching influence on several areas of thought, he influenced especially the fields of poetry and criticism in the Anglo-American world. The publication of "The Wasteland" (1922) is generally regarded as a landmark in the history of poetry, and his many critical essays have been only slightly less influential.

This particular poem and the critical essays should really be considered together because the poem is simply an affirmation of its author's critical beliefs. Above all, it is an example of Eliot's view of poetry as an intellectual exercise, both for the poet and the reader, as well as an embodiment of the techniques which Eliot deems necessary for poetic expression. In addition to being one of the most challenging poems in all literature, it demands of the reader a careful recognition of many devices of impressionism and other approaches commonly associated with modern poetry. The reward for the reader is a penetrating examination of many of the fundamental questions of existence—as well as a rich and powerful study in the use of imagery.

Among the doctrines most successfully propounded by Eliot is his concept of criticism as an interpretation of the work of art under discussion and an agent to correct taste. Hence criticism must embrace other studies—particularly theology, ethics, and philosophy—and it must operate at all times on a high level of *thought. Further, poetry is to be judged in terms of the poetic "tradition"—that is, the emphasis is to be placed on the poem, not the poet, as it forms part of the great flow of poetry down through the ages. (This idea is treated in the passage below.)*

Although Eliot later modified somewhat his insistence that criticism focus its attention solely on the work itself, the New Critics still quote him approvingly on this point. Thus he has had an impact on that particular group.

Thomas Stearns Eliot was born in St. Louis, Missouri, of New England forbears. After receiving the baccalaureate degree from Harvard, he studied in France, Germany, and England in an effort to enrich his background in philosophy, literature, language, and related disciplines. Later, he met all the requirements for a doctorate in philosophy at Harvard but never completed the mechanics of presenting his dissertation for the degree.

Although born and reared in the United States, Eliot spent the majority of his years abroad. Most of this time he lived in England where he worked as teacher, book reviewer, official in Lloyd's Bank, and editorial employee and director in the publishing house of Faber and Faber. In 1927, he became a British citizen.

Tradition and the Individual Talent

I

In English writing we seldom speak of tradition, though we occasionally apply its name in deploring its absence. We cannot refer to 'the tradition' or to 'a tradition'; at most, we employ the adjective in saying that the poetry of So-and-so is 'traditional' or even 'too traditional.' Seldom, perhaps, does the word appear except in a phrase of censure. If otherwise, it is vaguely approbative, with the implication, as to the work approved, of some pleasing archæological reconstruction. You can hardly make the word agreeable to English ears without this comfortable reference to the reassuring science of archæology.

Certainly the word is not likely to appear in our appreciations of living or dead writers. Every nation, every race, has not only its own creative, but its own critical turn of mind; and is even more oblivious of the shortcomings and limitations of its critical habits than of those of its creative genius. We know, or think we know, from the enormous mass of critical writing that has appeared in the French language, the critical method or habit of the French; we only conclude (we are such unconscious people) that the French are 'more critical' than we, and sometimes even plume ourselves a little with the fact, as if the French were the less spontaneous. Perhaps they are; but we might remind ourselves that criticism is as inevitable as breathing, and that we should be none the worse for articulating what passes in our minds when we read a book and feel an emotion about it, for criticizing our own minds in their work of criticism. One of the facts that might come to light in this process is our tendency to insist, when we praise a poet, upon those aspects of his work in which he least resembles anyone else. In these aspects or parts of his work we pretend to find what is individual, what is the peculiar essence of the man. We dwell with satisfaction upon the poet's difference from his predecessors, especially his immediate predecessors; we endeavour to find something that can be isolated in order to be enjoyed. Whereas if we approach a poet without this prejudice we shall often find that not only the best, but the most individual parts of his work may be those in which the dead poets, his ancestors, assert their immortality most vigorously. And I do not mean the impressionable period of adolescence, but the period of full maturity.

Yet if the only form of tradition, of handing down, consisted in following the ways of the immediate generation before us in a blind or timid adherence to its successes, 'tradition' should positively be discouraged. We have seen many such simple currents soon lost in the sand; and novelty is better than repetition. Tradition is a matter of much wider significance. It cannot be inherited, and if you want it you must obtain it by great labour. It involves, in the first place, the historical sense, which we may call nearly indispensable to anyone who would continue to be a poet beyond his twenty-fifth year; and the historical sense involves a perception, not only of the pastness of the past, but of its presence; the historical sense compels a man to write not merely with his own generation in his bones, but with a feeling that the whole of the literature of Europe from Homer and within it the whole of the literature of his own country has a simultaneous existence and composes a simultaneous order. This historical sense, which is a sense of the timeless as well as of the temporal and of the timeless and of the temporal together, is what makes a writer traditional. And it is at the same time what makes a writer most acutely conscious of his place in time, of his own contemporaneity.

No poet, no artist of any art, has his complete meaning alone. His significance, his appreciation is the appreciation of his relation to the dead poets and artists. You cannot value him alone; you must set him, for contrast and comparison, among the dead. I mean this as a principle of æsthetic, not merely historical, criticism. The necessity that he shall conform, that he shall cohere, is not onesided; what happens when a new work of art is created is something that happens simultaneously to all the works of art which preceded it. The existing monuments form an ideal order among themselves, which is modified by the introduction of the new (the really new) work of art among them. The existing order is complete before the new work arrives; for order to persist after the supervention of novelty, the *whole* existing order must be, if ever so slightly, altered; and so the relations, proportions, values of each work of art toward the whole are readjusted; and this is conformity between the old and the new. Whoever has approved this idea of order, of the form of European, of English literature will not find it preposterous that the past should be altered by the present as much as the present is directed by the past. And the poet who is aware of this will be aware of great difficulties and responsibilities.

In a peculiar sense he will be aware also that he must inevitably be judged by the standards of the past. I say judged, not amputated, by them; not judged to be as good as, or worse or better than, the dead; and certainly not judged by the canons of dead critics. It is a judgment, a comparison, in which two things are measured by each other. To conform merely would be for the new work not really to conform at all; it would not be new, and would therefore not be a work of art. And we do not quite say that the new is more valuable because it fits in; but its fitting in is a test of its value—a test, it is true, which can only be slowly and cautiously applied, for we are none of us infallible judges of conformity. We say: it appears to conform, and is perhaps individual, or it appears individual, and may conform; but we are hardly likely to find that it is one and not the other.

To proceed to a more intelligible exposition of the relation of the poet to the past: he can neither take the past as a lump, an indiscriminate bolus, nor can he form himself wholly on one or two private admirations, nor can he form himself wholly upon one preferred period. The first course is inadmissible, the second is an important experience of youth, and the third is a pleasant and highly desirable supplement. The poet must be very conscious of the main current, which does not at all flow invariably through the most distinguished reputations. He must be quite aware of the obvious fact that art never improves, but that the material of art is never quite the same. He must be aware that the mind of Europe—the mind of his own country—a mind which he learns in time to be much more important than his own private mind—is a mind which changes, and that this change is a development which abandons nothing *en route*, which does not superannuate either Shakespeare, or Homer, or the rock drawing of the Magdalenian draughtsmen. That this development, refinement perhaps, complication certainly, is not, from the point of view of the artist, any improvement. Perhaps not even an improvement from the point of view of the psychologist or not to the extent which we imagine; perhaps only in the end based upon a complication in economics and machinery. But the difference between the present and the past is that the conscious present is an awareness of the past in a way and to an extent which the past's awareness of itself cannot show.

Someone said: 'The dead writers are remote from us because we *know* so much more than they did.' Precisely, and they are that which we know.

I am alive to a usual objection to what is clearly part of my programme for the *métier* of poetry. The objection is that the doctrine requires a ridiculous amount of erudition (pedantry), a claim which can be rejected by appeal to the lives of poets in any pantheon. It will even be affirmed that much learning deadens or perverts poetic sensibility. While, however, we persist in believing that a poet ought to know as much as will not encroach upon his necessary receptivity and necessary laziness, it is not desirable to confine knowledge to whatever can be put into a useful shape for examinations, drawing-rooms, or the still more pretentious modes of publicity. Some can absorb knowledge, the more tardy must sweat for it. Shakespeare acquired more essential history from Plutarch than most men could from the whole British Museum. What is to be insisted upon is that the poet must develop or procure the consciousness of the past and that he should continue to develop this consciousness throughout his career.

What happens is a continual surrender of himself as he is at the moment to something which is more valuable. The progress of an artist is a continual self-sacrifice, a continual extinction of personality.

There remains to define this process of depersonalization and its relation to the sense of tradition. It is in this depersonalization that art may be said to approach the condition of science. I therefore invite you to consider, as a suggestive analogy, the action which takes place when a bit of finely filiated platinum is introduced into a chamber containing oxygen and sulphur dioxide.

II

Honest criticism and sensitive appreciation is directed not upon the poet but upon the poetry. If we attend to the confused cries

of the newspaper critics and the *susurrus* of popular repetition
that follows, we shall hear the names of poets in great numbers;
if we seek not Blue-book knowledge but the enjoyment of poetry,
and ask for a poem, we shall seldom find it. I have tried to point
out the importance of the relation of the poem to other poems by
other authors, and suggested the conception of poetry as a living
whole of all the poetry that has ever been written. The other
aspect of this Impersonal theory of poetry is the relation of the
poem to its author. And I hinted, by an analogy, that the mind
of the mature poet differs from that of the immature one not
precisely in any valuation of 'personality,' not being necessarily
more interesting, or having 'more to say,' but rather by being a
more finely perfected medium in which special, or very varied,
feelings are at liberty to enter into new combinations.

The analogy was that of the catalyst. When the two gases
previously mentioned are mixed in the presence of a filament of
platinum, they form sulphurous acid. This combination takes place
only if the platinum is present; nevertheless the newly formed
acid contains no trace of platinum, and the platinum itself is
apparently unaffected: has remained inert, neutral, and unchanged. The mind of the poet is the shred of platinum. It may
partly or exclusively operate upon the experience of the man
himself; but, the more perfect the artist, the more completely
separate in him will be the man who suffers and the mind which
creates; the more perfectly will the mind digest and transmute
the passions which are its material.

The experience, you will notice, the elements which enter the
presence of the transforming catalyst, are of two kinds: emotions
and feelings. The effect of a work of art upon the person who
enjoys it is an experience different in kind from any experience
not of art. It may be formed out of one emotion, or may be a
combination of several; and various feelings, inhering for the
writer in particular words or phrases or images, may be added
to compose the final result. Or great poetry may be made without
the direct use of any emotion whatever: composed out of feelings
solely. Canto XV of the *Inferno* (Brunetto Latini) is a working

up of the emotion evident in the situation; but the effect, though single as that of any work of art, is obtained by considerable complexity of detail. The last quatrain gives an image, a feeling attaching to an image, which 'came,' which did not develop simply out of what precedes, but which was probably in sus-pension in the poet's mind until the proper combination arrived for it to add itself to. The poet's mind is in fact a receptacle for seizing and storing up numberless feelings, phrases, images, which remain there until all the particles which can unite to form a new compound are present together.

If you compare several representative passages of the greatest poetry you see how great is the variety of types of combination, and also how completely any semi-ethical criterion of 'sublimity' misses the mark. For it is not the 'greatness,' the intensity, of the emotions, the components, but the intensity of the artistic process, the pressure, so to speak, under which the fusion takes place, that counts. The episode of Paolo and Francesca employs a definite emotion, but the intensity of the poetry is something quite differ-ent from whatever intensity in the supposed experience it may give the impression of. It is no more intense, furthermore, than Canto XXVI, the voyage of Ulysses, which has not the direct dependence upon an emotion. Great variety is possible in the process of transmutation of emotion: the murder of Agamemnon, or the agony of Othello, gives an artistic effect apparently closer to a possible original than the scenes from Dante. In the *Agamem-non*, the artistic emotion approximates to the emotion of an actual spectator; in *Othello* to the emotion of the protagonist himself. But the difference between art and the event is always absolute; the combination which is the murder of Agamemnon is probably as complex as that which is the voyage of Ulysses. In either case there has been a fusion of elements. The ode of Keats contains a number of feelings which have nothing particular to do with the nightingale, but which the nightingale, partly perhaps because of its attractive name, and partly because of its reputation, served to bring together.

The point of view which I am struggling to attack is perhaps related to the metaphysical theory of the substantial unity of the soul: for my meaning is, that the poet has, not a 'personality' to express, but a particular medium, which is only a medium and not a personality, in which impressions and experiences combine in peculiar and unexpected ways. Impressions and experiences which are important for the man may take no place in the poetry, and those which become important in the poetry may play quite a negligible part in the man, the personality.

I will quote a passage which is unfamiliar enough to be regarded with fresh attention in the light—or darkness—of these observations:

> And now methinks I could e'en chide myself
> For doating on her beauty, though her death
> Shall be revenged after no common action.
> Does the silkworm expend her yellow labours
> For thee? For thee does she undo herself?
> Are lordships sold to maintain ladyships
> For the poor benefit of a bewildering minute?
> Why does yon fellow falsify highways,
> And put his life between the judge's lips,
> To refine such a thing—keeps horse and men
> To beat their valours for her? . . .

In this passage (as is evident if it is taken in its context) there is a combination of positive and negative emotions: an intensely strong attraction toward beauty and an equally intense fascination by the ugliness which is contrasted with it and which destroys it. This balance of contrasted emotion is in the dramatic situation to which the speech is pertinent, but that situation alone is inadequate to it. This is, so to speak, the structural emotion, provided by the drama. But the whole effect, the dominant tone, is due to the fact that a number of floating feelings, having an affinity to this emotion by no means superficially evident, have combined with it to give us a new art emotion.

It is not in his personal emotions, the emotions provoked by particular events in his life, that the poet is in any way remarkable or interesting. His particular emotions may be simple, or crude, or flat. The emotion in his poetry will be a very complex thing, but not with the complexity of the emotions of people who have very complex or unusual emotions in life. One error, in fact, of eccentricity in poetry is to seek for new human emotions to express; and in this search for novelty in the wrong place it discovers the perverse. The business of the poet is not to find new emotions, but to use the ordinary ones and, in working them up into poetry, to express feelings which are not in actual emotions at all. And emotions which he has never experienced will serve his turn as well as those familiar to him. Consequently, we must believe that 'emotion recollected in tranquillity'[1] is an inexact formula. For it is neither emotion, nor recollection, nor, without distortion of meaning, tranquillity. It is a concentration, and a new thing resulting from the concentration, of a very great number of experiences which to the practical and active person would not seem to be experiences at all; it is a concentration which does not happen consciously or of deliberation. These experiences are not 'recollected,' and they finally unite in an atmosphere which is 'tranquil' only in that it is a passive attending upon the event. Of course this is not quite the whole story. There is a great deal, in the writing of poetry, which must be conscious and deliberate. In fact, the bad poet is usually unconscious where he ought to be conscious, and conscious where he ought to be unconscious. Both errors tend to make him 'personal.' Poetry is not a turning loose of emotion, but an escape from emotion; it is not the expression of personality, but an escape from personality. But, of course, only those who have personality and emotions know what it means to want to escape from these things.

III

This essay proposes to halt at the frontier of metaphysics or mysticism, and confine itself to such practical conclusions as can

[1] In this instance, Eliot is referring to an oft-quoted line from William Wordsworth's definition of poetry as given in the preface to *Lyrical Ballads*.

be applied by the responsible person interested in poetry. To divert interest from the poet to the poetry is a laudable aim: for it would conduce to a juster estimation of actual poetry, good and bad. There are many people who appreciate the expression of sincere emotion in verse, and there is a smaller number of people who can appreciate technical excellence. But very few know when there is an expression of *significant* emotion, emotion which has its life in the poem and not in the history of the poet. The emotion of art is impersonal. And the poet cannot reach this impersonality without surrendering himself wholly to the work to be done. And he is not likely to know what is to be done unless he lives in what is not merely the present, but the present moment of the past, unless he is conscious, not of what is dead, but of what is already living.

John Crowe Ransom

(b. 1888)

John Crowe Ransom has enjoyed a distinguished career as poet, critic, and university teacher. In all three areas, he has had the opportunity to propound his critical theory, and he has taken an extensive advantage of that opportunity.

Although merely one of several important figures in the New Criticism, he is often regarded as the central personality because of his spirited defense of the tenets therein and because of his The New Criticism *(1941). However, in thinking of Ransom and the New Critics, one must remember that while they agree, for the most part, on basic principles, they often disagree on secondary matters. In the instance of Ransom, one finds a note of individuality in a deep commitment to the old South with its special kind of social system and its espousal of agrarianism.*

Ransom has been particularly successful as a polemic critic. He has advanced and defended several ideas regarding ontological criticism; he has clearly distinguished the function of poetry as opposed to that of science; and he has made some discriminating distinctions between the form and the technique of poetry.

In reading Ransom, one must be especially careful in interpreting the language—as for example, in the "structure–texture" distinction. Ransom sees the "structure" of the poem as a rational "core" around which an "irrelevant texture" is placed. One is then to analyze the poem by using these entities as his base.

Also noticeable in Ransom is an emphasis on things rather than ideas. Poetry, he insists, must examine the thing of which it speaks by looking completely inward. The poem cannot rep-

*resent mere surface observation; it must be a penetrating exam-
ination that reaches the very center of the object.*

*As Ransom envisions the criticism of poetry, the critic must
first consider the total matter of structure. Then, he must focus
on an appreciation and an evaluation of the peculiar meaning of
the poem. Throughout all, Ransom argues for an objectivity that
makes criticism more of a science and less of a subjective venture
than that endorsed by most other critics.*

*Ransom, born in Pulaski, Tennessee, received his early educa-
tion in Nashville and his undergraduate degree from Vanderbilt
University in 1909. One year later, he was awarded a Rhodes
Scholarship which led to a B.A. degree from Christ College,
Oxford, with a specialty in classics. After teaching for one year
in a Mississippi secondary school, Ransom joined the faculty at
Vanderbilt, remaining there until 1937. In that year, he accepted
the position of Carnegie Professor of English at Kenyon College,
as well as the first editorship of the well known* Kenyon Review.
*Now retired, he confines his efforts to writing and occasional
lecturing.*

*In the selection below, Ransom elucidates both his conception
of the role of the critic and the manner in which the critic is to
proceed.*

From Criticism as Pure Speculation[1]

When we inquire into the "intent of the critic," we mean: the
intent of the generalized critic, or critic as such. We will concede
that any professional critic is familiar with the technical practices
of poets so long as these are conventional and is expert in judging
when they perform them brilliantly, and when only fairly, or
badly. We expect a critical discourse to cover that much, but
we know that more is required. The most famous poets of our
own time, for example, make wide departures from conventional
practices: how are they to be judged? Innovations in poetry, or
even conventions when pressed to their logical limits, cause the

[1] An essay in *The Intent of the Critic,* Princeton University Press, 1941.

ordinary critic to despair. He tries the poem against his best philosophical conception of the peculiar character that a poem should have.

Mr. T. S. Eliot is an extraordinarily sensitive critic. But when he discusses the so-called "metaphysical" poetry, he surprises us by refusing to study the so-called "conceit" which is its reputed basis; he observes instead that the metaphysical poets of the seventeenth century are more like their immediate predecessors than the latter are like the eighteenth and nineteenth century poets, and then he goes into a very broad philosophical comparison between two whole "periods" or types of poetry. I think it has come to be understood that his comparison is unsound; it has not proved workable enough to assist critics who have otherwise borrowed liberally from his critical principles. (It contains the famous dictum about the "sensibility" of the earlier poets, it imputes to them a remarkable ability to "feel their thought," and to have a kind of "experience" in which the feeling cannot be differentiated from the thinking.) Now there is scarcely another critic equal to Eliot at distinguishing the practices of two poets who are closely related. He is supreme as a comparative critic when the relation in question is delicate and subtle; that is, when it is a matter of close perception and not a radical difference in kind. But this line of criticism never goes far enough. In Eliot's own range of criticism the line does not always answer. He is forced by discontinuities in the poetic tradition into sweeping theories that have to do with esthetics, the philosophy of poetry; and his own philosophy probably seems to us insufficient, the philosophy of the literary man.

The intent of the critic may well be, then, first to read his poem sensitively, and make comparative judgments about its technical practice, or, as we might say, to emulate Eliot. Beyond that, it is to read and remark the poem knowingly; that is, with an esthetician's understanding of what a poem generically "is."

●　●　●

The ostensible substance of the poem may be anything at all

which words may signify: an ethical situation, a passion, a train of thought, a flower or landscape, a thing. This substance receives its poetic increment. It might be safer to say it receives some subtle and mysterious alteration under poetic treatment, but I will risk the cruder formula: the ostensible substance is increased by an x, which is an increment. The poem actually continues to contain its ostensible substance, which is not fatally diminished from its prose state: that is its logical core, or paraphrase. The rest of the poem is x, which we are to find.

We feel the working of this simple formula when we approach a poetry with our strictest logic, provided we can find deliverance from certain inhibiting philosophical prepossessions into which we have been conditioned by the critics we have had to read. Here is Lady Macbeth planning a murder with her husband:

> When Duncan is asleep—
> Whereto the rather shall his hard day's journey
> Soundly invite him—his two chamberlains
> Will I with wine and wassail so convince,
> That memory, the warder of the brain,
> Shall be a fume, and the receipt of reason
> A limbec only; when in swinish sleep
> Their drenched natures lie as in a death,
> What cannot you and I perform upon
> The unguarded Duncan? what not put upon
> His spongy officers, who shall bear the guilt
> Of our great quell?

It is easy to produce the prose argument or paraphrase of this speech; it has one upon which we shall all agree. But the passage is more than its argument. Any detail, with this speaker, seems capable of being expanded in some direction which is not that of the argument. For example, Lady Macbeth says she will make the chamberlains drunk so that they will not remember their charge, nor keep their wits about them. But it is indifferent to this argument whether memory according to the old psychology is located at the gateway to the brain, whether it is to be dis-

integrated into fume as of alcohol, and whether the whole receptacle of the mind is to be turned into a still. These are additions to the argument both energetic and irrelevant—though
they do not quite stop or obscure the argument. From the point
of view of the philosopher they are excursions into particularity.
They give, in spite of the argument, which would seem to be
perfectly self-sufficient, a sense of the real density and contingency of the world in which arguments and plans have to be
pursued. They bring out the private character which the items
of an argument can really assume if we look at them. This
character spreads out in planes at right angles to the course of
the argument, and in effect gives to the discourse another dimension, not present in a perfectly logical prose. We are expected
to have sufficient judgment not to let this local character take us
too far or keep us too long from the argument.

All this would seem commonplace remark, I am convinced,
but for those philosophically timid critics who are afraid to think
that the poetic increment is local and irrelevant, and that poetry
cannot achieve its own virtue and keep undiminished the virtues
of prose at the same time. But I will go a little further in the hope
of removing the sense of strangeness in the analysis. I will offer a
figurative definition of a poem.

A poem is, so to speak, a democratic state, whereas a prose
discourse—mathematical, scientific, ethical, or practical and ver-
nacular—is a totalitarian state. The intention of a democratic
state is to perform the work of state as effectively as it can perform it, subject to one reservation of conscience: that it will not
despoil its members, the citizens, of the free exercise of their
own private and independent characters. But the totalitarian
state is interested solely in being effective, and regards the
citizens as no citizens at all; that is, regards them as functional
members whose existence is totally defined by their allotted contributions to its ends; it has no use for their private characters,
and therefore no provision for them. I indicate of course the
extreme or polar opposition between two polities, without denying that a polity may come to us rather mixed up.

In this trope the operation of the state as a whole represents of course the logical paraphrase or argument of the poem. The private character of the citizens represents the particularity asserted by the parts in the poem. And this last is our x.

For many years I had seen—as what serious observer has not—that a poem as a discourse differentiated itself from prose by its particularity, yet not to the point of sacrificing its logical cogency or universality. But I could get no further. I could not see how real particularity could get into a universal. The object of esthetic studies became for me a kind of discourse, or a kind of natural configuration, which like any other discourse or configuration claimed universality, but which consisted actually, and notoriously, of particularity. The poem was concrete, yet universal, and in spite of Hegel I could not see how the two properties could be identified as forming in a single unit the "concrete universal." It is usual, I believe, for persons at this stage to assert that somehow the apparent diffuseness or particularity in the poem gets itself taken up or "assimilated" into the logic, to produce a marvelous kind of unity called a "higher unity," to which ordinary discourse is not eligible. The belief is that the "idea" or theme proves itself in poetry to be even more dominating than in prose by overcoming much more energetic resistance than usual on the part of the materials, and the resistance, as attested in the local development of detail, is therefore set not to the debit but to the credit of the unifying power of the poetic spirit. A unity of that kind is one which philosophers less audacious and more factual than Hegel would be loath to claim. Critics incline to call it, rather esoterically, an "imaginative" rather than a logical unity, but one supposes they mean a mystical, an ineffable, unity. I for one could neither grasp it nor deny it. I believe that is not an uncommon situation for poetic analysts to find themselves in.

It occurred to me at last that the solution might be very easy if looked for without what the positivists call "metaphysical prepossessions." Suppose the logical substance remained there all the time, and was in no way specially remarkable, while the particularity came in by accretion, so that the poem turned out partly universal, and partly particular, but with respect to different parts. I began to remark the dimensions of a poem, or other work of art. The poem was not a mere moment in time, nor a mere point in space. It was sizeable, like a house. Apparently it had a "plan," or a central frame of logic, but it had also a huge wealth of local detail, which sometimes fitted the plan functionally or served it, and sometimes only subsisted comfortably under it; in either case the house stood up. But it was the political way of thinking which gave me the first analogy which seemed valid. The poem was like a democratic state, in action, and observed both macroscopically and microscopically.

The house occurred also, and provided what seems to be a more negotiable trope under which to construe the poem. A poem is a logical structure having a local texture. These terms have been actually though not systematically employed in literary criticism. To my imagination they are architectural. The walls of my room are obviously structural; the beams and boards have a function; so does the plaster, which is the visible aspect of the final wall. The plaster might have remained naked, aspiring to no character, and purely functional. But actually it has been painted, receiving color; or it has been papered, receiving color and design, though these have no structural value; and perhaps it has been hung with tapestry, or with paintings, for "decoration." The paint, the paper, the tapestry are texture. It is logically unrelated to structure. But I indicate only a few of the textural possibilities in architecture. There are not fewer of them in poetry.

The intent of the good critic becomes therefore to examine and define the poem with respect to its structure and its texture. If he has nothing to say about its texture he has nothing to say about it specifically as a poem, but is treating it only insofar as it is prose.

I do not mean to say that the good critic will necessarily employ my terms.

• • •

Many critics today are writing analytically and with close

intelligence, in whatever terms, about the logical substance or structure of the poem, and its increment of irrelevant local substance or texture. I believe that the understanding of the ideal critic has to go even further than that. The final desideratum is an ontological insight, nothing less. I am committed by my title to a representation of criticism as, in the last resort, a speculative exercise. But my secret committal was to speculative in the complete sense of—ontological.

There is nothing especially speculative or ontological in reciting, or even appraising, the logical substance of the poem. This is its prose core—its science perhaps, or its ethics if it seems to have an ideology. Speculative interest asserts itself principally when we ask why we want the logical substance to be compounded with the local substance, the good lean structure with a great volume of texture that does not function. It is the same thing as asking why we want the poem to be what it is.

It has been a rule, having the fewest exceptions, for estheticians and great philosophers to direct their speculations by the way of overstating and overvaluing the logical substance. They are impressed by the apparent obedience of material nature, whether in fact or in art, to definable form or "law" imposed upon it. They like to suppose that in poetry, as in chemistry, everything that figures in the discourse means to be functional, and that the poem is imperfect in the degree that it contains items, whether by accident or intention, which manifest a private independence. It is a bias with which we are entirely familiar, and reflects the extent to which our philosophy hitherto has been impressed by the successes of science in formulating laws which would "govern" their objects. Probably I am here reading the state of mind of yesterday rather than of today. Nevertheless we know it. The world-view which ultimately forms itself in the mind so biassed is that of a world which is rational and intelligible. The view is sanguine, and naive. Hegel's world-view, I think it is agreed, was a subtle version of this, and if so, it was what determined his view of art. He seemed to make the handsomest concession to realism by offering to knowledge a kind of universal which was not restricted to the usual abstracted aspects of the material, but included all aspects, and was a concrete universal. The concreteness in Hegel's handling was not honestly, or at any rate not fairly, defended. It was always represented as being in process of pointing up and helping out the universality. He could look at a work of art and report all its substance as almost assimilated to a ruling "idea." But at least Hegel seemed to distinguish what looked like two ultimate sorts of substance there, and stated the central esthetic problem as the problem of relating them. And his writings about art are speculative in the sense that he regarded the work of art not as of great intrinsic value necessarily, but as an object-lesson or discipline in the understanding of the world-process, and as its symbol.

I think of two ways of construing poetry with respect to its ultimate purpose; of which the one is not very handsome nor speculatively interesting, and the other will appear somewhat severe.

The first construction would picture the poet as a sort of epicure, and the poem as something on the order of a Christmas pudding, stuffed with what dainties it will hold. The pastry alone, or it may be the cake, will not serve; the stuffing is wanted too. The values of the poem would be intrinsic, or immediate, and they would include not only the value of the structure but also the incidental values to be found in the texture. If we exchange the pudding for a house, they would include not only the value of the house itself but also the value of the furnishings. In saying intrinsic or immediate, I mean that the poet is fond of the precise objects denoted by the words, and writes the poem for the reason that he likes to dwell upon them. In talking about the main value and the incidental values I mean to recognize the fact that the latter engage the affections just as truly as the former. Poetic discourse therefore would be more agreeable than prose to the epicure or the literally acquisitive man; for prose has but a single value, being about one thing only; its parts have no values of their own, but only instrumental values, which might be reckoned as fractions of the single value pro-

portionate to their contributions to it. The prose is one-valued
and the poem is many-valued. Indeed, there will certainly be
poems whose texture contains many precious objects, and ag-
gregates a greater value than the structure.

So there would be a comfortable and apparently eligible view
that poetry improves on prose because it is a richer diet. It
causes five or six pleasures to appear, five or six good things,
where one had been before; an alluring consideration for ro-
bustious, full-blooded, bourgeois souls. The view will account
for much of the poem, if necessary. But it does not account for
all of it, and sometimes it accounts for less than at other times.

The most impressive reason for the bolder view of art, the
speculative one, is the existence of the "pure," or "abstractionist,"
or non-representational works of art; though these will probably
occur to us in other arts than poetry. There is at least one art,
music, whose works are all of this sort. Tones are not words, they
have no direct semantical function, and by themselves they mean
nothing. But they combine to make brilliant phrases, harmonies,
and compositions. In these compositions it is probable that the
distinction between structure of functional content, on the one
hand, and texture or local variation and departure, on the other,
is even more determinate than in an impure art like poetry. The
world of tones seems perfectly inhuman and impracticable;
there is no specific field of experience "about which" music is
telling us. Yet we know that music is powerfully affective. I take
my own musical feelings, and those attested by other audients,
as the sufficient index to some overwhelming human importance
which the musical object has for us. At the same time it would
be useless to ask the feelings precisely what they felt; we must
ask the critic. The safest policy is to take the simplest construction, and try to improvise as little fiction as possible. Music
is not music, I think, until we grasp its effects both in structure
and in texture. As we grow in musical understanding the structures become always more elaborate and sustained, and the
texture which interrupts them and sometimes imperils them
becomes more bold and unpredictable. We can agree in saying

about the works of music that these are musical structures, and they are richly textured; we can identify these elements, and perhaps precisely. To what then do our feelings respond? To music as structural composition itself; to music as manifesting the structural principles of the world; to modes of structure which we feel to be ontologically possible, or even probable. Schopenhauer construed music very much in that sense. Probably it will occur to us that musical compositions bear close analogy therefore to operations in pure mathematics. The mathematicians confess that their constructions are "non-existential"; meaning, as I take it, that the constructions testify with assurance only to the structural principles, in the light of which they are possible but may not be actual, or if they are actual may not be useful. This would define the mathematical operations as speculative: as motivated by an interest so generalized and so elemental that no word short of ontological will describe it.

But if music and mathematics have this much in common, they differ sharply in their respective world-views or ontological biasses. That of music, with its prodigious display of texture, seems the better informed about the nature of the world, the more realistic, the less naive. Perhaps the difference is between two ontological educations. But I should be inclined to imagine it as rising back of that point: in two ontological temperaments.

There are also, operating a little less successfully so far as the indexical evidences would indicate, the abstractionist paintings, of many schools, and perhaps also works of sculpture; and there is architecture. These arts have tried to abandon direct representational intention almost as heroically as music. They exist in their own materials and indicate no other specific materials; structures of color, light, space, stone—the cheapest of materials. They too can symbolize nothing of value unless it is structure or composition itself. But that is precisely the act which denotes will and intelligence; which becomes the act of fuller intelligence if it carefully accompanies its structures with their material textures; for then it understands better the ontological nature of materials.

Cleanth Brooks

(b. 1906)

In any discussion of the New Criticism, the name of Cleanth
Brooks is invariably singled out by adversaries for special attack.
The chief reasons seem to be that he has written often and confidently on his viewpoints; he has tended to leave himself open
to strong charges; and he has altered his position on occasions
by retreating from earlier stands. Meanwhile, however, he has
demonstrated a certain fundamental soundness of ideas, and he
has exerted a potent influence on the critical judgments of a
generation of readers of poetry.

Brooks has produced many articles and several books. Of
these, the most significant are Understanding Poetry (1938) with
Robert Penn Warren, Modern Poetry and the Tradition (1939),
and The Well Wrought Urn (1947). In Understanding Poetry,
Brooks and his co-author argue that the essence of criticizing
poetry is a painstaking, single-minded consideration of the poem
itself. One must not invoke biographical facts or other material
outside the poem in order to explicate or evaluate. Instead, he
must consider the poem as an independent unit. This particular
conclusion has proved the chink in Brooks' critical armor, and
other critics have been quick to strike. Although Brooks qualifies
his position rather noticeably in later writings, he remains a
popular target on this score.

A more significant retreat by Brooks, however, is evidenced
in his Literary Criticism: A Short History (1957), written in
collaboration with William K. Wimsatt, Jr. In this work, Brooks
praises Sigmund Freud for contributing to criticism valuable
terminology and insights into symbolism. This praise comes, of

242

course, from the man who earlier ruled out psychology as an extraneous matter.

Against these shortcomings, however, one must recognize Brooks' distinct contribution in fastening attention on the work itself and in insisting on a more disciplined critical procedure to replace subjective judgments. He also demonstrates clearly the presence of paradox (as he defines the term) as a major element in the function of poetry; and he defends quite capably his contention that poetry expresses through metaphor certain truths which lie beyond the possibilities of science or of prose.

Cleanth Brooks, born in Murray, Kentucky, received the Bachelor of Arts degree from Vanderbilt (1928), where he studied under John Crowe Ransom, and the Master of Arts from Tulane (1929). He then continued his formal education as a Rhodes Scholar at Oxford. In addition to early periods of teaching at the University of Louisiana, the University of Texas, and the University of Southern California, Brooks has also been a full-time editor of literary magazines, a cultural attaché at the American embassy in London (1964–66), and a professional writer. Currently, he is Gray Professor of Rhetoric at Yale.

Below is a passage which exemplifies ideas by which Brooks has made his critical judgments. It is also a competent analysis of the situation in criticism at the time of its appearance.

Modern Criticism[1]

"Modern criticism, through its exacting scrutiny of literary texts, has demonstrated with finality that in art beauty and truth are indivisible and one." So writes Mark Schorer in a recent essay on criticism, and he continues as follows:[2]

The Keatsian overtones of these terms are mitigated and an old dilemma solved if for beauty we substitute form, and for truth, con-

---

[1] First published as a Foreword to *Critiques and Essays in Criticism 1920– 1948*, selected by Robert Wooster Stallman. The Ronald Press, New York, 1949.
[2] From *The Hudson Review*, I (Spring, 1948), 67. [Brooks' note]

tent. We may, without risk of loss, narrow them even more, and speak
of technique and subject matter. Modern criticism has shown us that
to speak of content as such is not to speak of art at all, but of experience, and that it is only when we speak of the *achieved* content,
the form, the work of art as a work of art, that we speak as critics. The
difference between content, or experience, and achieved content, or
art, is technique.

When we speak of technique, then, we speak of nearly everything.
For technique is the means by which the writer's experience, which is
his subject matter, compels him to attend to it; technique is the only
means he has of discovering, exploring, developing his subject, of conveying its meaning, and, finally, of evaluating it.

I subscribe to all that is said here. It is an admirable summary
of what modern criticism has achieved. But I envy Schorer his
boldness of tone: "Modern criticism has demonstrated with
finality," "Modern criticism has shown us," etc. For I am conscious
that nearly every statement that he makes has been, and continues
to be, challenged; and further, that some of those who would
accept his summary as a statement of the accomplishment of
modern criticism, place a very different value on the accomplishment. Modern criticism has been blamed for strangling the
creative impulse, for producing an arid intellectualization of our
poetry, for perverting literary studies. If one is to provide a really
serviceable introduction to such a volume as this, he had better
not leave such charges out of account. Ignored, such charges
confuse the issues on every level.

There is something to be said, then, for a general stock-taking,
and particularly at the present time. The recent publication of
books like Stanley Hyman's *The Armed Vision,* and Eric Bentley's
The Importance of Scrutiny, or of essays like R. P. Blackmur's
A Burden for Critics and of Schorer's *Technique as Discovery,*
already mentioned—all suggest the sense of a period's having
been fulfilled. The criticism characteristic of our time has come
to fruition, or has arrived at a turning point, or, as some writers
hint, has now exhausted its energies. For those who would dwell
upon this darker note there are further corroborative signs: the

increasing tendency to talk about the "methods" of the "new" criticism; the growing academic respectability of the new criticism; the attempt to codify the new critics and to establish their sources and derivations. As it consolidates its gains, the new criticism ceases to be "new" and thus loses its romantic attractiveness, and with that, some of its more callow proponents. But, by the same token, it risks gaining the allegiance of another set of followers who hope to exploit it mechanically.

Yet, though a general stock-taking is in order, I shall not attempt it here. In the first place, it could hardly be done satisfactorily in a short introduction. In the second place, as a contributor to this volume, I do not wish to seem to sit in judgment upon my peers, defining what is central to the new criticism and what is peripheral. Suffice it to recognize that there is a large area of agreement among the critics represented in this volume. But they do not constitute a school—much less a guild. I have no wish to minimize their varying emphases and their active disagreements. It is even a question whether they are accurately described under a common name, and most of all under the name which has caught on—the "new criticism."

I suppose that when John Crowe Ransom chose the phrase a few years ago, he meant it to be a neutral and modest designation; i.e., the modern criticism, the contemporary criticism. Despite such intent, the name has hardly proved a happy choice. It has seemed to stress, perhaps arrogantly, the relative novelty of the criticism; and many popular reviewers and professors have been quick to sense in it a dangerous novelty. The typical professor of English is naturally and constitutionally opposed to change; the popular reviewer, in so far as his critical principles are concerned, only less so. Both have what amounts to a vested interest in a more desultory and less strenuous discussion of literature.

Yet much more than vested interests is of course involved. The misconceptions about modern criticism are too widespread and too persistent to be accounted for in such a fashion. They are very stubbornly rooted indeed. They are rooted, I believe, in an essentially romantic conception of poetry. This conception tends to take quite literally the view that poetry is the spontaneous overflow of emotion, and that its appreciation is best served by a corresponding overflow of emotion on the part of the reader. It conceives of the function of the intellect as only officious and meddling. The creation of poetry is magical, and if the intellect is brought into play at all in examining a poem, this is an attempt to expose the magic and thus do away with it.

Critical activity is therefore interpreted as somehow inimical to the creation of a robust poetry. Our own age, it is argued, is "Alexandrian," over-ingenious, self-conscious, and therefore cannot create anything but a kind of sophisticated intellectual poetry. The position is rarely argued: its strength is that it does not need to be argued. It is enough to catcall "Alexandrian." But a little argument may serve to take some of the sting out of the epithet. If ours is a critical age, it is not because of this fact an uncreative age. Measured against the poetry of the Victorians, say, the poetry of the twentieth century compares very favorably indeed. That will be the consensus, I think, even of those who are worried about what they take to be the twentieth century's excessive interest in criticism. As for those who would dispute the achievement of the twentieth century in poetry, they might be reminded that they dispute it on the basis of a critical judgment of their own, and so are begging the very question which they are deciding.

In brief, what is important about a "critical" age is the soundness of its criticism—the matter of whether its criticism is good or bad—and not the mere fact that the age is interested in criticism. Everything else being equal, the production of a great deal of criticism probably argues for an intense interest in the arts, and normally goes hand in hand with creative activity. For criticism does not compete with creative activity. The critic is not in his arrogance offering a scheme which explains the construction of poetry, a formula by which poems are to be written. Nor is he, on the other hand, concerned with reducing the poem to an intellectual scheme in order to "explain" the poem—that is, to explain the poem away—expose the magic—kill the emotional response.

In referring such misconceptions of criticism to a naively romantic view of the arts, I have perhaps made them seem over-naive—too simple to be held by practising writers. In that case it may be well to illustrate from a recent review which appeared in one of our metropolitan bookpages. Alfred Kazin, the reviewer, is concerned about the impersonality and technicality of the sort of criticism contained in this volume. Its very "expertness," for him, is damning:[3]

In our day the real princelings of criticism have been those who can manage, in some way or other, to sound like impersonal experts, and for whom the work before them is always an occasion for technical analysis or some sovereign redefinition of our lot. In one sense they have even set themselves up as the rivals to the works before them, and have sought by their expertness to replace them with their own. This is not . . . entirely due to the presumption of critics. We live in a time when an overwhelming sense of having come to the end of a period in man's total history has put a premium on intellectual revaluation rather than on the literature of "real" experience. But it certainly leads to arid intellectual pride, and even, as there is no lack of examples around us to prove, patronage of artists themselves.

Now the temptation of pride is a constant one, and in a fiercely competitive age like our own, men, including literary men, can never too often be warned against it. But to imply that the critics at whom Kazin points his finger are somehow especially susceptible as other critics (social, historical, etc.) are not, or, for that matter, as poets, novelists, and Saturday Reviewers of Literature are not, seems to me absurd. For the impersonality of the critic can just as fairly be interpreted as modesty rather than as arrogance—as an unwillingness to interpose his own personality between the reader and the work itself. Furthermore, the concern for technical analysis looks like a wholesome preoccupation with the work of art; that is, the critic is content to describe the work

[3] From *Books (New York Herald Tribune)*, May 30, 1948, p. 5. [Brooks' note]

as sensitively as he can rather than to dilate upon his emotional response to it. Rivalry with the work of art is in fact more likely to be instituted by a critic who is anxious to stress his personal response or to use the work he discusses as a peg upon which to hang his own commentary on morals or politics.

I cannot therefore accept Kazin's suggestion that the new critics are on principle arrogant, but his other suggestion, namely, that the pressures of our age have something to do with the characteristic development of criticism in our time, seems to me quite true. I should prefer, however, to state the matter in somewhat different fashion—certainly not as the result of some "overwhelming sense of [our] having come to the end of a period in man's total history." I should prefer to put the case more modestly, and, I think, more specifically, thus: the raveling out of the Victorian poetic conventions coincided with the final breakdown of the current theory of poetic statement, itself some centuries old. It coincided also with the near collapse of linguistic training in our schools and colleges. All three are doubtless aspects of a general breakdown of the means of communication, but it may be serviceable to notice them separately.

The going to seed of a particular literary period may seem unimportant. But in this case it was special and significant, for the Victorian conventions represented what could be salvaged from a pre-scientific age, or represented compromises with the new scientific symbolism which had undercut the older poetic symbols. The Victorian conventions were thus the product of a poetics which had come dangerously close to relegating the specifically poetic uses of language to decoration and embellishment. This general impoverishment was, and is, abundantly reflected in the educational system—whether in the elementary grades or in the graduate school.

It would be unfair to say that the new poetry impinged upon an audience of illiterates. But the discovery that it lacked an audience that could read it soon raised a further and more fundamental question: whether that same audience could read any poetry, including the poetry of the past. The audience, of course, assumed that it could; but in that case, what did the typical reader derive from the poetry of the past—if he read it, and when he read it? Noble sentiments? Ethical doctrine? An escape from a dull and stale world? He read poetry for pleasure, to be sure. But pleasure becomes an even more ambiguous term in a day of mass-produced entertainment. If he answered "for truth," that term too, in an age overawed by the tremendous structure of science, called for elaborate definition and qualification. How could methods so notoriously unscientific as those of poetry yield anything resembling truth?

Questions of this sort are not, of course, new. But in our time it has become increasingly difficult to evade answering them. Partial solutions will no longer work. Compromises which apparently served the nineteenth century are no longer practical. This is not to say that the twentieth century has found the answers: it is to explain why it has had to canvass such questions thoroughly and *de novo*.

Thus far I have dealt with criticism as related to the impact of poetry on the modern world. But the problem has to be seen in broader terms. The rise of modern criticism is part of a general intensification of the study of language and symbolism. The development of semantics, symbolic logic, cultural anthropology, and the psychology of Jung and Freud may all be taken as responses to the same general situation. How they are specifically related to each other and what contributions these studies have made, or may make, to criticism are topics that I shall not attempt to discuss here. Suffice it that they all bear upon the problem of symbolism (logical and extra-logical) and represent attempts to recover symbolic "languages" whose real importance has become evident to us only as the supporting cultural pattern breaks down.

It is no accident, therefore, that a great deal of modern criticism has occupied itself with the problem of how language actually works and specifically how it works in a piece of literature. Because of this, there is a tendency to identify the new criticism with "close textual reading" and to assume that it is limited to problems of what used to be called "diction." The essays here collected should supply a corrective to such a view. Modern critics, it is perfectly true, tend to force attention back to the text of the work itself: that is, to look at the poem as a poem, not as an appendage to the poet's biography, nor as a reflection of his reading, nor as an illustration of the history of ideas. Such an emphasis naturally stresses a close reading of the text, and, since poems are written in words, careful attention to language. But, though the text must provide the ultimate sanction for the meaning of the work, that does not mean that close textual reading is to be conceived of as a sort of verbal piddling. Words open out into the larger symbolizations on all levels—for example, into archetypal symbol, ritual, and myth. The critic's concern for "language" need not be conceived narrowly, even if his concern leads to an intensive examination: it can be extended to the largest symbolizations possible. A renewed respect for words and a sense of their complexities are matters for congratulation. The alternative does not liberate: it leads away from literature altogether.

I have dealt with some of the honest and some of the willful misunderstandings of modern criticism. But these are probably calculated to do less damage than extravagant claims made for criticism. I shall cite only one example, though I think that it is a significant one. Stanley Hyman writes:[4] ". . . modern criticism for the most part no longer accepts its traditional status as an adjunct to 'creative' or 'imaginative' literature. . . ." " 'No exponent of criticism . . . has, I presume, ever made the preposterous assumption that criticism is an autotelic art,' T. S. Eliot wrote in 1923, in 'The Function of Criticism.' Whether or not anyone had made that 'preposterous assumption' by 1923, modern criticism, which began more or less formally the following year with the publication of I. A. Richards's *Principles of Literary Criticism,* has been acting on it since."

I disagree. True, we can define art (Hyman suggests any

[4] From *The Armed Vision* (New York: Alfred A. Knopf, 1948), p. 7. [Brooks' note]

"creation of meaningful patterns of experience") broadly enough to include criticism. But I think that we lose more than we gain. In any case, we risk confusing the issues, and, as has been pointed out, the issues are sufficiently confused as it is. Better to assign to literary criticism a more humble and a more specific function: let us say that the task of literary criticism is to put the reader in possession of the work of art.

To read a work of art successfully involves, of course, a process of imaginative reconstruction. The good reader thus necessarily makes use of a process related to that by which the author has constructed the work. If the poet is a maker, the critic is at least a remaker; and I suppose that the successful critic is entitled to claim that his work is imaginative in this sense. (He had certainly better not be lacking in imagination!) But I do not think that the critic is entitled to claim more, nor do I think that he wishes to claim more.

To put the reader into possession of the work of art. Is this a mere reading of the work or is it a judgment of it? Frankly, I do not see how the two activities can be separated. For to possess the work implies a knowledge of it as a work of art, not merely the knowledge of it as a document (political, philosophical, etc.), nor merely the knowledge of something abstracted from it (a logical scheme or paraphrase). The critic inevitably judges, but how explicit he is to make his judgment will obviously depend upon the circumstances. In some cases, and for some readers, he may think it enough to show the pattern of tensions in the work and the way in which they are resolved, or the failure to resolve them. In other cases, he may wish to make his judgment very explicit. But if a full reading of a work implies a judgment on it, a responsible judgment on it ought to imply that a full reading lies behind the judgment, and if called for, can be set forth. The attempt to drive a wedge between close reading of the text and evaluation of the work seems to me confused and confusing.

The essays collected in this volume provide more than a mere sampling of modern criticism. They have not been chosen at random. If they show a real diversity, they also suggest a unity, making as they do a collective comment on the central problems of criticism. They represent an achievement, and taken even at the lowest discount, a worthy achievement.

I have little to say about the future of criticism. I shall not say that the future of criticism is immense. But I think that I can point out something that needs to be done (and is in process of being done): that is, to discriminate more closely among the various problems with which criticism in the large is concerned. To give an example: Beardsley and Wimsatt have pointed out that the genesis of the work (how it was composed, what went into its making, etc.) constitutes a problem distinct from what may be called the analysis of the work in terms of its formal properties.[5] This latter problem has in turn to be distinguished from the further problem which has to do with the actual effect of the work on various kinds of people and at various periods. All three problems are intimately related, and all may be worth discussion; but unless they are distinguished we shall get into trouble. For example, it is one thing to discuss *Uncle Tom's Cabin* in terms of its formal properties as a novel. It is a rather different thing to ask how Harriet Beecher Stowe came to write it, how it was shaped by the pressures of the time. It is still another thing to account for the way in which it affected men in the past, and to try to predict what further effects (if any) it may have in the future. Here the discriminations seem easy; but many who concede them here in this instance refuse to recognize them when we substitute for *Uncle Tom's Cabin, Paradise Lost,* or *Moby Dick, or The Four Quartets.*

To insist on a clearer marking of boundary lines, of course, may suggest more specialization, more technicalities, and the segregation of the critic into an even narrower compartment. But clearly marked boundary lines do not imply fences, barricades, or tariff walls. Nobody wants to restrict free trade—between scholarship and criticism, and least of all, between the various areas of criticism. But if the distinctions are real—if they

[5] See "The Intentional Fallacy," *Sewanee Review,* LIV (1946), 468–88.

actually exist—muddling of the boundary markers remedies nothing: it merely begets confusion. To indicate the boundaries clearly is actually to encourage free passage across them; for, as it is, we too often line up to defend them as national borders in the spirit of troops repelling an invasion. The critic occupied with the formal analysis of a work is damned for having offered an obviously inadequate account of the social pressures which played upon the author of the work, or for having left out of account the importance of the work as a political document, or he is reproached for having (or for not having) accounted for the composition of the work.

The ways in which we can view a poem or novel or drama are very nearly infinite. Some of them are of the highest importance. Some of them in our day have hardly got the attention which they deserve.

But instead of pining for the perfect critic who will do everything, it might be more sensible to see what the critics have actually done—to discriminate among the various "criticisms" in their proper relations to each other. Interrelated, they certainly are; but the ability to discriminate among them might allow us to make better use of the actual and limited, flesh-and-blood critics that we have.

Kenneth Burke

(b. 1897)

To understand the critical theories of Kenneth Burke, one should begin by noting Burke's vision of art in terms of its effect upon the beholder and his idea of art as an instrument in achieving social progress. Burke, armed with a commitment to a special brand of communism, discusses literary criticism within the spectrum of certain social and political changes which he sees as necessary for a soundly organized and functioning society.

In his Attitudes Toward History *(1937), he places the critic in the role of "propagandist and craftsman." He views the critic as a man with a mission, specifically equipped and trained for his task. He also emphasizes the effect which a work of art has on the collective consciousness of the audience, thereby demonstrating his interest in the beholder rather than the artist.*

Further, Burke is clearly aware of the multiplicity of meanings to be derived from a literary work. In fact, he often sees "image clusters" where others would deny them; and to these clusters he attaches considerable significance.

In reading Burke, one must be careful of barriers raised by individual vocabulary. In his "Psychology and Form," for example, he makes a heavy point of "form" which he explains as the producing and satisfying of an appetite in the listener's or the reader's mind. Also, one must learn the meaning of such expressions as "collective poems," "authority symbols," and "rituals of purification and rebirth"—to all of which he assigns meanings that fall outside the area of commonly accepted definitions.

Like many other critics, Burke has been praised and censured.

Many knowledgable writers, especially among the New Critics, have spoken approvingly of the sensitivity with which he has explained symbolism in literature. Still others have seen great merit in his concept of the social values of literature. Yet on the other side his detractors have attacked with considerable success his attempts to make criticism an all-encompassing entity. They have argued convincingly that criticism can scarcely accomplish all that Burke envisions.

Kenneth Burke was born in Pittsburgh, Pennsylvania, on May 5, 1897. Educated at the Ohio State University and Columbia University, he has spent his working life as a magazine editor, a lecturer, a translator, a college teacher, and above all, a writer. Although Burke's writing has centered primarily on history, contemporary affairs, and criticism, he has also produced a novel, Towards a Better Life *(1966), and a group of interesting essays. Presently, he restricts his activities to writing critical essays and lecturing, mostly on college campuses.*

Below is an essay which Burke wrote for The New York Review of Books *(Vol. I, No. 2, 1963) upon the death of William Carlos Williams. Although the work is primarily a tribute to Williams and his writings, it is also a clear revelation of Burke's theories rendered somewhat mellow, perhaps, by the circumstances of the occasion.*

William Carlos Williams, 1883–1963

William Carlos Williams, poet and physician. Trained to crises of sickness and parturition that often came at odd hours. An ebullient man, sorely vexed in his last years, and now at rest. But he had this exceptional good luck: that his appeal as a person survives in his work. To read his books is to find him warmly there, everywhere you turn.

In some respects, the physician and the poet might be viewed as opposites, as they certainly were at least in the sense that time spent on his patients was necessarily time denied to the writing of poetry. But that's a superficial view. In essence, this man was an imaginative physician and a nosological poet. His great humaneness was equally present in both roles, which contributed essentially to the development of each other.

"There is no thing that with a twist of the imagination cannot be something else," he said in an early work, whereby he could both use flowers as an image of lovely womanhood and speak of pathology as a "flower garden." The principle made for great mobility, for constant transformations that might affect a writer in late years somewhat like trying to run a hundred yards in ten seconds flat. At the same time, such shiftiness in the new country of the poet's mind allowed for imaginal deflections that could be at once secretive and expressive. Also (except that the simile fails to bring out the strongly personal aspect of the work) his "objectivism" was like inquiring into baseball not in terms of the rule book, but rather by noting the motions and designs which the players in some one particular game might make with reference to the trajectories of a sphere that, sometimes thrown, sometimes struck, took various courses across a demarcated field. Such constant attempts to see things afresh, as "facts," gave him plenty to do. For he proceeded circumstantially, without intellectualistic shortcuts—and with the combined conscientiousness of both disciplines, as man of medicine and medicine man.

An anecdote might help indicate what I have in mind about Williams. (For present purposes, I think, we should refer to him thus, though the usage does greatly misrepresent my personal attitude.) Some years after Williams had retired from his practice as a physician, and ailments had begun to cripple him, we were walking slowly on a beach in Florida. A neighbor's dog decided to accompany us, but was limping. I leaned down, aimlessly hoping to help the dog (which became suddenly frightened, and nearly bit me). Then Williams took the paw in his left hand (the right was now less agile) and started probing for the source of the trouble. It was a gesture at once expert and imaginative, something in which to have perfect confidence, as both the cur and I saw in a flash. Feeling between the toes lightly, quickly, and above all *surely*, he spotted a burr, removed it without the slightest cringe on the dog's part—and the three of us were again on our way along the beach.

I thought to myself (though not then clearly enough to say so): "And here I've learned one more thing about Williams' doctrine of 'contract.'" It concerned the *"tactus eruditus,"* and I quote words that he had tossed, as a line all by itself, into a somewhat rough-and-tumble outburst, "This is My Platform," he had written in the twenties.

Some forty years earlier, when I had first haggled with him about this slogan (which is as basic to an understanding of him as the statement of poetic policy he makes several times in his writings, "No ideas but in things"), the talk of "contact" had seemed most of all to imply that an interest in local writing and language should replace my absorption in Thomas Mann's German and André Gide's French. Next, it suggested a cult of "Amurricanism" just at the time when many young writers, copying Pound and Eliot, were on the way to self-exile in Europe while more were soon to follow. (I mistakenly thought that I was to be one of them.) Further, it seemed to imply the problematical proposition that one should live in a small town like Rutherford rather than in the very heart of Babylon (or in some area that, if not central to the grass roots of the nation, was at least close to the ragweed).

But over the years, as Williams persisted unstoppably in his ways, the nature of his writings gradually made it clear that the implications of "contact" and its particular kind of "anti-poetry" were quite different, and went much deeper. I feel sure that, whatever may be our uncertainties about the accidents of his doctrine, its essence resides in the kind of physicality imposed upon his poetry by the nature of his work as a physician. Thus, as with the incident of the dog, my understanding of his slogan took a notable step forward when, some time after giving up his practice, he said explosively that he missed the opportunity to get his hands on things (and he made gestures to do with the delivering of a child). However, my thesis is not made any easier by the fact that, while including Aaron Burr among his band because

Burr felt the need "to touch, to hear, to see, to smell, to taste" (thus being "intact" in the ways of contact), at the same time Williams disapproved of Franklin, "the face on the penny stamp," and complained with regard to Franklin's perpetual tinkering: "To want to touch, not to wish anything to remain clean, aloof—comes always of a kind of timidity, from fear."

The point is this: For Williams any natural or poetic concern with the body as a sexual object was reinforced and notably modified by a professional concern with the body as a suffering or diseased object. (Think how many of his stories testify to his sympathetic yet picturesquely entertaining encounters with wide areas of both physical and social morbidity.) The same relation to the human animal in terms of bodily disabilities led him to a kind of democracy quite unlike Whitman's, despite the obvious influence of Whitman upon him. "After some years of varied experience with the bodies of the rich and the poor a man finds little to distinguish between them, bulks them as one and bases his working judgments on other matters." (In any case, the political editorializing in Whitman's come-one-come-all attitude had lost its meaning, other than as a pleasant sentiment, in proportion as Congress erected legal barriers to the flow of immigrants by a quota system.)

The same stress upon the all-importance of the bodily element accounts also for the many cruel references to subsidence that are scattered through *The Collected Later Poems*. (We shall later get to the earlier, more athletic stages.) Consider "The Night Rider," for instance, that begins, "scoured like a conch/or the moon's shell/I ride from my love/through the damp night," and ends: "the pulse a remembered pulse/of full-tide gone." The theme naturally lends itself to other kinds of imagery: "The old horse dies slow": the portrait of an old goat, "listless in its assured sanctity"; a time of drought ("The Words Lying Idle"); the tree, stretched on the garage roof, after a hurricane; homage to the woodpecker, "stabbing there with a barbed tongue which *succeeds*"; apostrophizing the self, "why do you try/so hard to be a man? You are/a lover! Why adopt/the reprehensible absurdities

of/an inferior attitude?"; with the mind like a tidal river, "the
tide will/change/and rise again, maybe"; there is the theme of
"The Thoughtful Lover" who finds that "today/the particulars of
poetry" require his "whole attention"; and of a "Bare Tree" he
writes, "chop it down/and use the wood/against this biting cold."
In this group, certainly, would belong "The Injury," an account
of the poet lying in a hospital bed; he hears "an engine/breath-
ing—somewhere/in the night:—soft coal, soft coal,/soft coal"; in
terms of the laboring engine's sounds as he interprets them, he
makes plans for the next phase, "the slow way . . . if you can find
any way." This expression of dispiritedness wells up so simply, so
spontaneously, it is itself a poignantly beautiful instance of spirit.
And for a happy and charming variation on such themes, there is
"Spring is Here Again, Sir," ending:

> We lay, Floss and I, on
> the grass together, in
> the warm air a bird flew
> into a bush, dipped our
> hands in the cold running water—
> cold, too cold; but found
> it, to our satisfaction,
> as in the past, still wet.

The sudden reference (already quoted) to using the "bare tree"
as firewood reminds us that whereas in an early poem fires came
"out of the bodies/Of all men that walk with lust at heart," in
later poems the theme of fire could be modified by merging with
connotations of the purgative. Thus, there is the ecstatic section to
do with fire in *Paterson*. And his rightly well-known piece, "Burning the Christmas Greens," interweaves this elation of the purgative with the color that is always the best of omens in Williams'
work. I have at times got courage from the thought that a poem
of his, entitled "At Kenneth Burke's Place," has for its ending a
reference to a greening apple, "smudged with/a sooty life that
clings, also,/with the skin," and despite a bit of rot "still good/
even unusual compared with the usual."

But this moves us to a further step in his benignly nosological approach to the subject matter of poetry. I refer to his interest in the sheer survival of things, so that he would record the quality of an ungainly apple from a gnarled old unpruned, unsprayed tree, "as if a taste long lost and regretted/had in the end, finally, been brought to life again." Thus it seems almost inevitable that he should get around to writing a long poem, "The Desert Music." Along these lines, I have thought that an ideal subject for a poem by him would be a gallant description of weeds, wild-flowers, bushes and low trees gradually carving out a livelihood for themselves in the slag piles around Scranton. This would be done without sentimentality. (Poems of his like that can't be sentimental, for they say what's actually there in front of him, as with his lines on the rat, surviving even infections deliberately imposed by the hellish ingenuity of man-made plagues, an animal "well/suited to a world/conditioned to such human 'tropism/for order' at all cost.") Here would belong his many poems that, by the very accuracy of their description, testify to his delight in scattered, improvised bits of beauty, as with things one can see during that most dismal of transitions, "Approach to a City" (tracks in dirty snow, "snow/pencilled with the stubble of old/weeds," dried flowers in a barroom window, while "The flags in the heavy/air move against a leaden/ground"). In such observations, he says, he can "refresh" himself. Cannot one easily see how his doctoring figured here, teaching him never to overlook "a mud/livid with decay and life," and where the doctor had found sheer life, challenging the poet to go a step further and spontaneously find it beautiful, as a theologian might have striven to find it good?

See, on this point, "The Hard Core of Beauty," describing things on "the/dead-end highway, abandoned/when the new bridge went in finally." Just stop for a while, go back over that line, ponder on each moment—and I'm sure you'll agree that, whatever its cruel, spare sharpness, there's something softly nostalgic like a voice heard through a mist. Within it there's the thought that never left him, the beauty and cleanness of the river around the falls at Paterson, before its rape by the drastic combination of raw politics, raw technics, and raw business. (In earlier years, he referred to the area as "the origin today of the vilest swillhole in christendom, the Passaic river.") All the time the poet-doctor is pointing out, again and again, what survives, there is also the poignancy of what is lost. And in *Paterson*, along with the love, there is the tough, unanswerable, *legalistic documentation* of man's brutal errors, and their costliness to man. As he put it in another book, "Poised against the *Mayflower* is the slave ship." This too was *contact*. And he has done for that damned botched area just west of the Hudson (that hateful traffic-belching squandering of industrial power atop the tidal swamps) something quite incredible: he has made it poignantly songful. He went on singing, singing, singing, while the rivers and the soil and the air and the fires became progressively more polluted in the name of Progress, while more and more of the natural beauties were ripped apart, singing while each year there spread inexorably farther west a cancerous growth of haphazard real-estating that came to enclose his own fine old house in some measure of the general urban sprawl. When the sun rises behind "the moody/water-loving giants of Manhattan," eight miles to the east, they must cast their shadows for a time on the houses west of the Meadows. And in any case the troublous monsters at a distance, magical in the morning or evening mist, did unquestionably cast their shadows on his work.

I have said that Williams was never "sentimental." But I must say more on this point, in view of Wallace Stevens' remark in his preface to Williams' *Collected Poems 1921–1931:* " 'The Cod Head' is a bit of pure sentimentalization; so is 'The Bull.' " But, as you must expect of Stevens, the word is used in a quite alembicated sense, to name "what vitalizes Williams," and to serve as a proper accompaniment to his "anti-poetic" side. To see most quickly how the two motives work together, one needs but think of a gruffly beautiful line like "the moon is in/the oak tree's crotch." Or "Little frogs/with puffed-out throats,/singing in the slime."

I meant that Williams' typical use of imagery does not involve *false* or *forced* sentiment. If I correctly interpret Wallace Stevens' "Nuances of a Theme by Williams" (in *Harmonium*), Stevens meant by sentiment any personal identification with an object, as distinct from an appreciation of it in its pure singularity, without reference to its possible imaginary role as a mirror of mankind.

In this sense, Williams is "sentimental." For all his "objectivist" accuracy, Williams' details are not in essence descriptions of things but portraits of personalities. Typically in his poems the eye (like a laying on of hands), by disguised rituals that are improvised constantly anew, inordinates us into the human nature of things.

As regards the two poems that Stevens specifically mentions, the ending of "The Cod Head" ("a severed codhead between two/green stones—lifting/falling") involves associations that might ultimately fit better with a title somehow combining "severed godhead" and "codpiece"—and something similar is obviously afoot at the end of the poem "The Bull": "Milkless/he nods the hair between his horns/and eyes matted/with hyacinthine curls." As with Marianne Moore, Williams' observations about animals or things are statements about notable traits in people. Along with their ostensible nature, the sympathetic reader gets this deeper dimension as a bonus, an earned increment. Let's be specific. I shall quote a brief item that, if it doesn't seem almost like nonsense, must seem like what it is, a marvel:

> *As the cat*
> *climbed over*
> *the top of*
>
> *the jamcloset*
> *first the right*
> *forefoot*
>
> *carefully*
> *then the hind*
> *stepped down*

into the pit of
the empty
flowerpot

Here is the account of a consummate moment in the motions of an
unassuming cat, an alleycat (I like to think) that just happened
to have a home—plus the inanity of the consummation, as hinted
by the empty flowerpot. How differently a dog would have man-
aged, barging in and doubtless bumping the flowerpot over! What
trimness the poet brings to his representation of trimness! And
in its perfectly comic study of perfection, it is so final, I could
easily imagine it being used as the epilogue to something long
and arduous. Inevitably, he called the lines just "Poem."

Stevens' point led us away from our main point. But in his own
way he leads us back again, when he ends by observing that an
alternative preface might have been written presenting Williams
as "a kind of Diogenes of contemporary poetry." Diogenes wrote
when Greek culture was decidedly in a valetudinarian condition;
and though neither poet nor medico, in his proverbial down-
rightness he could properly be taken to stand for Williams' particular combination of the two.

There are many cases where Williams' diagnostic eye, modified
by an urge toward encouragement, becomes the sheerly appreciative eye. (Cf. Stevens: "He writes of flowers exquisitely.") But
it's also a fact, for instance, that whenever Williams bears down
on the description of a flower, connotations of love and lovely
woman are there implicitly, and quite often explicitly. Thus, in
Stevens' sense, the poems are inherently "sentimentalized." Whatever the gestures of *haecceitas* (the sense of an object in its sheer
thisness), with Williams lyric utterance is essentially a flash of
drama, a fragment of narrative, a bit of personal history mirrored
as well in talk of a thing as in talk of a person.

And for this reason, given his initial medical slant, the tendency always is towards a matter of welfare. Dante said that
the proper subjects for poetry are *venus, virtus* and *salus.* The
"anti-poetic" strain in Williams' poetry gives us a medical variant

of *salus,* nowhere more startlingly contrived than in this neat abruptness:

> *To*
>
> *a child (a boy) bouncing*
> *a ball (a blue ball)—*
>
> *He bounces it (a toy racket*
> *in his hand) and runs*
>
> *and catches it (with his*
> *left hand) six floors*
> *straight down—*
> *which is the old back yard*

When the child, successfully clutching the ball, hits "the old back yard," by God he is home.

Stevens' use of imagery is more airy than Williams', quite as the world of a part-time insurance man differs from the world of a part-time medical doctor, though each of these poets in his way is strongly aware of the appetites. That great "heavy" of Williams, "The Clouds," is interesting in this regard. The deathy horses, in a "charge from south to north" while a writhing black flag "fights/to be free," are racing in a gigantic turmoil (something like a visual analogue of Wagner's Valkyrs). It's a vision of such death as goes with fire, famine, plague and slaughter. That's how it starts. The second section is a kind of inventory, a quick sampling of the great dead, and done somewhat haphazardly, like glances at the scurrying clouds themselves. It brings the poet forcefully close to a vision of pure spirit despite himself: "The intellect leads, leads still! Beyond the clouds." Part three is a "scherzo," a kind of joke, grisly in this context, about a "holy man" who, while "riding/the clouds of his belief" (that is, officiating at a service) had "turned and grinned" at him. And the final stanza gets torn into unfinished uncertainty, quite like "the disordered heavens, ragged, ripped by winds." It is a gorgeous poem, at times almost ferocious, and stopped abruptly, in the middle of a sentence, as with the boy who had conscientiously caught the ball.

Elsewhere Williams aims at less drastic kinds of spirit, the most puzzling or puzzled contrivance being perhaps at the end of the long late poem, "Asphodel, that Greeny Flower." To be sure, the flower is green, and that's all to the good. But a few lines before the close we are informed, "Asphodel/has no odor, save to the imagination." Yet in an earlier poem we had been assured: "Time without/odor is Time without me." And one of Williams' most amusing early poems was an itemized rebuke to his nose for the "ardors" of its smelling.

At this point, another personal anecdote occurs to me, for its bearing upon Williams' character. On one occasion, when visiting us, he told me ruefully of misbehavior on his part (an incident that also falls under the head of "contact"). A little delegation of solemn admirers had come to pay him homage. Naturally, he was grateful to them. But as his poems overwhelmingly testify, he was also mercurial. And in the very midst of their solemnity at parting, since one of the little band happened to be a pretty young woman he gave her a frank, good-natured smack on the fanny. It was all part of the game, done on the spur of the moment, and it had seemed quite reasonable. It was the *tactus eruditus* in capricious relaxation. But his visitors were horrified, and he realized that he had spoiled the whole show. He confessed to me his gloom at such unruly ways. But is it not a simple scientific fact that the poet they had come to honor owed much of his charm to precisely such whimsicality as this? One might class it with another occasion when, in a talk at a girls' school, he earnestly exhorted them, "You must learn to be a man." Maybe some of them did—but all were furious. How were they to be reminded precisely then that he was also the man who has written: "Anyone who has seen 2,000 infants born as I have and pulled them one way or another into the world must know that man, as such, is doomed to disappear in not too many thousand years. He just can't go on. No woman will stand for it. Why should she?"

I wish that, to commemorate Williams, some publisher would now reissue his *Al Que Quiere,* just as it was in the original 1917 edition. It shows with such winsomeness this quirky aspect of his genius. Consider the crazy "Danse Russe," for instance, a poem delightfully alien to the pomposities that Eliot did so much to encourage; yet in their way the verse and prose of this "Diogenes" have been written into the very constitution of our country:

> *If I when my wife is sleeping*
> *and the baby and Kathleen*
> *are sleeping*
> *and the sun is a flame-white disc*
> *in silken mists*
> *above shining trees,—*
> *if I in my north room*
> *danse naked, grotesquely*
> *before my mirror*
> *waving my shirt round my head*
> *and singing softly to myself:*
> *"I am lonely, lonely.*
> *I was born to be lonely.*
> *I am best so!"*
> *If I admire my arms, my face*
> *my shoulders, flanks, buttocks*
> *against the yellow drawn shades,—*
> *who shall say I am not*
> *the happy genius of my household?*

Here also was first published the well-known "Tract," his instructions to his "townspeople," on "how to perform a funeral," lines that were read by the minister, as a final goodbye, at the side of Williams' own grave. That was exactly right. And at the end of the book there is a long poem ("The Wanderer, a Rococo Study") which, though it was written before the poet had fully got his stride, and is a kind of romantic allegorizing that he would later outlaw, yet is in its way notable, particularly as a stage in Williams' development. For after several preparatory steps which it would require too much space to detail here, it leads up to a ritualistic transformation involving an imaginary baptism in the waters of "The Passaic, that filthy river." These lines should be enough to indicate how the merger of poet and physician initially involved a somewhat magical process, thus:

> *Then the river began to enter my heart,*
> *Eddying back cool and limpid*
> *Into the crystal beginning of its days.*
> *But with the rebound it leaped forward:*
> *Muddy, then black and shrunken*
> *Till I felt the utter depth of its rottenness*
> *The vile breath of its degradation*
> *And dropped down knowing this was me.*

Here, surely, was the essential ritualistic step by which he began his "contact" with "anti-poetry"—and though often, in later years, he turned to the sheerly beautiful, even sheerly decorative, here we see the tubes and coils and sluices of the powerhouse. Or am I but tricked by the occasion into going back forty-plus years, and seeing him too much as I saw him then? Yet recall (in *Journey to Love*) that late poem, "The Sparrow," dedicated to his father, "a poetic truth/more than a natural one," and thus a delightful contribution to the *comédie humaine.* As you follow the great variety of *aperçus* that use as their point of departure this busy mutt-bird, his ways of congregation, his amours and family life, you heartly agree it's "a pity/there are not more oats eaten now-a-days." Here is no less than Aesop singing.

In the course of doing this piece, I found among my notes a letter dated May 10, 1940. Presumably I had sent Williams some pages which he had read with his usual mixture of friendliness and resistance. He writes (enclosing a poem):

If I hadn't been reading your essay and thinking my own thoughts against it—I shouldn't have stepped on the word "prebirth" and so the poem (completely independent of the whole matter otherwise) might not have been written.

THEREFORE the poem belongs to you. I like it as well as anything I have written—

Then, after some other matters, he returns to the subject abruptly: "All I wanted to do was to send you the poem."

At the time I assumed that he meant the gift figuratively. But after inquiring of John Thirlwall, who has spent so much effort tracking down Williams' scattered work, I think it possible that friendly Wm. C. Wms., strong man two-gun Bill, may have meant the gift literally, and I may possess the only copy of the poem. In any case, I append it here, since it is a lovely thing to end on. It has a kind of reversal which crops up somewhat mystically, every now and then, among his poems, and which is probably implicit in many other passages. In the light of such forms, when he writes "It is merely pure luck that gets the mind turned inside out in a work of art," we may take it that he had such reversals in mind:

CHERRY BLOSSOMS AT EVENING

In the prebirth of the evening
the blue cherry blossoms
on the blue tree
from this yellow, ended room—
press to the windows
inside shall be out
the clustered faces of the flowers
straining to look in

(Signed) William Carlos Williams.

Allen Tate

(b. 1899)

Allen Tate—college teacher, poet, and essayist—has proved to be one of the most respected personalities within the New Criticism. From his earliest writings, he has held a wide audience among those subscribing to the tenets of this group, and because of his persuasiveness of argument, he has won many advocates to his beliefs.

However, Tate, like Ransom and others associated with the New Criticism, should be viewed somewhat as a man apart. The reason is that Tate emphasizes certain viewpoints ignored by other leading members. Especially notable is his concern for the plight of man. He does not see criticism as a narrow function, separate from the mainstream of day-to-day living. Rather, he sees it as an entity that must serve to raise man aesthetically, morally, and spiritually. In fact, these concerns—especially that of the spiritual element—form the foundation of Tate's critical precepts.

Tate's insistence on a religious element in criticism relates him to T. S. Eliot. Each maintains that poetry and literature in general must recognize a Christian tradition.

Because of his concern for a religious character in art, Tate advocates a correlation between literature and the upright life. Hence he gives, at best, only small quarter to any doctrine that grants an open or tacit approval of the licentious or the immoral. Always, he insists on a high-minded purpose, controlled by lofty procedures and guided by a finely developed intellect.

Throughout his years of critical writing, Tate has seldom favored any middle positions. He takes firm stands, and he de-

fends them in a forthright manner. Yet he is not the dogmatist so much as he is the careful, deliberate thinker who feels no need to apologize for his convictions. Hence a reading of Tate's essays becomes an encounter with a strongly moving argument.

Allen Tate was born in Clarke County, Kentucky, on November 19, 1899. After receiving his Bachelor of Arts degree from Vanderbilt in 1922, he turned immediately to writing, eventually earning wide acclaim as a poet, critic, and lecturer. Over the years, he has also taught at several colleges and universities, among them being Vanderbilt, New York University, the University of Chicago, and the University of Minnesota. Although now at an age when most men are disposed to rest, Tate maintains a busy schedule as a lecturer.

In the essay below, Tate undertakes to present both an explanation and a defense of his appraisal of modern poetry. This selection is typical of his principal views and his critical approaches.

Understanding Modern Poetry

About every six months I see in the *New York Times Book Review* the confident analogy between the audience of the modern poet and the audience that the English Romantics had to win in the early nineteenth century. Only wait a little while, and T. S. Eliot will be as easy for high-school teachers as "The Solitary Reaper." There may be some truth in this; but I think there is very little truth in it, and my reasons for thinking so will be the substance of this essay. There is a great deal of confusion about this matter, and not a little of it comes from the comfortable habit of citing a passage in the "Preface" to *Lyrical Ballads*, in which Wordsworth says that, as soon as the objects of modern life (meaning the physical changes wrought in society life by the Industrial Revolution) become as familiar to the people as the old mythologies of poetry, the difficulties of apprehension and communication will disappear. But this has not happened. It is true that no modern poet has succeeded in knowing all the physical features of modern industrial society; but neither has "society" succeeded in knowing them. It may be doubted that any poet in the past ever made a special point of studying the "techniques of production" of his time or of looking self-consciously at the objects around him as mere objects. Wordsworth himself did not.

Dante knew the science of the thirteenth century, and he was intensely aware of the physical features of his time— the ways of living, the clothing, the architecture, the implements of war, the natural landscape. But it was not a question of his becoming "familiar" with objects though it cannot be denied that a relatively unchanging physical background, since it can be taken for granted, is an advantage to any poet. It is rather that *all* that he knew came under a philosophy which was at once dramatic myth, a body of truths, and a comprehensive view of life.

Now Wordsworth's point of view is still the point of view of the unreflecting reader, and it is a point of view appropriate and applicable to the poets of the Romantic movement who are still, to the general reader, all that poets ought to be or can be. But the modern poetry that our general reader finds baffling and obscure is a radical departure from the Romantic achievement; it contains features that his "education" has not prepared him for; neither in perception nor in intellect is he ready for a kind of poetry that does not offer him the familiar poetical objects alongside the familiar poetical truths.

Let us say, very briefly and only for the uses of this discussion, that the Romantic movement taught the reader to look for inherently poetical objects, and to respond to them "emotionally" in certain prescribed ways, these ways being indicated by the "truths" interjected at intervals among the poetical objects.

Certain modern poets offer no inherently poetical objects, and they fail to instruct the reader in the ways he must feel about the objects. All experience, then, becomes potentially the material of poetry—not merely the pretty and the agreeable—and the modern poet makes it possible for us to "respond" to this material in all the ways in which men everywhere may feel and think. On the ground of common sense—a criterion that the reader invokes against the eccentric moderns—the modern poet has a little the better of the argument, for to him poetry is not a special package tied up in pink ribbon: it is one of the ways that we have of knowing the world. And since the world is neither wholly pretty nor wholly easy to understand, poetry becomes a very difficult affair, demanding both in its writing and in its reading all the intellectual power that we have. But it is very hard for people to apply their minds to poetry, since it is one of our assumptions that come down from the early nineteenth century that our intellects are for mathematics and science, our emotions for poetry.

Who are these modern poets? Some twenty years ago they were supposed to be Mr. Lindsay, Mr. Masters, and Mr. Carl Sandburg. When Mr. Sandburg's poetry first appeared, it was said to be both ugly and obscure; now it is easy and beautiful to high-school students, and even to their teachers, whose more advanced age must have given them a prejudice in favor of the metrical, the pretty, and the "poetical" object. Doubtless the "obscure" moderns are the poets whom Mr. Max Eastman has ridiculed in *The Literary Mind,* and whom Mr. Cleanth Brooks, in *Modern Poetry and the Tradition,* distinguishes as the leaders of a poetic revolution as far-reaching as the Romantic revolution brought in by *Lyrical Ballads* in 1798.

The volumes by Mr. Eastman and Mr. Brooks are of uneven value, but I recommend them to be read together; and I would suggest that it is exceedingly dangerous and misleading to read Mr. Eastman alone. Yet, although Mr. Eastman is aggressive, sensational, and personal in his attacks, he has been widely read; while Mr. Brooks, who is sober, restrained, and critical, will win one reader for Mr. Eastman's fifty. Mr. Eastman is a debater, not a critic; and he is plausible because, like the toothpaste manu-facturer, he offers his product in the name of science. Reading his book some years ago, I expected on every page to see the picture of the white-coated doctor with the test tube and the goatee, and under it the caption: "Science says . . ." But why science? Simply because Mr. Eastman, being still in the Romantic movement, but not knowing that he is, insists that the poet get hold of some "truths" that will permit him to tell the reader what to think about the new poetical objects of our time: he must think scientifically or not at all. Eastman's *The Literary Mind* is an interesting document of our age; Brooks's *Modern Poetry and the Tradition* will probably survive as an epoch-making critical synthesis of the modern movement.

The poets of the new revolution range all the way from the greatest distinction to charlatanism—a feature of every revolution, literary or political. Mr. Eastman can make the best moderns sound like the worst—as no doubt he could make the great passages of "The Prelude" sound like "Peter Bell" if he set his hand to it; and he found, as he confesses with candor and chagrin, that certain passages in the later works of Shakespeare strongly resemble some of the poetry of the modern "Cult of Unintelligibility"; but this hot potato, because he doesn't know what to do with it, he quickly drops. It is not my purpose to make Mr. Eastman the whipping-boy of a school of critics; of his school, he is one of the best. What I wish to emphasize is the negative of his somewhat sly contention that an admirer of Eliot's *Ash Wednesday* must also be an admirer of Miss Stein's *Geography and Plays,* that there is only a great lump of modernist verse in which no distinctions are possible. By such tactics we could discredit Browning with quotations from Mrs. Hemans. I notice this palpable nonsense because Mr. Eastman has been widely read by professors of English, who are really rather glad to hear this sort of thing, since it spares them the trouble of reading a body of poetry for which there are no historical documents and of which generations of other professors have not told them what to think.

In this essay I cannot elucidate a great many modern poems— a task that at the present time would be only a slight service to the reader; for in the state of his education and mine, we should have to undertake the infinite series of elucidations. We have no critical method; we have no principles to guide us. Every poem being either a unique expression of personality or a response to an environment, we should know at the end of the tenth difficult poem only what we knew at the end of the first; we could only cite the personalities and the environments. What I wish to do here, then, is not to explain certain modern poems but rather to discuss the reasons, as I see them, why certain kinds of poetry are difficult today.

The most pervasive reason of all is the decline of the art of reading—in an age in which there is more print than the world has been seen before. If you ask why this is so, the answer is that impressionistic education in all its varieties, chiefly the variety known as "progressive education," is rapidly making us a nation of illiterates: a nation of people without letters. For you do not have to attend to the letters and words on the page in order to "read" what is there. In an essay entitled "The Retreat of the Humanities" (*English Journal,* February, 1939, p. 127), Mr. Louis B. Wright quotes an interesting passage from another essay, "Supervising the Creative Teaching of Poetry," whose author Mr. Wright mercifully leaves anonymous:

The teaching of poetry divides itself naturally into two areas of enterprise, each with its essential conditioning validities. . . . Comprehending a poem need not involve any intellectual or formal concern with its technique, prose content, type, moral, diction, analysis, social implications, etc. Comprehending a poem is essentially an organic experience, essentially a response to the poetic stimulus of the author. Poetic comprehension may be verbalized or it may not.

In short, poetic comprehension does not involve anything at all, least of all the poem to be comprehended. Mr. Wright remarks that this is "equivalent to the emotion that comes from being tickled on the ear with a feather. . . . Before such ideas and such jargon, sincere advocates of learning sometimes retreat in despair." Yes; but for the sake of the good people whose "education" has doomed them to teach poetry with this monstrous jargon, I wish to examine the quotation more closely, and more in contempt than in despair. We have here, then, an offensive muddle of echoes ranging from business jargon through sociological jargon to the jargon of the Watsonian behaviorists. One must be more pleased than disappointed to find that poetry "naturally divides" itself, without any intellectual effort on our part, into "areas" having "conditioning validities" that are "essential"—an adjective that our Anonymity repeats twice adverbially in a wholly different non-sense. Now, if technique, diction, analysis, and the others are irrelevant in the reading of poetry, in what respect does poetry differ from automobiles: cannot one be conditioned to automobiles? No, that is not the answer. One is conditioned by responding to the "poetic stimulus of the author." One gets the poet's personality; and there's no use thinking about the poet's personality, since one cannot think, "verbalization" now being the substitute for thought—as indeed it is, in our Anonymity.

I am sure that thoughtful persons will have perceived, beyond this vulgar haze, an "idea" curiously resembling something that I have already alluded to in this essay: it is astonishing how regularly the pseudo-scientific vocabularies are used in order to reach a poetic theory that the most ignorant "man in the street" already holds. That theory I call "decadent Romanticism," but I should like it to be plainly understood that I am not attacking the great Romantic poets. Romanticism gave us the "Ode to a Nightingale"; decadent Romanticism is now giving us the interminable ballads and local-color lyrics of Mr. Coffin and Mr. Stephen Benét—as it gave us, some twenty-five years ago, Joyce Kilmer's "Trees," the "favorite poem" of the American people, taught piously by every high-school teacher, and sometimes aggressively by college professors when they want to show what poetry ought to be; surely one of the preposterously bad lyrics in any language.

What I said earlier that I should like to call attention to again is: The weakness of the Romantic sensibility is that it gave us a poetry of "poetical" (or *poetized*) objects, predigested perceptions; and in case there should be any misunderstanding about the poetical nature of these objects, we also got "truths" attached to them—truths that in modern jargon are instructions to the reader to "respond" in a certain way to the poetical object, which is the "stimulus." And in the great body of nineteenth-century lyrical poetry—whose worst ancestor was verse like Shelley's "I arise from dreams of thee"—the poet's personal emotions became the "poetic stimulus." The poem as a formal object to be looked at, to be studied, to be construed (in more than the grammatical sense, but first of all in that sense), dissolved into biography and history, so that in the long run the poetry was only a misunderstood pretext for the "study" of the sexual life of the poet, of the history of his age, of anything else that the scholar wished to "study"; and he usually wished to study anything but poetry.

Now our Anonymity has said that prose content, morals, and social implications are irrelevant in reading poetry, and it looks as if there were a fundamental disagreement between him and the biographical and historical scholars. There is no such disagreement. Once you arrive with Anonymity at the "poetic stimulus of the author," you have reached his biography and left his poetry behind; and, on principle, Anonymity cannot rule out the morals and the social implications (however much he may wish to rule them out), because morals and social implications are what you get when you discuss personality.

At this point I ought to enter a *caveat* to those persons who are thinking that I would dispense with historical scholarship. It is, in fact, indispensable; it is pernicious only when some ham actor in an English department uses it to wring tears from the Sophomores, by describing the sad death of Percy Shelley. Let me illustrate one of its genuine uses. Here are the first two stanzas of Donne's "Valediction: forbidding mourning":

> As virtuous men passe mildly away,
>   And whisper to their soules, to goe,
> Whilst some of their sad friends doe say,
>   The breath goes now, and some say, no:

Soe let us melt, and make no noise,
  No teare-floods, nor sigh-tempests move,
  T'were prophanation of our joyes
  To tell the layetie our love.

The elaborate simile here asserts on several planes the analogy between the act of love and the moment of death. But if you happen to know that in Middle English and down through the sixteenth century the verb *die* has as a secondary meaning, "to perform the act of love," you are able to extend the analogy into a new frame of reference. The analogy contains a concealed pun. But we are detecting the pun not in order to show that a man in the late sixteenth century was still aware of the early, secondary meaning of *die;* we are simply using this piece of information to extend our knowledge of what happens in the first eight lines of the poem. It is of no interest to anybody that Donne knew how to make this pun; it is of capital interest to know what the pun does to the meaning of the poem.

I have seemed to be talking about what I consider bad poetic theory; but I have also been talking about something much larger, that cannot here be adequately discussed: I have been talking about a bad theory of education. If only briefly, I must notice it because it abets the bad poetic theory and is at the bottom of the popular complaint that modern poetry is difficult. The complainant assumes that he understands all English poetry up to, say, about 1917—a date that I select because in that year Eliot's *Prufrock and Other Observations* was published. But, as a matter of fact, the complainant does not understand Marvel and Donne any better than he understands Eliot; and I doubt that he can read Sidney any better than he can read Pound; he could not read Raleigh at all, and he has never heard of Fulke Greville.

So it is not "modern" poetry which is difficult; it is rather a certain kind of poetry as old, in English, as the sixteenth century, and, in Italian, much older than that. It is a kind of poetry that requires of the reader the fullest co-operation of all his intellectual resources, all his knowledge of the world, and all the per-sistence and alertness that he now thinks only of giving to scientific studies.

This kind of poetry must have the direct and *active* participation of a reader who today, because he has been pampered by bad education, expects to lie down and be *passive* when he is reading poetry. He admits, for some obscure reason, that poetry is a part of his education; but he has been taught to believe that education is *conditioning*: something is being done to him, he is not doing anything himself. And that is why he cannot read poetry.

A conditioning theory of education may be good enough for animals in the zoo, but it is not good enough for human beings; and it is time that this symptom of decadence were known for what it is, and not as enlightenment, "science," liberalism, and democracy. I do not know whether we are living in a democracy; it is, at any rate, an anomaly of democratic theory that it should produce, in education, a theory that we are bundles of reflexes without intelligence.

The theory assumes, first of all, that education is a process of getting adjusted to an environment. Something known as "personality" is making *responses* to things known as *stimuli*. In the educational environment there are *stimuli* called "poems," to which you make responses.

Now while you are making a response, you are not doing more than a chimpanzee or a Yahoo would be doing. But should you do more than respond, you might perform an act of intelligence, of knowing, of cognition. In the conditioning theory there is no cognition because there is no intelligence. Of what use is intelligence? It does not at all help to describe the "behavior" of persons who are getting responses from the *stimuli* of poems. What the poem is in itself, what it says, is no matter. It is an irrelevant question. But if you can imagine it not to be irrelevant, if you can imagine "Lycidas" to be something more than the stimulation of "drives," "appetites," "attitudes," in certain "areas," then you have got to use your intelligence, which, after you have been progressively educated, you probably no longer have.

As I conceive this gloomy situation, it is far more complicated than the violent synopsis of it that I have just sketched. The complications would distribute the blame to many historical villains, of whom the teachers'-college racketeers (some of them misguided idealists) are only a conspicuous contemporary group. The trouble goes far back, farther even than the Romantic movement, when, for the first time in Western art, we had the belief that poetry is chiefly or even wholly an emotional experience.

Does poetry give us an emotional experience? What is an "emotional experience"? And what is an "intellecual experience"?

These are difficult questions. We are proceeding today as if they were no longer questions, as if we knew the answers, and knew them as incontestable truth. If by "an emotional experience" we mean one in which we find ourselves "moved," then we mean nothing; we are only translating a Latin word into English: a tautology. If by "an intellectual experience" we mean that we are using our minds on the relations of words, the relation of words and rhythm, the relation of the abstract words to the images, all the relations together—and if, moreover, we succeed in reducing all these things to the complete determination of logic, so that there is nothing left over, then this intellectual experience is a tautology similar to that of the emotional experience: we are intellectually using our intellects, as before we were emotionally being moved. But if on the other hand, as in the great seventeenth-century poets, you find that exhaustive analysis applied to the texture of image and metaphor fails to turn up any inconsistency, and at the same time fails to get all the meaning of the poem into a logical statement, you are participating in a poetic experience. And both intellect and emotion become meaningless in discussing it.

I have had to make that statement abstract, or not at all; it needs many pages of illustration. I can cite only three examples of poetry, which I hope will somewhat illuminate it. The first example is William Browne's slight "Epitaph on the Countesse Dowager of Pembroke," a favorite anthology piece, and one that is neither in the metaphysical style of its period nor romantically modern:

> Underneath this sable Herse
> Lyes the subject of all verse:
> Sydney's sister, Pembroke's Mother:
> Death, ere thou hast slaine another
> Faire and learned and good as she,
> Time shall throw a dart at thee.

I find this poem perennially moving (exciting, interesting), and it is plain that we cannot be moved by it until we understand it; and to understand it we have got to *analyze* the meaning of the difference here asserted as existing between Time and Death, who are dramatically personified and in conflict. Since, in one of the major modes of poetry, Death is conceived as the work of Time, we must perform a dissociation of ideas, and see Time as turning against himself, so that the destruction of Death is actually the destruction of Time. However far you may take these distinctions, no inconsistency appears; nothing contradicts anything else that is said in the poem; yet we have not reduced the poem to strict logic. Browne has offered certain particulars that are irreducible: the Sydney and Pembroke families (for the sake of whose dignity this upheaval of the order of nature will occur); and then there is the dart, a dramatic and particular image that does not contradict, yet cannot be assimilated into, a logical paraphrase of the poem. Is this poem an emotional experience? And yet it is not an "intellectual" experience.

The second quotation must be slighted, but it is so familiar that a few lines will bring the whole poem before the reader—Shelley's "When the lamp is shattered"; I quote the last stanza:

> Its [Love's] passions will rock thee,
> As the storms rock the ravens on high:
> Bright reason will mock thee,
> Like the sun from a wintry sky.
> From thy nest every rafter.

> Will rot, and thine eagle home
> Leave thee naked to laughter,
> When leaves fall and cold winds come.

The general "argument" is that the passing of spiritual communion from lovers leaves them sad and, in this last stanza,
the prey of lust and self-mockery, and even of the mockery
of the world ("naked to laughter"). The first line sets the tone
and the "response" that the reader is to maintain to the end:
we are told in advance what the following lines will mean:
an abstraction that will relieve us of the trouble of examining
the particular instances. Indeed, when these appear, the development of their imagery is confused and vague. The ravens
in the second line are eagles in the sixth; but, after all, they are
only generically birds; greater particularity in them would have
compromised their poeticism as objects, or interfered with the
response we are instructed to make to them. I pass over "Bright
reason," the self-mockery, for the mockery of the world. Are
we to suppose that other birds come by and mock the raven
(eagle), or are we to shift the field of imagery and see "thee" as
a woman? Now in the finest poetry we cannot have it both ways.
We can have a multiple meaning through ambiguity, but we cannot have an incoherent structure of images. Shelley, in confusion,
or carelessness, or haste, could not sustain the nest-bird metaphor
and say all that he wished to say; so, in order to say it, he changed
the figure and ruined the poem. The more we track down the
implications of his imagery, the greater the confusion; the more
we track down the implications of the imagery in the best verse
of Donne, Marvel, Raleigh, Milton, Hopkins, Yeats, Eliot, Ransom, Stevens, the richer the meaning of the poem. Shelley's poem
is confused. Are we to conclude that therefore it offers an emotional experience?

In conclusion, one more poem—this one by W. H. Auden:

> Our hunting fathers told the story
> Of the sadness of the creatures,
> Pitied the limits and the lack

Set in their finished features;
Saw in the lion's intolerant look,
   Behind the quarry's dying glare
Love raging for the personal glory
   That reason's gift would add,
The liberal appetite and power,
   The rightness of a god.

Who nurtured in that fine tradition
   Predicted the result,
Guessed love by nature suited to
   The intricate ways of guilt;
That human company could so
   His southern gestures modify
And make it his mature ambition
   To think no thought but ours,
To hunger, work illegally,
   And be anonymous?

In this poem there is an immense complication of metaphor, but I do not propose to unravel it. I would say just this: that all the complications can be returned without confusion or contradiction to a definite, literal, and coherent field of imagery; that when the poet wishes to extend his meaning, he does it by means of this field of metaphor, not by changing the figure, which is: the hunter debases his human nature (Love) in his arrogant, predatory conquest of the world, and Love itself becomes not merely morally bad but evil. The field of imagery, to which all the implications refer, is that of the hunting squire, who by a deft ambiguity quickly becomes predatory man.

I halt the analysis here because, as I have already said, we need something more fundamental in reading poetry than the occasional analyses of poems. I would say then, in conclusion, that modern poetry is difficult because we have lost the art of reading any poetry that will not read itself to us; that thus our trouble is a fundamental problem of education, which may be more fundamental than education. We may be approaching the time when we shall no longer be able to read anything and shall be subject to passive conditioning. Until this shall happen, however, we might possibly begin to look upon language as a field of study, not as an impressionistic debauch. If we wish to understand anything, there is only the hard way; if we wish to understand Donne and Eliot, perhaps we had better begin, young, to read the classical languages, and a little later the philosophers. There is probably no other way.

Edmund Wilson

(b. 1895)

Among the critics writing from the 1920's onward, few have enjoyed the unqualified respect given Edmund Wilson, whose prestige seems to rise with each passing day. Wilson's success has resulted principally from his finely honed critical sense, fortified by a wide reading and a deep sensitivity. It further stems from a remarkable ability to defend his opinions in a clear, readable style.

In achieving his high position, Wilson has accomplished the difficult feat of pleasing both the specialist and the general reader. He is commonly regarded as a great critic in literary circles and academia, meanwhile receiving the unreserved approval of the reader of the popular journal.

Wilson's main concern has always been the relevance of literature to the world from which it emanates. He has aligned himself undeviatingly with those who consider literary production as an integral part of life rather than a mere expression of life. He believes, therefore, that criticism must study life and the forces that shape life as a prelude to all else.

In writing criticism, Wilson exhibits a pleasant balance between the objective and the subjective. He displays the master's knowledge of principles of criticism; he invokes an extensive background of knowledge; and he approaches his work with a scientific restraint. Yet he also introduces an element of the personal reaction that is clearly appealing. He seems, in short, to reflect simultaneously the best attributes of the scientific school of criticism and the devotees of personal evaluation.

Wilson is often linked with the Marxist critics of the 1930's *because of his endorsement of the philosophy of Lenin. One should note, however, that Wilson had reservations about this philosophy and that he became clearly disillusioned with the Stalinism that replaced Leninism in Soviet Russia. One should further note that Wilson's political convictions have had only a small influence on his idea of the artist as a free personality moving without restraint in a free society.*

Edmund Wilson, born in Red Bank, New Jersey, on May 8, 1895, received his formal education at the Hill School, Pottstown, Pennsylvania, and Princeton University, from which he earned the A.B. degree in 1916. Not satisfied with his "banker's education," he began a lifetime effort in a carefully devised program of self-study. As a result, he is almost incredibly knowledgeable in the fields of comparative literature, literary history, and art—as well as being one of the most widely read of all critics in other disciplines.

At Princeton, Wilson formed several longtime friendships, the most notable of which was with novelist F. Scott Fitzgerald, with whom he constantly exchanged opinions and ideas on literature. Throughout his working life, Wilson has served as newspaperman, editor, and free-lance writer—in addition to producing novels, poems, and essays on many topics. His most important achievements, however, have been his critical essays. At present, Wilson resides in Wellfleet, Massachusetts, where he restricts his writing to critical essays.

Below is one of Wilson's most enlightening essays. It is an address delivered at Princeton University on October 23, 1940, as part of the topic "The Intent of the Critic," which was the theme of the particular occasion.

The Historical Interpretation of Literature

I want to talk about the historical interpretation of literature— that is, about the interpretation of literature in its social, economic and political aspects.

To begin with, it will be worth while to say something about the kind of criticism which seems to be furthest removed from this. There is a kind of comparative criticism which tends to be non-historical. The essays of T. S. Eliot, which have had such an immense influence in our time, are, for example, fundamentally non-historical. Eliot sees, or tries to see, the whole of literature, so far as he is acquainted with it, spread out before him under the aspect of eternity. He then compares the work of different periods and countries, and tries to draw from it general conclusions about what literature ought to be. He understands, of course, that our point of view in connection with literature changes, and he has what seems to me a very sound conception of the whole body of writing of the past as something to which new works are continually being added, and which is not thereby merely increased in bulk but modified as a whole—so that Sophocles is no longer precisely what he was for Aristotle, or Shakespeare what he was for Ben Jonson or for Dryden or for Dr. Johnson, on account of all the later literature that has intervened between them and us. Yet at every point of this continual accretion, the whole field may be surveyed, as it were, spread out before the critic. The critic tries to see it as God might; he calls the books to a Day of Judgment. And, looking at things in this way, he may arrive at interesting and valuable conclusions which could hardly be reached by approaching them in any other way. Eliot was able to see, for example—what I believe had never been noticed before—that the French Symbolist poetry of the nineteenth century had certain fundamental resemblances to the English poetry of the age of Donne. Another kind of critic would draw certain historical conclusions from these purely esthetic findings, as the Russian D. S. Mirsky did; but Eliot does not draw them.

Another example of this kind of non-historical criticism, in a somewhat different way and on a somewhat different plane, is the work of the late George Saintsbury. Saintsbury was a connoisseur of wines; he wrote an entertaining book on the subject. And his attitude toward literature, too, was that of the connoisseur. He tastes the authors and tells you about the vintages; he distinguishes the qualities of the various wines. His palate was as fine as could be, and he possessed the great qualification that he knew how to take each book on its own terms without expecting it to be some other book and was thus in a position to appreciate a great variety of kinds of writing. He was a man of strong social prejudices and peculiarly intransigent political views, but, so far as it is humanly possible, he kept them out of his literary criticism. The result is one of the most agreeable and most comprehensive commentaries on literature that have ever been written in English. Most scholars who have read as much as Saintsbury do not have Saintsbury's discriminating taste. Here is a critic who has covered the whole ground like any academic historian, yet whose account of it is not merely a chronology but a record of fastidious enjoyment. Since enjoyment is the only thing he is looking for, he does not need to know the causes of things, and the historical background of literature does not interest him very much.

There is, however, another tradition of criticism which dates from the beginning of the eighteenth century. In the year 1725, the Neapolitan philosopher Vico published *La Scienza Nuova,* a revolutionary work on the philosophy of history, in which he asserted for the first time that the social world was certainly the work of man, and attempted what is, so far as I know, the first social interpretation of the work of literature. This is what Vico says about Homer: 'Homer composed the *Iliad* when Greece was young and consequently burning with sublime passions such as pride, anger and vengeance—passions which cannot allow dissimulation and which consort with generosity; so that she then admired Achilles, the hero of force. But, grown old, he composed the *Odyssey,* at a time when the passions of Greece were already somewhat cooled by reflection, which is the mother of prudence— so that she now admired Ulysses, the hero of wisdom. Thus also, in Homer's youth, the Greek people liked cruelty, vituperation, savagery, fierceness, ferocity; whereas, when Homer was old, they were already enjoying the luxuries of Alcinoüs, the delights of

Calypso, the pleasures of Circe, the songs of the sirens and the pastimes of the suitors, who went no further in aggression and combat than laying siege to the chaste Penelope—all of which practices would appear incompatible with the spirit of the earlier time. The divine Plato is so struck by this difficulty that, in order to solve it, he tells us that Homer had foreseen in inspired vision these dissolute, sickly and disgusting customs. But in this way he makes Homer out to have been but a foolish instructor for Greek civilization, since, however much he may condemn them, he is displaying for imitation these corrupt and decadent habits which were not to be adopted till long after the foundation of the nations of Greece, and accelerating the natural course which human events would take by spurring the Greeks on to corruption. Thus it is plain that the Homer of the *Iliad* must have preceded by many years the Homer who wrote the *Odyssey;* and it is plain that the former must belong to the northeastern part of Greece, since he celebrates the Trojan War, which took place in his part of the country, whereas the latter belongs to the southeastern part, since he celebrates Ulysses, who reigned there.'

You see that Vico has here explained Homer in terms both of historical period and of geographical origin. The idea that human arts and institutions were to be studied and elucidated as the products of the geographical and climatic conditions in which the people who created them lived, and of the phase of their social development through which they were passing at the moment, made great progress during the eighteenth century. There are traces of it even in Dr. Johnson, that most orthodox and classical of critics—as, for example, when he accounts for certain characteristics of Shakespeare by the relative barbarity of the age in which he lived, pointing out, just as Vico had done, that 'nations, like individuals, have their infancy.' And by the eighties of the eighteenth century Herder, in his *Ideas on the Philosophy of History,* was writing of poetry that it was a kind of 'Proteus among the people, which is always changing its form in response to the languages, manners, and habits, to the temperaments and climates, nay even to the accents of different nations.' He said—

what could still seem startling even so late as that—that 'language was not a divine communication, but something men had produced themselves.' In the lectures on the philosophy of history that Hegel delivered in Berlin in 1822–23, he discussed the national literatures as expressions of the societies which had produced them—societies which he conceived as great organisms continually transforming themselves under the influence of a succession of dominant ideas.

In the field of literary criticism, this historical point of view came to its first complete flower in the work of the French critic Taine, in the middle of the nineteenth century. The whole school of historian-critics to which Taine belonged—Michelet, Renan, Sainte-Beuve—had been occupied in interpreting books in terms of their historical origins. But Taine was the first of these to attempt to apply such principles systematically and on a large scale in a work devoted exclusively to literature. In the Introduction to his *History of English Literature,* published in 1863, he made his famous pronouncement that works of literature were to be understood as the upshot of three interfusing factors: *the moment, the race and the milieu.* Taine thought he was a scientist and a mechanist, who was examining works of literature from the same point of view as the chemist's in experimenting with chemical compounds. But the difference between the critic and the chemist is that the critic cannot first combine his elements and then watch to see what they will do: he can only examine phenomena which have already taken place. The procedure that Taine actually follows is to pretend to set the stage for the experiment by describing the moment, the race and the milieu, and then to say: 'Such a situation demands such and such a kind of writer.' He now goes on to describe the kind of writer that the situation demands, and the reader finds himself at the end confronted with Shakespeare or Milton or Byron or whoever the great figure is—who turns out to prove the accuracy of Taine's prognosis by precisely living up to this description.

There was thus a certain element of imposture in Taine; but it was the rabbits he pulled out that saved him. If he had really

been the mechanist that he thought he was, his work on literature would have had little value. The truth was that Taine loved
literature for its own sake—he was at his best himself a brilliant
artist—and he had very strong moral convictions which give his
writing emotional power. His mind, to be sure, was an analytic
one, and his analysis, though terribly oversimplified, does have an
explanatory value. Yet his work was what we call creative. Whatever he may say about chemical experiments, it is evident when
he writes of a great writer that the moment, the race and the
milieu have combined, like the three sounds of the chord in
Browning's poem about Abt Vogler, to produce not a fourth
sound but a star.

To Taine's set of elements was added, dating from the middle
of the century, a new element, the economic, which was introduced into the discussion of historical phenomena mainly by
Marx and Engels. The non-Marxist critics themselves were at the
time already taking into account the influence of the social classes.
In his chapters on the Norman conquest of England, Taine shows
that the difference between the literatures produced respectively
by the Normans and by the Saxons was partly the difference between a ruling class, on the one hand, and a vanquished and
repressed class, on the other. And Michelet, in his volume on
the Regency, which was finished the same year that the *History
of English Literature* appeared, studies the *Manon Lescaut* of
the Abbé Prévost as a document representing the point of view
of the small gentry before the French Revolution. But Marx and
Engels derived the social classes from the way that people made
or got their livings—from what they called the *methods of production;* and they tended to regard these economic processes as
fundamental to civilization.

The Dialectical Materialism of Marx and Engels was not really
so materialistic as it sounds. There was in it a large element of
the Hegelian idealism that Marx and Engels thought they had
got rid of. At no time did these two famous materialists take so
mechanistic a view of things as Taine began by professing; and

their theory of the relation of works of literature to what they called the *economic base* was a good deal less simple than Taine's theory of the moment, the race and the milieu. They thought that art, politics, religion, philosophy and literature belonged to what they called the *superstructure* of human activity; but they saw that the practioners of these various professions tended also to constitute social groups, and that they were always pulling away from the kind of solidarity based on economic classes in order to establish a professional solidarity of their own. Furthermore, the activities of the superstructure could influence one another, and they could influence the economic base. It may be said of Marx and Engels in general that, contrary to the popular impression, they were tentative, confused and modest when it came down to philosophical first principles, where a materialist like Taine was cocksure. Marx once made an attempt to explain why the poems of Homer were so good when the society that produced them was from his point of view—that is, from the point of view of its industrial development—so primitive; and this gave him a good deal of trouble. If we compare his discussion of this problem with Vico's discussion of Homer, we see that the explanation of literature in terms of a philosophy of social history is becoming, instead of simpler and easier, more difficult and more complex.

Marx and Engels were deeply imbued, moreover, with the German admiration for literature, which they had learned from the age of Goethe. It would never have occurred to either of them that *der Dichter* was not one of the noblest and most beneficent of humankind. When Engels writes about Goethe, he presents him as a man equipped for 'practical life,' whose career was frustrated by the 'misery' of the historical situation in Germany in his time, and reproaches him for allowing himself to lapse into the 'cautious, smug and narrow' philistinism of the class from which he came; but Engels regrets this, because it interfered with the development of the 'mocking, defiant, world-despising genius,' 'der geniale Dichter,' 'der gewaltige Poet,' of whom Engels would not even, he says, have asked that he should have been a political liberal if Goethe had not sacrificed to his bourgeois shrinkings his truer esthetic sense. And the great critics who were trained on Marx—Franz Mehring and Bernard Shaw—had all this reverence for the priesthood of literature. Shaw deplores the absence of political philosophy and what he regards as the middle-class snobbery in Shakespeare; but he celebrates Shakespeare's poetry and his dramatic imagination almost as enthusiastically as Swinburne does, describing even those potboiling comedies, *Twelfth Night* and *As You Like It*—the themes of which seem to him most trashy—as 'the Crown Jewels of English dramatic poetry.' Such a critic may do more for a writer by showing him as a real man dealing with a real world at a definite moment of time than the impressionist critic of Swinburne's type who flourished in the same period of the late nineteenth century. The purely impressionist critic approaches the whole of literature as an exhibit of belletristic jewels, and he can only write a rhapsodic catalogue. But when Shaw turned his spotlight on Shakespeare as a figure in the Shavian drama of history, he invested him with a new interest as no other English critic had done.

The insistence that the man of letters should play a political role, the disparagement of works of art in comparison with political action, were thus originally no part of Marxism. They only became associated with it later. This happened by way of Russia, and it was due to special tendencies in that country that date from long before the Revolution or the promulgation of Marxism itself. In Russia there have been very good reasons why the political implications of literature should particularly occupy the critics. The art of Pushkin itself, with its marvelous power of implication, had certainly been partly created by the censorship of Nicholas I, and Pushkin set the tradition for most of the great Russian writers that followed him. Every play, every poem, every story, must be a parable of which the moral is *implied*. If it were stated, the censor would suppress the book as he tried to do with Pushkin's *Bronze Horseman*, where it was merely a question of the packed implications protruding a little too plainly. Right down through the writings of Chekhov and up almost to the Revolution, the imaginative literature of Russia presents the peculiar paradox of an art that is technically objective and yet charged with social messages. In Russia under the Tsar, it was inevitable that social criticism should lead to political conclusions, because the most urgent need from the point of view of any kind of improvement was to get rid of the tsarist regime. Even the neo-Christian moralist Tolstoy, who pretended to be non-political, was to exert a subversive influence, because his independent preaching was bound to embroil him with the Church, and the Church was an integral part of the tsardom. Tolstoy's pamphlet called *What Is Art?*, in which he throws overboard Shakespeare and a large part of modern literature, including his own novels, in the interest of his intransigent morality, is the example which is most familiar to us of the moralizing Russian criticism; but it was only the most sensational expression of a kind of approach which had been prevalent since Belinsky and Chernyshevsky in the early part of the century. The critics, who were usually journalists writing in exile or in a contraband press, were always tending to demand of the imaginative writers that they should dramatize bolder morals.

Even after the Revolution had destroyed the tsarist government, this state of things did not change. The old habits of censorship persisted in the new socialist society of the Soviets, which was necessarily made up of people who had been stamped by the die of the despotism. We meet here the peculiar phenomenon of a series of literary groups that attempt, one after the other, to obtain official recognition or to make themselves sufficiently powerful to establish themselves as arbiters of literature. Lenin and Trotsky and Lunacharsky had the sense to oppose these attempts: the comrade-dictators of Proletcult or Lev or Rapp would certainly have been just as bad as the Count Benckendorff who made Pushkin miserable, and when the Stalin bureaucracy, after the death of Gorky, got control of this department as of everything else, they instituted a system of repression that made Benckendorff and Nicholas I look like Lorenzo de' Medici. In the meantime,

Trotsky, who was Commissar of War but himself a great political writer with an interest in belles-lettres, attempted, in 1924, apropos of one of these movements, to clarify the situation. He wrote a brilliant and valuable book called *Literature and Revolution,* in which he explained the aims of the government, analyzed the work of the Russian writers, and praised or rebuked the latter as they seemed to him in harmony or at odds with the former. Trotsky is intelligent, sympathetic; it is evident that he is really fond of literature and that he knows that a work of art does not fulfill its function in terms of the formulas of party propaganda. But Mayakovsky, the Soviet poet, whom Trotsky had praised with reservations, expressed himself in a famous joke when he was asked what he thought of Trotsky's book—a pun which implied that a Commissar turned critic was inevitably a Commissar still*; and what a foreigner cannot accept in Trotsky is his assumption that it is the duty of the government to take a hand in the direction of literature.

This point of view, indigenous to Russia, has been imported to other countries through the permeation of Communist influence. The Communist press and its literary followers have reflected the control of the Kremlin in all the phases through which it has passed, down to the wholesale imprisonment of Soviet writers which has been taking place since 1935. But it has never been a part of the American system that our Republican or Democratic administration should lay down a political line for the guidance of the national literature. A recent gesture in this direction on the part of Archibald MacLeish, who seems a little carried away by his position as Librarian of Congress, was anything but cordially received by serious American writers. So long as the United States remains happily a non-totalitarian country, we can very well do without this aspect of the historical criticism of literature.

Another element of a different order has, however, since Marx's time been added to the historical study of the origins of works

---

* . . . *The first pancake lies like a narkom* (people's commissar)—a parody of the Russian saying, . . . *The first pancake lies like a lump.*

of literature. I mean the psychoanalysis of Freud. This appears as an extension of something which had already got well started before, which had figured even in Johnson's *Lives of the Poets,* and of which the great exponent had been Sainte-Beuve: the interpretation of works of literature in the light of personalities behind them. But the Freudians made this interpretation more exact and more systematic. The great example of the psychoanalysis of an artist is Freud's own essay on Leonardo da Vinci; but this has little critical interest: it is an attempt to construct a case history. One of the best examples I know of the application of Freudian analysis to literature is in Van Wyck Brooks's book, *The Ordeal of Mark Twain,* in which Mr. Brooks uses an incident of Mark Twain's boyhood as a key to his whole career. Mr. Brooks has since repudiated the method he resorted to here, on the ground that no one but an analyst can ever know enough about a writer to make a valid psychoanalytic diagnosis. This is true, and it is true of the method that it has led to bad results where the critic has built a Freudian mechanism out of very slender evidence, and then given us what is really merely a romance exploiting the supposed working of this mechanism, in place of an actual study that sticks close to the facts and the documents of the writer's life and work. But I believe that Van Wyck Brooks really had hold of something important when he fixed upon that childhood incident of which Mark Twain gave so vivid an account to his biographer— that scene at the deathbed of his father when his mother had made him promise that he would not break her heart. If it was not one of those crucial happenings that are supposed to determine the complexes of Freud, it has certainly a typical significance in relation to Mark Twain's whole psychology. The stories that people tell about their childhood are likely to be profoundly symbolic even when they have been partly or wholly made up in the light of later experience. And the attitudes, the compulsions, the emotional 'patterns' that recur in the work of a writer are of great interest to the historical critic.

These attitudes and patterns are embedded in the community and the historical moment, and they may indicate its ideals and its diseases as the cell shows the condition of the tissue. The recent scientific experimentation in the combining of Freudian with Marxist method, and of psychoanalysis with anthropology, has had its parallel development in criticism. And there is thus another element added to our equipment for analyzing literary works, and the problem grows still more complex.

The analyst, however, is of course not concerned with the comparative values of his patients any more than the surgeon is. He cannot tell you why the neurotic Dostoevsky produces work of immense value to his fellows while another man with the same neurotic pattern would become a public menace. Freud himself emphatically states in his study of Leonardo that his method can make no attempt to account for Leonardo's genius. The problems of comparative aristic value still remain after we have given attention to the Freudian psychological factor just as they do after we have given attention to the Marxist economic factor and to the racial and geographical factors. No matter how thoroughly and searchingly we may have scrutinized works of literature from the historical and biographical points of view, we must be ready to attempt to estimate, in some such way as Saintsbury and Eliot do, the relative degrees of success attained by the products of the various periods and the various personalities. We must be able to tell good from bad, the first-rate from the second-rate. We shall not otherwise write literary criticism at all, but merely social or political history as reflected in literary texts, or psychological case histories from past eras, or, to take the historical point of view in its simplest and most academic form, merely chronologies of books that have been published.

And now how, in these matters of literary art, do we tell the good art from the bad? Norman Kemp Smith, the Kantian philosopher, whose courses I was fortunate enough to take at Princeton twenty-five years ago, used to tell us that this recognition was based primarily on an emotional reaction. For purposes of practical criticism this is a safe assumption on which to proceed. It is possible to discriminate in a variety of ways the elements that in any given department go to make a successful work of literature. Different schools have at different times demanded different things of literature: *unity, symmetry, universality, originality, vision, inspiration, strangeness, suggestiveness, improving morality, socialist realism,* etc. But you could have any set of these qualities that any school of writing has called for and still not have a good play, a good novel, a good poem, a good history. If you identify the essence of good literature with any one of these elements or with any combination of them, you simply shift the emotional reaction to the recognition of the element or elements. Or if you add to your other demands the demand that the writer must have *talent*, you simply shift this recognition to the talent. Once people find some grounds of agreement in the coincidence of their emotional reactions to books, they may be able to discuss these elements profitably; but if they do not have this basic agreement, the discussion will make no sense.

But how, you may ask, can we identify this élite who know what they are talking about? Well, it can only be said of them that they are self-appointed and self-perpetuating, and that they will compel you to accept their authority. Impostors may try to put themselves over, but these quacks will not last. The implied position of the people who know about literature (as is also the case in every other art) is simply that they know what they know, and that they are determined to impose their opinions by main force of eloquence or assertion on the people who do not know. This is not a question, of course, of professional workers in literature—such as editors, professors and critics, who very often have no real understanding of the products with which they deal —but of readers of all kinds in all walks of life. There are moments when a first-rate writer, unrecognized or out of fashion with the official chalkers-up for the market, may find his support in the demand for his work of an appreciative cultivated public.

But what is the cause of this emotional reaction which is the critic's divining rod? This question has long been a subject of study by the branch of philosophy called esthetics, and it has recently been made a subject of scientific experimentation. Both these lines of inquiry are likely to be prejudiced in the eyes of the literary critic by the fact that the inquiries are sometimes conducted by persons who are obviously deficient in literary feeling or taste. Yet one should not deny the possibility that something of value might result from the speculations and explorations of men of acute minds who take as their given data the esthetic emotions of other men.

Almost everybody interested in literature has tried to explain to himself the nature of these emotions that register our approval of artistic works; and I of course have my own explanation.

In my view, all our intellectual activity, in whatever field it takes place, is an attempt to give a meaning to our experience— that is, to make life more practicable; for by understanding things we make it easier to survive and get around among them. The mathematician Euclid, working in a convention of abstractions, shows us relations between the distances of our unwieldy and cluttered-up environment upon which we are able to count. A drama of Sophocles also indicates relations between the various human impulses, which appear so confused and dangerous, and it brings out a certain justice of Fate—that is to say, of the way in which the interaction of these impulses is seen in the long run to work out—upon which we can also depend. The kinship, from this point of view, of the purposes of science and art appears very clearly in the case of the Greeks, because not only do both Euclid and Sophocles satisfy us by making patterns, but they make much the same kind of patterns. Euclid's *Elements* takes simple theorems and by a series of logical operations builds them up to a climax in the square on the hypotenuse. A typical drama of Sophocles develops in a similar way.

Some writers (as well as some scientists) have a different kind of explicit message beyond the reassurance implicit in the mere feat of understanding life or of molding the harmony of artistic form. Not content with such an achievement as that of Sophocles—who has one of his choruses tell us that it is better not to be born, but who, by representing life as noble and based on law, makes its tragedy easier to bear—such writers attempt, like

Plato, to think out and recommend a procedure for turning it into something better. But other departments of literature—lyric poetry such as Sappho's, for example—have *less* philosophical content than Sophocles. A lyric gives us nothing but a pattern imposed on the expression of a feeling; but this pattern of metrical quantities and of consonants and vowels that balance has the effect of reducing the feeling, however unruly or painful it may seem when we experience it in the course of our lives, to something orderly, symmetrical and pleasing; and it also relates this feeling to the more impressive scheme, works it into the larger texture, of the body of poetic art. The discord has been resolved, the anomaly subjected to discipline. And this control of his emotion by the poet has the effect at second-hand of making it easier for the reader to manage his own emotions. (Why certain sounds and rhythms gratify us more than others, and how they are connected with the themes and ideas that they are chosen as appropriate for conveying, are questions that may be passed on to the scientist.)

And this brings us back again to the historical point of view. The experience of mankind on the earth is always changing as man develops and has to deal with new combinations of elements; and the writer who is to be anything more than an echo of his predecessors must always find expression for something which has never yet been expressed, must master a new set of phenomena which has never yet been mastered. With each such victory of the human intellect, whether in history, in philosophy or in poetry, we experience a deep satisfaction: we have been cured of some ache of disorder, relieved of some oppressive burden of uncomprehended events.

This relief that brings the sense of power, and, with the sense of power, joy, is the positive emotion which tells us that we have encountered a first-rate piece of literature. But stay! you may at this point warn: are not people often solaced and exhilarated by literature of the trashiest kind? They are: crude and limited people do certainly feel some such emotion in connection with work that is limited and crude. The man who is more highly organized and has a wider intellectual range will feel it in connection with work that is finer and more complex. The difference between the emotion of the more highly organized man and the emotion of the less highly organized one is a matter of mere gradation. You sometimes discover books—the novels of John Steinbeck, for example—that seem to mark precisely the borderline between work that is definitely superior and work that is definitely bad. When I was speaking a little while back of the genuine connoisseurs who establish the standards of taste, I meant, of course, the people who can distinguish Grade A and who prefer it to the other grades.

Ronald S. Crane

(1886–1967)

When the New Critics were enjoying widespread respect in the 1930's and 40's, other groups arose to challenge their doctrines. Sometimes the challenges were merely attempts to discredit without offering any substitute for the particular concept under attack. At other times, however, the opponents offered carefully reasoned conclusions as replacements. Among the most thoughtful opponents of the New Critics were the "neo-Aristotelians" or "Chicago Critics," as they are often called. The first designation resulted from the emphasis which this group places on critical dicta from Classical Antiquity—especially those of Aristotle. The second name has been employed because the leading members of the group were on the faculty of the University of Chicago.

The dominant figure in the neo-Aristotelians was Ronald S. Crane, longtime professor of English at Chicago, who was backed vigorously by such colleagues as Elder Olson, W. R. Yeast, Richard McKeon, and Bernard Weinberg.

Crane, an able scholar and writer, was disturbed by the basic approach of the New Critics, even though he endorsed their intensity of scholarship and close attention to detail. Especially, he scored the New Critics for failing to build their theory and practice upon the ideas laid down by Aristotle in his Poetics. This failure, Crane argued, can lead only to seriously flawed conclusions.

In Crane's judgment, criticism must exist as a mode of thought, seeking primarily to develop a theory for making sound critical judgments. In the introduction to Critics and Criticism (1952)—which is a collection of essays by Crane and his colleagues, *written from the 1930's onward—Crane presents the ideas upon which his conclusions rest. They are as follows: (1) any critical statement is necessarily relative to the critic's theory; (2) the critic's theory is always determined by his responses; (3) because literature, by its very nature, admits of a variety of responses, the critic's theory varies accordingly; and (4) even though there must be, of necessity, a "plurality of distinct critical methods," a competent person can still "discriminate between critical systems," all designed, of course, to "permit a reasonably many-sided or comprehensive discussion of literary phenomena."*

Crane, born in Tecumseh, Michigan, on January 5, 1886, earned his A.B. degree from the University of Michigan (1908) and his Ph.D. from the University of Pennsylvania (1911). He also was awarded honorary doctorates from the University of Michigan and Northwestern University. Crane taught at Northwestern from 1911 to 1924, leaving to become Professor of English at the University of Chicago where he served in that role until 1950. During the academic year 1950–51, he was Distinguished Service Professor at Chicago, assuming the following year the designation of "Emeritus Distinguished Professor." In addition to his regular teaching assignments, Crane taught and lectured at many other colleges and universities throughout the United States, meanwhile producing his numerous significant writings.

The selection below is a speech delivered by Crane in 1953 at Carleton College at a regional conference of college teachers of English. In this selection, one finds Crane's concepts reduced to their simplest form. Herein Crane states directly the essence of his entire critical viewpoint.

Questions and Answers in the Teaching of Literary Texts

In this essay I want to deal particularly with the teaching of literature at a fairly elementary level to students of whom a few will, but most will not, become specialists in our subject. (I must say at once, however, that I cannot think of any general principles applicable to this earlier stage of literary study that are not relevant also to later undergraduate stages and even to graduate work on its less technical side.) And I shall restrict the treatment of the subject still further. The problem of subject matter—of what authors or works, and how many of each, we should include in our general courses—is one we all have to face annually, or at least whenever we get tired of our current syllabi. But it is hardly a subject for fruitful public debate, and even if it were, the necessary criteria for talking intelligently about it depend (as I hope to make clear) upon our first having made up our minds about something else. Nor can I see any profit in recanvassing the problem of our objectives. It may be needful at times to indoctrinate students with the faith that they are not wasting their time in studying literature. But the best indoctrination, after all, is a good course; and as for ourselves, however much we may like to dispute, in the abstract, about the ends of English study, I suspect that we are all pretty well agreed on what, in a concrete sense, we should like to see result from our endeavors, in the way of newly acquired skill and knowledge in our students. We want these students, whatever their intentions in life, not only to have fixed in their memories a certain number of excellent literary works and a certain body of essential facts about their historical relations, but also to carry away from their experience with us a more eager inclination to read literature for its own sake than they brought to it. All this of course; and beyond this, as something again which few will question, we want them to become sufficiently educated in the elements of a critical approach to literature so that, in their later studies and in life, they will know how to interpret and judge for themselves, appropriately and independently, whatever new works they may read.

To specify such a training of critical habits as one of our agreed aims, however, is at once to raise the crucial question of what it is that a good elementary critical education consists in and how it may most effectually be given to our students. The important practical problem for us, in short, is the problem of method; and I mean this not in the pedagogical sense of the relations between lectures and discussions, oral recitation and writing, close reading and extensive reading, organization by periods and organization by literary types, and so on, but rather in the intellectual sense of the kinds of questions about literary works we ask students and train them to ask themselves, and of the techniques we cultivate in them for getting and justifying answers. It is with this restricted aspect of our general subject, at any rate, that I wish to deal.

I shall group my remarks under two principal heads: first, the varieties of questions that seem most pertinent and necessary to the development of a rounded understanding and appreciation of literary works; second, the conditions of formulation and testing under which warranted answers to such questions are to be sought.

The view of critical questions I want to suggest is based on the simple premise that no statement we make about literature in general or a given literary work can have any determinate meaning or relevance, or permit of any intelligent appraisal of its validity, so long as it is considered merely as an isolated statement. This ought to be obvious to everyone; but unfortunately the history of criticism has been so written, for the most part, as to blind us to both its truth and its implications. The majority of histories of criticism have been constructed on the assumption that we can give an adequate account of what critics in the past have done by summarizing, and comparing directly with one another, the explicit doctrinal conclusions they have set forth concerning art, literature, poetry, or particular parts and species of these, and by treating similarly their judgments on individual writers and works. The immediate effect of such a procedure is to resolve the development of criticism into a succession of arbitrary and hopelessly conflicting dogmas, only a few of which need be taken seriously, plus an accumulation of equally arbitrary and conflicting pronouncements in "practical criticism" that seem well deserving of the satire bestowed upon them in Henri Peyre's witty lectures on *Writers and Their Critics*. And the ultimate effect is to encourage in us one or the other of two attitudes toward the existing body of critical statements, both of them severely limiting in their practical consequences. On the one hand, we may very well conclude, from the history of criticism as thus told, that any serious concern with the principles of literature, or systematic application of principles to works, is a futile business; or, on the other hand, we may restrain our skepticism to the limited extent of pinning our faith to one particular system out of the many systems of criticism available to us in the past, or now being constructed, and treat the others either as modern corruptions of ancient truths or as ancient errors sufficiently refuted by the discoveries of later times.

To respond in either of these ways, however—as a skeptic or as a dogmatic adherent to one system or "approach"—is enormously to restrict our resources as critics and teachers of literature. Fortunately, neither response is justified by the nature of critical statements when that nature is fully understood. The trouble with the historians I have been speaking of is that they have disregarded the simple premise I stated a moment ago. They have consistently taken the declarations of critics, on both general and particular subjects, as if they were capable of being interpreted, and their truth or falsity pronounced upon, as self-contained assertions, without prior consideration of their logical status and functions in the critical discourse in which they appear. But all statements in criticism have logical contexts, apart from which nothing significant can be said about them; and the immediate context of any statement is the precise question (often not explicitly formulated at all) to which it is an intended answer. Wherefore it follows that two critical doctrines cannot be sensibly compared, no matter how similar their verbal forms, or be judged in relation to one another, until we are sure that both are conceived as answers to exactly the same question. Thus we have no right to say that Croce either refuted or made obsolete the doctrine of poetic genres unless we are prepared to show— which cannot, I think, be done—that his conclusions represent a solution of the very same theoretical problem, or problems, that faced the earlier critics who upheld that doctrine; and conversely, of course, as well.

But we can, and indeed must, go further than this. For no critical question, in turn, is an isolable thing. Just as statements are relative to the questions to which they are answers, so questions are relative, so far as their meanings and the conditions of their proper answering are concerned, to the still larger context of primary terms, distinctions, and premises which make up the conceptual "framework" (as we say nowadays) of the critic's writing, and determine both what questions he will think it possible or important to ask and what kinds of answers he will seek for them. Wherefore it follows, very often, that what appear to be hopeless doctrinal conflicts in criticism are not really doctrinal conflicts at all, but simply expressions of preference among different, but equally defensible, frameworks, within any two of which the seemingly common referents of the critics' statements may be only nominally the same. This is the case, for instance, with Plato as compared with Aristotle (there is no sense in which Aristotle can be said to have refuted Plato on poetry), with the German idealist critics of the early nineteenth century as compared with these ancients, and with the contemporary school of "semantic" critics as compared with their Victorian predecessors.

If all this is true, it has important practical consequences for our initial problem of determining the kinds of questions we will want to ask, and encourage students to ask for themselves, in our literary teaching. It would doubtless be desirable, from one point of view, if we could forget about literary theory altogether and give our attention wholly to the concrete particulars of the poems, novels, and dramas before us. But we cannot do that, since everything we say, every question we ask, about literary works is inevitably dependent upon some assumption as to what such things are and as to how knowledge and appreciation of them is to be obtained. Whether we like it or not, we are inescapably bound to theory; but once we have recognized this, we can, I think, do two things, both of them clearly implied in the view of critical statements and questions I have been trying to suggest. We can accustom ourselves, in the first place, to looking upon the theoretical statements of critics, from Aristotle to the authors of *Understanding Poetry,* not as doctrines to be taught, but rather as more or less useful tools of our trade—as sources of concepts and distinctions from which we and our students may derive significant questions to ask about works in the hope of generating observations on them that might not otherwise be made. We can form the habit, in a word, of treating critical theories heuristically. And having done this, we can emancipate ourselves from the stultifying notion, which is still widespread, that there must be some "proper" or "right" approach to literature, poetry, or Shakespeare, which we are justified in opposing to other approaches and insisting on as the one true way to critical salvation, whether this is contained in the textbook we are using or not.

The truth is that all the critical systems that have been devised, or that can be devised, are finite bodies of ideas, restricted, by the very nature of critical discourse, to one particular selection of aspects out of the many different ones which literary works present. Each has its peculiar power of stimulating observation and making possible understanding; but each, at the same time, has its characteristic limitations, beyond which its utility ceases. The special concern of Aristotle in the *Poetics,* for example, is with those aspects of certain kinds of poems—the kinds which, as he says, "happen to be imitations"—that emerge when we ask what are the principles of artistic reasoning presupposed by their obviously different structures and effects; it is with these aspects, but only with these, that the conceptual apparatus he provides will permit us to deal.[1] The special concern of Coleridge, again, is with those aspects of poems and poetry, considered generally not specifically, and in terms not so much of artistic principles as of natural causes, that appear when we ask about the effects pro-

[1] See Elder Olson, "The Poetic Method of Aristotle: Its Powers and Limitations," *English Institute Essays, 1951* (New York, 1952), pp. 70–94.

duced on the mind by poems as distinct from other modes of
composition and especially about the degree of participation
achieved by poets in the universal synthetic workings of the
imagination; it is to these aspects that he consistently directs our
attention and it is with respect to these, but these only, that he is
a useful and inspiring guide. The special concern, finally, of
Brooks and Warren in *Understanding Poetry* is with those aspects
of poetry, considered as one homogeneous kind of thing, that are
isolated when we make poetry a mode of discourse sharply
opposed in its materials and methods to science, and ask questions mainly about the characteristics of "poetic" form and meaning which this comparison discloses; what is valuable and
suggestive in their approach is strictly relative to this basic
decision as to the aspect of poetry they will talk about.[2]

We have here three critical systems that neither overlap nor
contradict one another at any significant points; and there are
many others, both past and contemporary, of which the same can
be said. I think this is a great reason for self-congratulation—that
we have available for our needs in teaching, if only we will take
advantage of the fact, so many different and well-tested instru-
ments for helping our students see more in works of literature
than they have been accustomed to seeing. It should be our
obligation as teachers, therefore, first to try to grasp what is
positive and still valuable, within the limits of their respective
frameworks, in at least the major critical systems of the past
and present. We ought then to bring this understanding to bear
on the problem of devising a general scheme of critical questions
that will include, and set in significant relation to each other,
the different fundamental aspects of literary works which our
predecessors and contemporaries have defined, and which our
students ought to be led to consider.

I want to propose such a scheme here, but without implying

[2] For this general view of critical questions and statements, see further *Critics and Criticism: Ancient and Modern*, edited by R. S. Crane (Chicago, 1952), especially pp. 2–12, 63–64, 148–49, 174–75, 317–18, 463–66, 522–23, 530–45, 546–52, 594; and Crane, *The Languages of Criticism and the Structure of Poetry* (Toronto, 1953).

that I think no other equally useful schemes could be devised for the same purpose. It consists of five groups of critical questions, corresponding to five distinguishable aspects of literary works— their verbal elements and the actions, thoughts, and feeling revealed by these; their overall forms; the qualities of thought and sensibility in their authors which they reflect; the circumstances of their composition; and the moral, social, or intellectual effects they are capable of exerting. I shall speak of them in ascending order of complexity.

1. We may ask questions, in the first place, that depend for their content and for the data of their answers, merely on a consideration of literary works, irrespective of their specific kinds, in their common aspect as verbal compositions. This is the distinctive sphere of *explication de textes*, in its various lexicographical, syntactical, prosodical, logical, and stylistic applications. We may call the results, for short, the criticism of elements and devices.

The objects of such criticism are literary works considered from the point of view of their basic literary constituents—their words, lines, sentences, paragraphs, speeches, and so on; and the categories which determine its questions are, first, meaning or content and, second, diction or style. Meaning (as I use the term here) is the immediate power exerted by the language of a composition as selected and arranged by the writer; it embraces everything from the individual significations of the words and metaphors, through the implications which these set up, to the structure and import of arguments or actions, and the signs, in the discourse, of character, emotion, and action. The meanings to be discovered by our questions are not just any possible meanings we may wish to give to the words but the meanings of the authors. The devices by which these are expressed, and hence the procedures necessary for their recovery, are not essentially different in prose and verse, or in essays, histories, lyrics, dramas, and novels; for meaningful language exists as such and becomes poetic, scientific, or rhetorical only by virtue of the specific uses to which it is put. Diction or style (as I use the term here) is that aspect of discourse which appears when we ask about the kinds of words, among the alternatives available for a given purpose to the writer, which he has selected to convey his meanings, the particular phonetic, rhythmical, and syntactical patterns in which he has chosen to arrange his words, and the devices of imagery, metaphor, antithesis, paradox, and so on, which give to his writing such dynamic quality as it has. We teach an appreciation of diction whenever we call attention by our questions to these things and train our students to make ever more discriminating judgments between appropriate and inappropriate uses by writers of their stylistic resources, and especially between styles that have distinction, no matter of what kind, and styles that have not.

Such an education in the recovery of content and in the perception of dictional devices and qualities may be termed the grammar of literary study. It is an indispensable foundation for whatever else we may attempt to do; and that is why those contemporary critics, in the line of I. A. Richards, who have insisted so constantly on the all-importance of close textual reading are surely right. We need to make one distinction, however. The great virtue of a textbook like *Understanding Poetry* is the exercise it gives in the sensitive grammatical interpretation of texts; its shortcoming is that it superimposes on this a partial and one-sided theory of poetic form, with the result that the student is insensibly conditioned to see only those meanings and stylistic devices in poems which the theory selects as important. Interpretation is one thing, and formal analysis another; it is well, I think, not to allow the first to be controlled by the second, so that our students become adept in finding instances of "ambiguity," "irony," "paradox," "symbol," or "myth" before they are able to say, independently of such notions, what the words and sentences actually mean, what the actions or the arguments are as stated or implied, and how such distinction as the language has is brought about. The criticism of elements, in short, is likely to be most fruitful in education when it is directed by its own special principles, uncontaminated by presuppositions about what the writer, as lyric poet or novelist or historian, *should* be saying; it can then most effectually serve as basis and control in the consideration of questions beyond its scope.

2. The elements and devices of literary works, however, are never there for their own sake merely but ultimately for the sake of what is done with them in the making of concrete literary wholes. Therefore the criticism of elements needs to be completed and reoriented, for any work, by a second kind of criticism —that of structure or form. By form I mean simply the overall principle, whatever it may be, that makes of the materials of a work a single definite thing. It is the aspect of literary works which comes into view when we ask ourselves not simply what the meanings and the dictional devices are, and what are the immediate effects they produce, but why these meanings and devices and local effects are appropriately in the work (if they do indeed belong) and how, and how well, they function artistically with respect to one another and the whole—the meaning of "Why?" here being relative to the peculiar nature and end of the individual work before us rather than to the general intentions or historical circumstances of its author.

The categories which determine the questions to be asked in such criticism relate, on the one hand, to the structural parts and, on the other hand, to the principle by which the parts, in any work, are synthesized into an artistic whole. The basic structural parts of a literary work are its language and content and whatever these are so shaped as to do. The latter may be the inculcation of an argument of some sort, in which case the other parts are the component premises and devices of proof or persuasion; or it may be the representation of a human experience of some sort, for the sake of its effects on our emotions and the beauty of its rendering, in which case the other parts are such things as thought, character, plot, or whatever corresponds to plot in representational lyrics, and the various technical expedients by which thought, character, emotion, situation, action are brought before us. These can be discussed, up to a certain point, in and for themselves (as when we ask questions about the qualities of character present in a given novel or the special features of its narrative techniques); but our discussions are bound to remain incomplete, and the answers and judgments our questions provoke somewhat arbitrary, until we have considered what the informing principle is that makes of the work a distinctive whole, and how the requirements of this principle have helped to determine the conception and handling of the parts. I have attempted elsewhere, apropos of Fielding's *Tom Jones*, to suggest the types of questions such an inquiry into principles of form involves and how some of them may be answered,[3] and I will merely add now that I think the great need, in this part of our teaching, is for more numerous and more specifically discriminating notions of possible formal principles in literature than we now have. The suggestions contained in *Understanding Poetry* are applicable at best to only one class of poetic works—those designed to embody and give force to conceptual themes; and, generally speaking, the "new critics" who have concerned themselves with questions of poetic structure have looked for principles of structure, like Cleanth Brooks's "paradox" or "irony," that are common to all poems or at least to all good ones. The analysis of tragic plot form in the *Poetics* approaches more nearly the kind of thing we need, but it would be a mistake to try to fit to Aristotle's formula more than a few of the works we call tragedies; and most of the other common names for classes of literary structures, such as comedy, lyric, or novel, are far too general to be of much practical use. There is some hope, however, that more will be done in the future toward providing the fuller apparatus of distinctions we require for criticism of this kind,[4] and meanwhile we can do something ourselves, as teachers, by continuing to ask, about all sorts of literary works, the basic questions upon which it depends.

[3] Cf. *Critics and Criticism*, pp. 616–47.
[4] See now Olson's *Tragedy and the Theory of Drama* (Detroit, 1961) for a very full and useful apparatus of such distinctions (with illustrations from ancient and modern tragedy) which can be used in the discussion of works of prose fiction as well as in the criticism of plays.

3. The criticism of forms is clearly incapable by itself of telling us why a given poem, drama, or novel is a great work of literary art. On the other hand, when sensitively done, it can supply an indispensable foundation—in the appreciation it gives of the enormously varied formal and technical problems faced by writers—for further questions about other aspects of the works we wish to consider. Thus, although literary works, when viewed in and for themselves, are particular syntheses of elements governed immediately by principles of poetic, rhetorical, dialectical, or historical art, they are also, in their origins, the creative acts of men endowed by nature and education with certain qualities of soul or literary personality or "vision," which, as reflected in texts, are capable of stimulating responses not entirely to be accounted for by strictly formal considerations. Here then is another aspect, every bit as important as the others, which can be made the center of a third set of critical questions.

The objects of these are the traits of substance and expression in literary works, taken singly or by authors or schools, which make us feel the presence behind them of a particular kind or degree of genius or sensibility or of a particular way of seeing and ordering the conditions and values of life. We may call this kind of criticism, in distinction from the other two kinds, the criticism of qualities or of literary personality; it has had a long tradition from Longinus in antiquity, through Dryden, Addison, Pope, Johnson, Coleridge, Hazlitt, Lamb, Sainte-Beuve, Matthew Arnold, Pater, and Bradley, to contemporaries like Benedetto Croce, Middleton Murry, T. S. Eliot, F. R. Leavis, and Wilson Knight. The categories which determine its questions are the general categories, applicable in the discussion of all species of literary works, which Longinus made explicit in his account of the sources of the "sublime"—namely, thought, in the sense of the author's distinctive conceptions of things; emotion, in the sense of the characteristic qualities of his sensibility; and expression, in the sense of all the devices of language by which his thought and emotional responses are realized in his works or particular passages thereof; and the method of procedure is comparative, inasmuch as the only way in which particular literary qualities can be defined is through a consideration, supported by references to other authors and works, of what they are not. The criticism of qualities depends, therefore, to a much greater extent than the first two kinds, upon wide literary experience and developed powers of discrimination and analysis; the very generality of its categories, besides, is a constant invitation to impressionism and irresponsibility. That is no reason, however, for neglecting it in our programs, so long as we do not expect our students to become young Hazlitts or young Eliots at once, and so long as we encourage them to test their qualitative generalizations by reference to what the criticism of elements and of forms has shown them about the same works and to acquire the habit of specifying in the details of texts the particular devices through which the felt qualities of the writer are made manifest.

4. There can be no good teaching of literary history, I think, that does not presuppose and make constant use of the insights into literary works which can be given by the three critical modes already discussed; but these in turn need to be completed by means of the questions appropriate to literary history, or, as we may call it, the criticism of circumstances. The great danger here is, or at least has been in the past, that we will be too ambitious, and think that we have not done our duty by our students—or our degrees—until we have given them a rounded scheme of periods, movements, literary schools, and the like, with definitions of their respective dominant traits; for to do this is inevitably to implant formulas in our students' heads which they will unfortunately remember but never quite understand. The better way is to try to build up, informally and bit by bit, through our discussions of particular authors and texts, first of all a grasp of essential chronology; then what I should call a sense of period styles (by which I mean an ability to infer from the internal characteristics of texts, without other aids, the generation in which they must have been written); and finally a habit of asking questions about works that will yield such information

concerning their occasions, their sources or models, the philosophic "commonplaces" or artistic conventions they use, and the traditions they carry on, as will directly promote our students' understanding and appreciation of them in their aspect as permanently valuable works of art produced at a given time. A useful kind of training in literary history, I have often thought, would be one in which, for instance, we first brought our students to recognize that *Lycidas, An Elegy Written in a Country Churchyard, In Memoriam,* and *The Waste Land* are all works having essentially the same poetic form, and then asked them to consider how far and in what ways the striking differences among the four are to be accounted for by differences in the genius and "vision" of their writers, and how far and in what ways by differences in the conventions of subject matter, language, and technique which depend on the fact that the first poem was published in 1638, the second in 1751, the third in 1850, and the fourth in 1922.

5. With our last set of questions we return from the past to the present. They are the questions that give us what may be called the criticism of moral, social, political, and religious values; and they pertain to that aspect of literary works which is called to mind whenever we consider literature or poetry in the context of education or of the particular goods we are interested in realizing in the society of our time; they are concerned, in short, with the functions of literary works over and above the requirements of formal or qualitative excellence or the satisfaction of contemporary tastes.

In its generalized applications this is the kind of criticism practiced by Plato in his *Republic,* by Aristotle in his *Politics,* by Sidney and Shelley in their defenses of poetry, by Matthew Arnold in his "Function of Criticism" and his "Literature and Science," and by the many later critics who have continued Arnold's line of discussion; here also we may place the criticism of Tolstoi, of the Marxists, of Kenneth Burke. It is surely desirable that our students should be introduced to this great debate about the uses of literature through some of the texts in which it has been carried on; but what I have chiefly in mind here are questions of value in a more limited and particular sense. We cannot read a powerful or vividly convincing author without being influenced in some degree by him in our moral feelings and estimates of things, and we should not try to evade the consequences of this fact in our teaching. We ought to attempt, therefore, to raise questions with our students, and train them to raise questions for themselves, that will lead to discriminating judgments of authors, not only as to the excellences and defects of their art, but also as to the kinds of influence their works are calculated to exert, and more especially as to the relative comprehensiveness or narrowness, complexity or simplicity, humanity or abnormality, truth or falsity of the basic propositions about life and conduct which they set forth or assume. The danger of such criticism of course is its tendency to encourage displays of dogmatic provincialism in morals, politics, and religion, so that we fail, for example, to do justice to the extraordinary breadth and sanity of Shakespeare's moral insights by overemphasis on his undemocratic view of the state. We can do something to guard against this, however, partly by giving priority in our teaching to the other kinds of questions and partly by seeing to it that in discussing questions of this kind our students make clear the assumptions underlying their judgments and relate their statements always to what is really in the text they are reading.

I have presented these five kinds of criticism as so many distinct lines of inquiry into literary works, each with its characteristic questions, presuppositions, and data; and I regard them simply as so many distinct analytical tools at our disposal for making the most of the authors and writings we have to teach. Their distinctness in the account I have given of them, however, does not imply any necessity of keeping them separate in our practice as teachers. If we are at all skillful, indeed, we will move freely among them, with our attention centered not on this or any other scheme of critical topics but on the concrete problems presented by the authors or texts we happen to be dealing with, the scheme operating only as a useful reminder of the varied things we can do. The nature of critical questions and statements is such, moreover, that I should not want to attempt any theoretical defence of the type of scheme I have offered, with its five distinct sets of questions, against the objections of those who prefer to think of criticism as an organic whole that does not lend itself to division into sharply differentiated lines of inquiry. That is clearly a tenable view, since there is an important sense in which all aspects of literature are bound up inextricably with one another, but I should insist that my view is also tenable, since there is another and equally important sense in which they have independent status. The fact is that the two positions are complementary half-truths, the systematic espousal of either one of which necessarily entails leaving out, at least temporarily an essential aspect of literary reality. I do not see how this can be avoided, inasmuch as we can not very well do both things at once. Therefore we are faced with a choice for which the only ground must be the relative utility of the two ways of conceiving criticism for what we want to do; and looking at the matter in these practical terms, I can see important advantages for us as teachers in the style of approach I have adopted. For if we have in mind a reasonably exhaustive inventory of the more clear-cut differences among critical questions and statements, we can the more easily decide, along with other things, whether our program in literature is as complete, in its disciplinary aspects, as it might be, whether we have made a properly varied selection of texts and authors for study, and whether we are doing all that we should do that is appropriate to our place in the total curriculum.

Our success will depend ultimately, however, not only on the kinds of questions we habituate our students to ask of literary works but also on the standards we induce them to apply in deciding upon and testing their answers. This is too complex a subject to permit of more than fragmentary treatment at the end of a discourse like this, and I shall accordingly confine myself to one small part of it.

The five kinds of questions we are concerned with asking are primarily questions about texts, that is, about unique combinations of particular meanings and literary traits; and the general conditions under which a warranted answer to any of them is possible are of two sorts. The first condition I have already touched upon. It is the necessity, simply, that we know what question we are trying to answer before we venture on any statement of our own about a text, or before we accept, or reject, any statement about the same text made by another. "When you say this, just what question do you think you or the critic you are citing or quarreling with is attempting to answer?"—the more often we insist that our students declare themselves in these terms, the more progress we shall make, and the less talking at cross purposes we shall have to endure.

The second condition is more important still, at least on the assumption that we are interested in developing in our students a sense of responsibility in what they say about literary matters rather than merely in giving them uncontrolled exercise in expressing their opinions. There are, as I have argued, various possible and equally legitimate approaches to literary works, and hence, in criticism considered broadly, there is no one type of interpretation or judgment which can be insisted upon as peculiarly "proper" or "right." To say this, however, is not to say that within any one approach, after we are clear about the nature and reference of the questions we are asking, we need subscribe to the now fashionable doctrine of multiple truth. It is possible to attribute to *Oedipus Rex*, for instance, both a tragic plot form in the ordinary sense and also a form resembling that of a primitive religious ritual: the two conclusions are answers to quite different types of questions and have to be argued on the basis of quite different assumptions and evidence; they do not therefore really contradict one another, any more than do the statements that a given pipe is a smoking instrument of such and such a form and that it is a particular concentration of dancing atoms. But the case is clearly altered when we ask a question about this or any other literary work that presupposes a single framework of discussion. Here we may legitimately assume that there can be only one completely true answer to any question we may raise. The doctrine of multiple truth in criticism has arisen, I believe, from a confusion between the two kinds of situations—those in which the conclusions of fundamentally different approaches to the same works are directly opposed to one another and those in which, the questions being essentially of the same order, there is disagreement about what the case really is. And much disagreement of this second sort is of course to be expected in practical criticism, as a consequence of the fact that our objects in such study are always concrete particulars and that our aim is to know and appreciate them as such rather than to treat them simply as data for deriving general scientific laws. Therefore we cannot hope, strictly speaking, to demonstrate anything about literary works, but only to construct hypotheses concerning them which, because they can never be completely adequate to the literary actuality, are always in need of reconsideration or revision.

There are, however—and this is the crux of what I want to say—better and worse ways of going about the making of hypotheses in criticism and literary teaching. And the worse way, unfortunately, is much the commoner. It is what has been called, in science, the method of the favorite or "ruling" hypothesis. What does this passage in this poem or essay mean? Or what is going on in this lyric or this novel or drama? It is easy and natural to come to such questions with the essential formula of the answers already in our minds. We have built up a more or less fixed notion, from our earlier reading or from the study of other critics, of what a given author is characteristically trying to say, either because we have "placed" him as a certain kind of man or because we have assimilated him to a certain age or intellectual tradition. Or we have learned to think of the structure of lyrics or dramas in terms of a certain distinctive pattern of elements, as when we identify the structure of tragedy with the form described in chapter 13 of the *Poetics* or the structure of lyric with the form described, and attributed consistently to all short poems, in *Understanding Poetry*. Our procedure then consists in applying the favorite hypothesis thus obtained directly to the passage or the composition before us and in announcing our recognition, supported by particular references to the text, that it does indeed fit. But after all there is nothing strange or necessarily significant in the fact that, oftener than not, it does fit. For the complexity of all literary texts is such that it is hard to think of any self-consistent hypothesis of meaning or structure under which we cannot subsume enough of the details of a given passage or work to convince ourselves of its truth, so long as the hypothesis in question is the only one we take the trouble to consider. At the worst we can always invent secondary hypotheses, after the fashion of the Ptolemaic epicycles, to get us over the difficult spots.

It would be easy to collect many instances of such malpractice from contemporary and earlier criticism. And there is, I believe, only one available safeguard against it. That is to base our procedure, as consistently as we can, on the principle that the value of any hypothesis is always relative, not merely to the particulars it is intended to explain, but to all the other variant hypotheses which the same particulars might suggest if we gave them a chance: the best hypothesis is simply the best among several possible hypotheses, relevant to the same question about the same work, with which we have actually compared it, and unless we make such comparisons a regular part of our procedure we always court the danger of missing either slightly or fully what the facts really are. This is what has been called, in science, the method of "multiple hypotheses,"[5] and it can be adapted, easily and with great profit, I think, to the situations that constantly arise in our literary teaching.

Let us suppose that we have before us a passage in a poem of which the precise meaning is not obvious at first glance. Instead of asking our students directly what they think the passage means, we can ask them to tell us, first, what are the several different meanings it might possibly have, or that have been im-

[5] Cf. T. C. Chamberlin, *Journal of Geology*, 39 (1931): 155–65.

puted to it by different critics, and then to consider, impartially, which one of these conjectures, if any, adequately accounts for its actual wording and arrangement, its distinctive imagery, and its place in the context in which it occurs. Or let us suppose that the question is not one of meaning but of artistic structure: we have before us a short poem concerning which we need to be reasonably sure, before we can talk to any purpose about the functions and qualities of its parts, just what kind of whole its writer has sought to achieve. It will make all the difference, in both our analysis of the poem and our judgment of its success, how we conceive of its overall formal nature—whether we assume it to be that of a simple poetic statement, of the order of epigram, in which the mode of utterance is the chief thing (as, for instance, in Ben Jonson's "Still To Be Neat" or Yeats's "That the Night Come"), or that of an elaborated rhetorical argument (as in Dryden's "Alexander's Feast," Johnson's "Vanity of Human Wishes," or Pope's "Epistle to Dr. Arbuthnot"), or that of a poetically represented human experience, embodied in words for the sake of its emotional values and the beauty of the representation; and whether, if the poem appears to be of the last kind, we assume that the form of the represented experience, and hence of the poem, is that of a person in a state of emotion (as in Shelley's "Ode to the West Wind" or Tennyson's "Tears, Idle Tears"), or that of a certain disposition or mode of feeling about things (as in "L'Allegro" or "Il Penseroso"), or that of an internal activity involving either moral choice (as in Gray's "Elegy") or a process of coming to understand (as in Wordsworth's "Intimations" ode or Whitman's "When lilacs last in the dooryard bloomed"), or that of a particularized character manifesting itself in words and actions (as in "The Bishop Orders His Tomb"), or that of an overt act of persuading, threatening, or the like (as in Marvell's "To His Coy Mistress"); and so on through other similarly distinguishable forms of poetic construction.[6] For any given poem we can often eliminate at once some or many of

[6] Cf. Olson, *Critics and Criticism*, pp. 560, 563–66; Norman Maclean, *ibid.*, pp. 429–36, 448–49.

these possible principles, but it is never safe to proceed before we have canvassed explicitly, in our questioning, at least several alternative hypotheses for its form, and excluded all but the one which, after comparison with the others, appears to explain most fully and economically the details of the poem and to do most complete justice to its felt qualities and merits. That is the most we can do, but that is surely much.

And the advantages of such a method go considerably beyond its immediate benefits in a fuller understanding and appreciation of the particular passages or works to which it is applied. There is no better way than this of cultivating critical responsibility in our students and the habit of resisting their all-too-natural tendency to an easy acceptance of ready-made formulas and fashionable opinions. And there is no better way, also—since the very act of comparing hypotheses is bound to make us see more than we would otherwise have seen—of encouraging particularity of observation on texts and hence of sharpening our students' sensitivity to words and meanings, to the variety of forms which literature assumes, to the several ways of thinking and expressing himself which distinguish one writer from another, and similarly to all those other aspects of literary works which our scheme of critical questions, insofar as it is adequate, will bring into view.

Malcolm Cowley

(b. 1898)

On rare occasions, a critic startles the literary world by publishing an unusually competent reappraisal of a writer whose talent is considered, in most quarters, to be rather seriously limited. In these instances, the critic owes his success to an ability to discover elements undetected by other critics and to explain and evaluate the elements with originality of insight. Such a critic is Malcolm Cowley, who has been largely responsible for obtaining a new and loftier position for William Faulkner, now widely regarded as one of America's greatest novelists. The groundwork for this new recognition was laid by Cowley's introduction to the Portable Faulkner *(Viking, 1948), a portion of which is presented below.*

Cowley's proficiency in evaluating Faulkner results essentially from his ability to see the special meaning in Faulkner's work. He states that all the "books in the Yoknapatawpha saga are part of the same living pattern. It is this pattern, and not the printed volumes in which part of it is recorded, that is Faulkner's real achievement." He then enlarges upon this statement to demonstrate that "each novel, each long or short story, seems to reveal more than it states explicitly and to have a subject bigger than itself."

The meaning identified and explained by Cowley centers about a South decaying from within—socially, politically, economically— and the significance of life for the people inhabiting a small sector of that region. Particularly, Cowley elucidates Faulkner's understanding of these people as they grope, stumble, or shuffle re-

signedly along the road created by circumstances for them to travel.

Also noteworthy in this critical essay is Cowley's explanation of Faulkner's perceptions. Faulkner, as Cowley demonstrates, was able to comprehend in a strangely intuitive manner the "curious sense of submission to fate" experienced by the natives of Yoknapatawpha County. Faulkner seemed to have a genius-like ability to understand people like Miss Rosa Coldfield in Absalom, Absalom! *who, Faulkner tells us, accepted life as "that dream state in which you run without moving from a terror in which you cannot believe, toward a safety in which you have no faith."*

Cowley, a free-lance writer and editor, received the A.B. degree from Harvard in 1920 and the honorary D.Litt. degree from Franklin and Marshall College in 1961 and Colby College in 1962. He has also taught at the University of Washington, Stanford University, the University of Michigan, and Cornell University.

From Introduction to *Viking Portable Faulkner*

When the war was over—the other war—William Faulkner went back to Oxford, Mississippi. He had served in the Royal Air Force in 1918. Now he was home again and not at home, or at least not able to accept the postwar world. He was writing poems, most of them worthless, and dozens of immature but violent and effective stories, while at the same time he was brooding over his own situation and the decline of the South. Slowly the brooding thoughts arranged themselves into the whole interconnected pattern that would form the substance of his later novels.

This pattern, which almost all his critics have overlooked, was based on what he saw in Oxford or remembered from his child-hood; on scraps of family tradition (the Falkners, as they spelled the name, had played their part in the history of the state); on kitchen dialogues between the black cook and her amiable hus-band; on Saturday-afternoon gossip in Courthouse Square; on stories told by men in overalls squatting on their heels while they passed around a fruit-jar full of white corn liquor; on all the sources familiar to a small-town Mississippi boy—but the whole of it was elaborated, transformed, given convulsive life by his emotions; until, by the simple intensity of feeling, the figures in it became a little more than human, became heroic or diabolical, became symbols of the old South, of war and reconstruction, of commerce and machinery destroying the standards of the past. There in Oxford, Faulkner performed a labor of imagination that has not been equaled in our time, and a double labor: first, to invent a Mississippi county that was like a mythical kingdom, but was complete and living in all its details; second, to make his story of Yoknapatawpha County stand as a parable or legend of all the Deep South.

• • •

Faulkner's mythical kingdom is a county in northern Mississippi, on the border between the sand hills covered with scrubby pine and the black earth of the river bottoms. Except for the storekeepers, mechanics, and professional men who live in Jefferson, the county seat, all the inhabitants are farmers or woodsmen. Except for a little lumber, their only product is baled cotton for the Memphis market. A few of them live in big plantation houses, the relics of another age, and more of them in substantial wooden farmhouses; but most of them are tenants, no better housed than slaves on good plantations before the Civil War. Yoknapatawpha County—"William Faulkner, sole owner and proprietor," as he inscribed on one of the maps he drew—has a population of 15,611 persons scattered over 2400 square miles. It sometimes seems to me that every house or hovel has been described in one of Faulkner's novels; and that all the people of the imaginary county, black and white, townsmen, farmers, and housewives, have played their parts in one connected story.

He has so far written nine books wholly concerned with Yoknapatawpha County and its people, who also appear in parts of three others and in thirty or more uncollected stories. *Sartoris* was the first of the books to be published, in the spring of 1929; it is a romantic and partly unconvincing novel, but with many fine scenes in it, like the hero's visit to a family of independent pine-hill farmers; and it states most of the themes that the author would later develop at length. *The Sound and the Fury* was written before *Sartoris,* but wasn't published until six months later; it describes the fall of the Compson family, and it was the first of Faulkner's novels to be widely discussed. The books that followed, in the Yoknapatawpha series, are *As I Lay Dying* (1930), about the death and burial of Addie Bundren; *Sanctuary* (1931), always the most popular of his novels; *Light in August* (1932), in many ways the best; *Absalom, Absalom!* (1936), about Colonel Sutpen and his ambition to found a family; *The Unvanquished* (1938), a book of interrelated stories about the Sartoris dynasty; *The Wild Palms* (1939), half of which deals with a convict from back in the pine hills; *The Hamlet* (1940), a novel about the Snopes clan; and *Go Down, Moses* (1942), in which Faulkner's theme is the Negroes. There are also many Yoknapatawpha stories in *These Thirteen* (1931) and *Dr. Martino* (1934), besides other stories privately printed (like "Miss Zilphia Gant") or published in magazines and still to be collected or used as episodes in novels.

Just as Balzac, who seems to have inspired the series, divided his *Comédie Humaine* into "Scenes of Parisian Life," "Scenes of Provincial Life," "Scenes of Private Life," so Faulkner might divide his work into a number of cycles: one about the planters and their descendants, one about the townspeople of Jefferson, one about the poor whites, one about the Indians (consisting of stories already written but never brought together), and one about the Negroes. Or again, if he adopted a division by families, there would be the Compson-Sartoris saga, the still unfinished Snopes saga, the McCaslin saga, dealing with the white and black descendants of Carothers McCaslin, and the Ratliff-Bundren saga, devoted to the backwoods farmers of Frenchman's Bend. All the cycles or sagas are closely interconnected; it is as if each new book was a chord or segment of a total situation always existing in the author's mind. Sometimes a short story is the sequel to an earlier novel. For example, we read in *Sartoris* that Myron Snopes stole a packet of letters from Narcissa Benbow; and in "There Was a Queen," a story published five years later, we learn how Narcissa got the letters back again. Sometimes, on the other hand, a novel contains the sequel to a story; and we discover from an incidental reference in *The Sound and the Fury* that the Negro woman whose terror of death was described in "That Evening Sun" had later been murdered by her husband, who left her body in a ditch for the vultures. Sometimes an episode has a more complicated history. Thus, in the first chapter of *Sanctuary*, we hear about the Old Frenchman place, a ruined mansion near which the people of the neighborhood had been "digging with secret and sporadic optimism for gold which the builder was reputed to have buried somewhere about the place when Grant came through the country on his Vicksburg campaign." Later this digging for gold served as the subject of a story published in the *Saturday Evening Post:* "Lizards in Jamshyd's Courtyard." Still later the story was completely rewritten and became the last chapter of *The Hamlet*.

As one book leads into another, Faulkner sometimes falls into inconsistencies of detail. There is a sewing-machine agent named V.K. Suratt who appears in *Sartoris* and some of the later stories. By the time we reach *The Hamlet*, his name has changed to Ratliff, although his character remains the same (and his age, too, for all the twenty years that separate the backgrounds of the two novels). Henry Armstid is a likable figure in *As I Lay Dying* and *Light in August;* in *The Hamlet* he is mean and half-demented. His wife, whose character remains consistent, is called Lula in one book and Martha in another; in the third she is nameless. There is an Indian chief named Doom who appears in several stories; he starts as the father of Issetibeha and ends as his grandson. The mansion called Sutpen's Hundred was built of brick at the beginning of *Absalom, Absalom!* but at the end of the novel it is all wood and inflammable except for the chimneys. But these errors are comparatively few and inconsequential, considering the scope of Faulkner's series; and I should judge that most of them are afterthoughts rather than oversights.

All his books in the Yoknapatawpha saga are part of the same living pattern. It is this pattern, and not the printed volumes in which part of it is recorded, that is Faulkner's real achievement. Its existence helps to explain one feature of his work: that each novel, each long or short story, seems to reveal more than it states explicitly and to have a subject bigger than itself. All the separate works are like blocks of marble from the same quarry: they show the veins and faults of the mother rock. Or else—to use a rather strained figure—they are like wooden planks that were cut, not from a log, but from a still living tree. The planks are planed and chiseled into their final shapes, but the tree itself heals over the wound and continues to grow. Faulkner is incapable of telling the same story twice without adding new details. In the present volume I wanted to use part of *The Sound and the Fury*, the novel that deals with the fall of the Compson family. I thought that the last part of the book would be most effective as a separate episode, but still it depended too much on what had gone before. Faulkner offered to write a very brief introduction that would explain the relations of the characters. What he finally sent me is the much longer passage here printed as an appendix: a genealogy of the Compsons from their first arrival in this country. Whereas the novel is confined to a period of eighteen years ending in 1928, the genealogy goes back to the battle of Culloden in 1745, and forward to the year 1945, when Jason, last of the Compson males, has sold the family mansion, and Sister Caddy has last been heard of as the mistress of a German general. The novel that Faulkner wrote about the Compsons had long ago been given its final shape; but the pattern or body of legend behind the novel—and behind all his other books—was still developing.

Although the pattern is presented in terms of a single Mississippi county, it can be extended to the Deep South as a whole; and Faulkner always seems conscious of its wider application. He might have been thinking of his own novels when he described the ledgers in the commissary of the McCaslin plantation, in *Go Down, Moses*. They recorded, he said, "that slow trickle of molasses and meal and meat, of shoes and straw hats and overalls, of plowlines and collars and heelbolts and clevises, which returned each fall as cotton"—in a sense they were local and limited; but they were also "the continuation of that record which two hundred years had not been enough to complete and another hundred would not be enough to discharge; that chronicle which was a whole land in miniature, which multiplied and compounded was the entire South."

• • •

Faulkner's novels of contemporary Southern life continue the legend into a period that he regards as one of moral confusion and social decay. He is continually seeking in them for violent images to convey his sense of despair. *Sanctuary* is the most violent of all his novels; it is also the most popular and by no means the least important (in spite of Faulkner's comment that it was "a cheap idea . . . deliberately conceived to make money"). The story of Popeye and Temple Drake has more meaning than appears on a first hasty reading—the only reading that most of the critics have been willing to grant it. Popeye himself is one of several characters in Faulkner's novels who represent the mechanical civilization that has invaded and partly conquered the South. He is always described in mechanical terms: his eyes "looked like rubber knobs"; his face "just went awry, like the face of a wax doll set too near a hot fire and forgotten"; his tight suit and stiff hat were "all angles, like a modernistic lampshade"; and in general he had "that vicious depthless quality of stamped tin." Popeye was the son of a professional strikebreaker, from whom he had inherited syphilis, and the grandson of a pyromaniac. Like two other villains in Faulkner's novels, Joe Christmas and Januarius Jones, he had spent most of his childhood in an institution. He was the man "who made money and had nothing he could do with it, spend it for, since he knew that alcohol would kill him like poison, who had no friends and had never known a woman"—in other words, he was the compendium of all the hateful qualities that Faulkner assigns to finance capitalism. *Sanctuary* is not a connected allegory, as one critic explained it, but neither is it a mere accumulation of pointless horrors. It is an example of the Freudian method turned backward, being full of sexual nightmares that are in reality social symbols. It is somehow connected in the author's mind with what he regards as the rape and corruption of the South.

In all his novels dealing with the present, Faulkner makes it clear that the descendants of the old ruling caste have the wish but not the courage or the strength to prevent this new disaster. They are defeated by Popeye (like Horace Benbow), or they run away from him (like Gowan Stevens, who had gone to school at Virginia and learned to drink like a gentleman, but not to fight for his principles), or they are robbed and replaced in their positions of influence by the Snopeses (like old Bayard Sartoris, the president of the bank), or they drug themselves with eloquence and alcohol (like Quentin Compson's father), or they retire into the illusion of being inviolable Southern ladies (like Mrs. Compson, who says, "It can't be simply to flout and hurt me. Whoever God is, He would not permit that. I'm a lady."), or they dwell so much on the past that they are incapable of facing the present (like Reverend Hightower of *Light in August*), or they run from danger to danger (like young Bayard Sartoris) frantically seeking their own destruction. Faulkner's novels are full of well-meaning and even admirable persons, not only the grandsons of the cotton aristocracy, but also pine-hill farmers and storekeepers and sewing-machine agents and Negro cooks and sharecroppers; but they are almost all of them defeated by circumstances and they carry with them a sense of their own doom.

They also carry, whether heroes or villains, a curious sense of submission to their fate. "There is not one of Faulkner's characters," says André Gide in his dialogue on "The New American Novelists," "who properly speaking, has a soul"; and I think he means that not one of them exercises the faculty of conscious choice between good and evil. They are haunted, obsessed, driven forward by some inner necessity. Like Miss Rosa Coldfield, in *Absalom, Absalom!* they exist in "that dream state in which you run without moving from a terror in which you cannot believe, toward a safety in which you have no faith." Or, like the slaves freed by General Sherman's army, in *The Unvanquished*, they blindly follow the roads toward any river, believing that it will be their Jordan:

They were singing, walking along the road singing, not even looking to either side. The dust didn't even settle for two days, because all that night they still passed; we sat up listening to them, and the next morning every few yards along the road would be the old ones who couldn't keep up any more, sitting or lying down and even crawling along, calling to the others to help them; and the others—the young ones—not stopping, not even looking at them. "Going to Jordan," they told me. "Going to cross Jordan."

All Faulkner's characters, black and white, are a little like that. They dig for gold frenziedly after they have lost their hope of finding it (like Henry Armstid in *The Hamlet* and Lucas Beauchamp in *Go Down, Moses*); or they battle against and survive a Mississippi flood for the one privilege of returning to the state prison farm (like the tall convict in "Old Man"); or, a whole family together, they carry a body through flood and fire and corruption to bury it in the cemetery at Jefferson (like the Bundrens in *As I Lay Dying*); or they tramp the roads week after week in search of men who had promised but never intended to marry them (like Lena Grove, the pregnant woman of *Light in August*); or, pursued by a mob, they turn at the end to meet and accept death (like Joe Christmas in the same novel). Even when they seem to be guided by a conscious purpose, like Colonel Sutpen, it is not something they have chosen by an act of will, but something that has taken possession of them: Sutpen's great design was "not what he wanted to do but what he just had to do, had to do it whether he wanted to or not, because if he did not do it he knew that he could never live with himself for the rest of his life." In the same way, Faulkner himself writes, not what he wants to, but what he just has to write whether he wants to or not.

• • •

He is not primarily a novelist: that is, his stories do not occur to him in book-length units of 70,000 to 150,000 words. Almost all his novels have some weakness in structure. Some of them combine two or more themes having little relation to each other, like *Light in August*, while others, like *The Hamlet*, tend to resolve themselves into a series of episodes resembling beads on a string. In *The Sound and the Fury*, which is superb as a whole, we can't be sure that the four sections of the novel are presented in the most effective order; at any rate, we can't fully understand and perhaps can't even read the first section until we have read the other three. *Absalom, Absalom!* though pitched in too high a key, is structurally the soundest of all the novels in the Yoknapatawpha series; but even here the author's attention shifts halfway through the book from the principal theme of Colonel Sutpen's ambition to the secondary theme of incest and miscegenation.

Faulkner is best and most nearly himself either in long stories like "The Bear," in *Go Down, Moses*, and "Old Man," which was published as half of *The Wild Palms*, and "Spotted Horses," which was first printed separately, then greatly expanded and fitted into the loose framework of *The Hamlet*—all three stories are included in this volume; or else in the Yoknapatawpha saga as a whole. That is, he is most effective in dealing with the total situation that is always present in his mind as a pattern of the South; or else in shorter units that can be conceived and written in a single burst of creative effort. It is by his best that we should judge him, like every other author; and Faulkner at his best—even sometimes at his worst—has a power, a richness of life, an intensity to be found in no other American novelist of our time. He has—once more I am quoting from Henry James's essay on Hawthorne—"the element of simple genius, the quality of imagination."

Moreover, he has a brooding love for the land where he was

born and reared and where, unlike other writers of his generation, he has chosen to spend his life. It is ". . . this land, this South, for which God has done so much, with woods for game and streams for fish and deep rich soil for seed and lush springs to sprout it and long summers to mature it and serene falls to harvest it and short mild winters for men and animals." So far as Faulkner's country includes the Delta, it is also (in the words of old Ike McCaslin)

. . . this land which man has deswamped and denuded and derivered in two generations so that white men can own plantations and commute every night to Memphis and black men own plantations and ride in jimcrow cars to Chicago and live in millionaries' mansions on Lake Shore Drive, where white men rent farms and live like niggers and niggers crop on shares and live like animals, where cotton is planted and grows man-tall in the very cracks of the sidewalks, and usury and mortgage and bankruptcy and measureless wealth, Chinese and African and Aryan and Jew, all breed and spawn together.

Here are the two sides of Faulkner's feeling for the South: on the one side, an admiring and possessive love; on the other, a compulsive fear lest what he loves should be destroyed by the ignorance of its native serfs and the greed of traders and absentee landlords.

No other American writer takes such delight in the weather. He speaks in various novels of "the hot still pinewiney silence of the August afternoon"; of "the moonless September dust, the trees along the road not rising soaring as trees should but squatting like huge fowl"; of "the tranquil sunset of October mazy with windless wood-smoke"; of the "slow drizzle of November rain just above the ice point"; of "those windless Mississippi December days which are a sort of Indian summer's Indian summer"; or January and February when there is "no movement anywhere save the low constant smoke . . . and no sound save the chopping of axes and the lonely whistle of the daily trains." Spring in Faulkner's country is a hurried season, "all coming at once, pell mell and disordered, fruit and bloom and leaf, pied meadow and blossoming wood and the long fields shearing dark

out of winter's slumber, to the shearing plow." Summer is dust-
choked and blazing, and it lasts far into what should be autumn.
"That's the one trouble with this country," he says in *As I Lay
Dying*. "Everything, weather, all, hangs on too long. Like our
rivers, our land: opaque, slow, violet; shaping and creating
the life of man in its implacable and brooding image."

And Faulkner loves these people created in the image of the
land. After a second reading of his novels, you continue to be
impressed by his villains, Popeye and Jason and Joe Christmas
and Flem Snopes; but this time you find more place in your
memory for other figures standing a little in the background yet
presented by the author with quiet affection: old ladies like Miss
Jenny Du Pre, with their sharp-tongued benevolence; shrewd but
kindly bargainers like Ratliff, the sewing-machine agent, and Will
Varner, with his cotton gin and general store; long-suffering farm
wives like Mrs. Henry Armstid (whether her name is Lula or
Martha); and backwoods patriarchs like Pappy MacCullum, with
his six middle-aged but unmarried sons named after the generals
of Lee's army. You remember the big plantation houses that
collapse in flames as if a whole civilization were dying, but you
also remember men in patched and faded but quite clean overalls
sitting on the gallery—here in the North we should call it the
porch—of a crossroads store that is covered with posters advertising soft drinks and patent medicines; and you remember the
stories they tell while chewing tobacco until the suption is out
of it (everything in their world is reduced to anecdote, and every
anecdote is based on character). You remember Quentin Compson, not in his despairing moments, but riding with his father
behind the dogs as they quarter a sedge-grown hillside after
quail; and not listening to his father's story, but still knowing
every word of it, because, as he thought to himself, "You had
learned, absorbed it already without the medium of speech
somehow from having been born and living beside it, with it, as
children will and do: so that what your father was saying did not
tell you anything so much as it struck, word by word, the
resonant strings of remembering."

Faulkner's novels have the quality of being lived, absorbed, remembered rather than merely observed. And they have what is rare in the novels of our time, a warmth of family affection, brother for brother and sister, the father for his children—a love so warm and proud that it tries to shut out the rest of the world. Compared with that affection, married love is presented as something calculating, and illicit love as a consuming fire. And because the blood relationship is central in his novels, Faulkner finds it hard to create sympathetic characters between the ages of twenty and forty. He is better with children, Negro and white, and incomparably good with older people who preserve the standards that have come down to them "out of the old time, the old days."

In his later books, which have attracted so little attention that they seem to have gone unread, there is a quality not exactly new to Faulkner—it had appeared already in passages of *Sartoris* and *Sanctuary*—but now much stronger and no longer overshadowed by violence and horror. It is a sort of homely and sober-sided frontier humor that is seldom achieved in contemporary writing (except by Erskine Caldwell, another Southerner). The horse-trading episodes in *The Hamlet,* and especially the long story of the spotted ponies from Texas, might have been inspired by the Davy Crockett almanacs. "Old Man," the story of the convict who surmounted the greatest of all the Mississippi floods, might almost be a continuation of *Huckleberry Finn.* It is as if some older friend of Huck's had taken the raft and drifted on from Aunt Sally Phelps's farm into wilder adventures, described in a wilder style, among Chinese and Cajuns and bayous crawling with alligators. In a curious way, Faulkner combines two of the principal traditions in American letters: the tradition of psychological horror, often close to symbolism, that begins with Charles Brockden Brown, our first professional novelist, and extends through Poe, Melville, Henry James (in his later stories), Stephen Crane, and Hemingway; and the other tradition of frontier humor and realism, beginning with Augustus Longstreet's *Georgia Scenes* and having Mark Twain as its best example.

But the American author he most resembles is Hawthorne, for all their polar differences. They stand to each other as July to December, as heat to cold, as swamp to mountain, as the luxuriant to the meager but perfect, as planter to Puritan; and yet Hawthorne had much the same attitude toward New England that Faulkner has toward the South, together with a strong sense of regional particularity. The Civil War made Hawthorne feel that "the North and the South were two distinct nations in opinions and habits, and had better not try to live under the same institutions." In the spring of 1861, he wrote to his Bowdoin classmate Horatio Bridge, "We were never one people and never really had a country."—"New England," he said a little later, "is quite as large a lump of earth as my heart can really take in." But it was more than a lump of earth for him; it was a lump of history and a permanent state of consciousness. Like Faulkner in the South, he applied himself to creating its moral fables and elaborating its legends, which existed, as it were, in his solitary heart. Pacing the hillside behind his house in Concord, he listened for a voice; you might say that he lay in wait for it, passively but expectantly, like a hunter behind a rock; then, when it had spoken, he transcribed its words—more slowly and carefully than Faulkner, it is true; with more form and less fire, but with the same essential fidelity. If the voice was silent, he had nothing to write. "I have an instinct that I had better keep quiet," he said in a letter to his publisher. "Perhaps I shall have a new spirit of vigor if I wait quietly for it; perhaps not." Faulkner is another author who has to wait for the spirit and the voice. Essentially he is not a novelist, in the sense of not being a writer who sets out to observe actions and characters, then fits them into the architectural framework of a story. For all the weakness of his own poems, he is an epic or bardic poet in prose, a creator of myths that he weaves together into a legend of the South.

Gary J. Scrimgeour

(b. 1934)

At present, many persons involved in teaching and in literary scholarship are writing critical essays for scholarly and professional journals. These writers, generally speaking, focus their attention on questions of explication or viewpoints on controversial subjects.

The explicative essays usually attempt to cast new light on a well-known poem or other literary work. A writer, for example, may have found another explanation for a familiar passage, or he may suddenly have discovered, he believes, a fresh insight into the total work. The essays treating controversial questions resemble the argument of the lawyer before the bar of the court; they state a thesis and then attempt to substantiate it. Consequently, they are, in essence, either defenses or attacks.

This latter kind of essay provides wonderfully interesting reading. One peruses it as he follows the arguments of the exciting legal case. He weighs and considers with the advocate; he admires strengths and scores flaws in reasoning; and he endorses and dismisses deductions and conclusions as he evaluates the supporting evidence. In short, he plays the role of judge and jury, eventually agreeing in whole or in part with the case as presented.

The service provided by this type of essay is invaluable. In its most powerful form, it may overturn one's settled viewpoint. In lesser situations, it may alter a smaller part of one's opinion. In all situations, however, it forces one to re-examine his basis for holding a specific conclusion. Hence it serves as a kind of testing or hardening agent within the field of criticism.

In the essay below, Gary J. Scrimgeour challenges widespread conclusions regarding the merits of F. Scott Fitzgerald's The Great Gatsby *(1925). Not only does he disagree with the prevailing estimate of this novel but he advances and strives to defend a less favorable evaluation.*

The approach of this essay is a common one. The author has chosen another novel as a measuring rod and has made comparisons and contrasts in an effort to prove his point.

Professor Scrimgeour, who has taught and lectured at several colleges and universities in the United States, holds the A.B. degree from the University of Sydney (Australia), the A.M. from Washington University, and the Ph.D. from Princeton University. Currently, he is engaged in editing a 100-volume edition of nineteenth century British and American plays.

Against *The Great Gatsby*

Since the Fitzgerald revival took shape, we have all tended to regard *The Great Gatsby* as the redemption for the manifest sins of Fitzgerald's other works. It is just good enough, just lyrical enough, just teachable-to-freshmen enough (and more than "American" enough) for unwary souls to call it a classic. Its superiority is seen in its craftsmanship, especially in a tighter structure that gives much greater depth and integrity to its content. It is usually difficult to evaluate the truth of claims that an author is both a fine technician and an intelligent moralist, but in this case Joseph Conrad's *Heart of Darkness* offers an appropriate measuring-stick. Conrad, as is well known, stood persistently firm in Fitzgerald's disorderly pantheon. There is evidence especially in *The Great Gatsby* that Fitzgerald's admiration extended as far as imitation, and the similarity between these two works enables us to challenge claims for Fitzgerald's intellectual and artistic merit by showing how much better Conrad could think and write.[1]

[1] This essay brings a new point of view and fresh material to a controversy raised by previous critics. Rather than expressing my agreements or disagree-

The most important of the similarities between the two novels is the use of the first-person narrator as a character in his own story. In both novels a thoughtful man (Carraway, Marlow) recounts his moralized tale of the fate of an exceptional man (Gatsby, Kurtz). Their tales are essentially adventure stories. Both narrators are stirred by restlessness to seek exotic experience, encounter their "hero" by chance, become unwillingly intrigued by him, and are caught up in an intimacy which ends with the hero's death. Both are forced to pay tribute to their dead in the form of resounding lies (Marlow to Kurtz's fiancée; Carraway at the inquest), and then they retire for wound-licking and the later creation of their understated moralizations. Marlow and Carraway are alike in nature as well as function. Neither story would be about men possessed of absurd but enormous romantic dreams unless both narrators were of the kind of sensitivity that enabled them to see *la condition humaine* in the fates of irritating and egocentric individuals. Both feel a simultaneous repulsion and attraction for their heroes, dislike for their personality countered by admiration for their magnitude. Both men pretend to open-mindedness, modesty, and honesty. It is certain Marlow learns something from Kurtz's fate; it is claimed that Carraway learns from Gatsby's failure.

I give special emphasis to the use of the first-person narrator in

---

ments in a series of footnotes, I refer the reader to the following articles: R. W. Stallman, "Gatsby and the Hole in Time," *Modern Fiction Studies,* I (Nov. 1955), 2–16; T. Hanzo, "The Theme and the Narrator of *The Great Gatsby,*" *Modern Fiction Studies,* II (Winter, 1956–57), 183–190; J. Thale, "The Narrator as Hero," *Twentieth Century Literature,* III (July 1957), 69–73. On Conrad's influence on Fitzgerald see James E. Miller, *F. Scott Fitzgerald: His Art and His Technique* (New York, 1964), especially pp. 92–95, 106–113; R. W. Stallmann, "Conrad and *The Great Gatsby,*" *Twentieth Century Literature,* I (April, 1955), 5–12; John Kuehl, "Scott Fitzgerald's Reading," *Princeton University Library Chronicle,* XXII (Winter, 1961), 58–59. Miller writes: "Probably the greatest influence on Fitzgerald during the gestation period of *The Great Gatsby* was Joseph Conrad" (p. 92). The parallels between *Heart of Darkness* and *The Great Gatsby* are sufficiently striking to suggest direct influence, but even if Conrad were not the source of Fitzgerald's technique, the Marlow stories would remain valid as a standard of comparison for the use of first-person narration.

the two novels for a particular reason. One forgets how recently we have come to see that Marlow is a character in the story he tells, rather than a translucent medium for transmitting a tale. In some novels the first-person narrator is merely a convenience in achieving selectivity, and in others at the opposite extreme the narrator himself is the object of our study. In *Heart of Darkness* both purposes are served; Marlow is both a technical device and part of the subject-matter. In *The Great Gatsby* the situation of Carraway is the same as that of Marlow, but I believe that Fitzgerald, never a great critical theorist, did not realize the dual nature of his narrator and therefore handled him very clumsily— and very revealingly.

When a narrator is also a character, with all that this implies of personality, individuality, and responsibility, we readers are forced to be more alert. We must question the accuracy of the narrator's account. When he makes judgments, we have to decide whether his special interests betray the truth and whether the meaning of each particular event and of the whole fable differs from the interpretation he offers. In *Heart of Darkness* Conrad is highly conscious of these problems and takes steps to solve them. Not all of the novel is in Marlow's words. He is presented and characterized by another narrator. He is given a setting, and he tells his story for an audience. He interrupts his own narrative several times, once to comment that "Of course in this you fellows see more than I could then. You see me, whom you know . . . ." By thus drawing attention to his existence as a character in the story he tells, he refuses to allow us to ignore his subjectivity, so that it becomes difficult to read *Heart of Darkness* without realizing that it is not just a fable about universals but also an interpreted personal experience.

Things are otherwise with *The Great Gatsby*. The entire novel is the narrator's written word, and with peril do we underestimate the significance of the change in manner from Marlow's oral delivery, full of hesitations, temporizings, and polished lack of polish, to the smooth veneer of Carraway's public, written narrative. It is quite legitimate to ask why Fitzgerald should follow

Conrad closely in narrative technique except for those elements which warn us that the narrator may be giving us a truth which is anything but unvarnished. Why remove Conrad's surrogate audience and inset narrative? Why exchange the honest hesitancy of Marlow's manner for Carraway's literary imitation of charming spontaneity? Carraway is a disarmingly frank chap, and, as with most such fellows, his self-revelations are highly contrived. Is his opening characterization of himself as accurate as it is influential? During the narrative he tells us what to think of his actions, but should we judge by what he says or what he does? It is an obvious enough point, but it is exactly here that readers go astray and that Fitzgerald's artistic and ethical inferiority lie. Conrad knew that problems would arise and provided material to alert the reader. Fitzgerald promptly abandoned that material and led readers to follow Carraway's interpretation of events without realizing that there should be a difference, a gap, a huge gulf, between Carraway's and their conceptions of the affair.

Let us examine the relationship between the two novels more deeply. In *Heart of Darkness* the point of the use of a first-person narrator is that what has happened to the central figure is explained by what we see happen to the narrator; and, reciprocally, the weakness evident in the central figure reveals a similar but unsuspected flaw in the character of the narrator. Kurtz is presented to us at the moment when failure overwhelms him, and it is in the development of Marlow that we see the causes of Kurtz's defeat. Marlow feels and explains to us his awareness of the same decay that overcame Kurtz. The melodrama accompanying Kurtz's magnificence prevents its direct presentation, but it can be comprehended through the more life-size abilities and weaknesses of Marlow. In return, the fate of Kurtz reveals the peril of weaknesses which Marlow shares, and we thus realize that the same destruction could overcome the balanced, "normal" Marlow, and by corollary, any human being.

A very similar relationship exists between narrator and central figure in *The Great Gatsby*, but, unless Fitzgerald was much subtler than anyone has yet suggested, I do not think he realized it. While he tried to create a Marlovian narrator by asserting that Carraway has all of Marlow's desirable characteristics, his abandonment of the material which would allow an objective evaluation of his narrator's character shows that he understood neither the full purpose of Conrad's technique nor that Carraway's character is in fact very different from what Carraway claims it to be. Indeed Fitzgerald reveals a fault frequent in romantic writers, the inability to understand the true natures of the characters he created.

Take, for example, Gatsby himself, a character who usually and despite Carraway's warnings wins grudging admiration from readers. Like all romantic ideals, he is what personally we would not be so foolish as to imitate but nonetheless admire for its grandeur. It is refreshing to see, without Carraway's intervening intelligence, exactly to what sort of person we are giving our sympathy. Gatsby is a boor, a roughneck, a fraud, a criminal. His taste is vulgar, his behavior ostentatious, his love adolescent, his business dealings ruthless and dishonest. He is interested in people—most notably in Carraway himself—only when he wants to use them. His nice gestures stem from the fact that, as one character comments, "he doesn't want any trouble with *any*body." Like other paranoiacs, he lives in a childish tissue of lies and is unaware of the existence of an independent reality in which other people have separate existences. What lifts him above ordinary viciousness is the magnitude of his ambition and the glamor of his illusion. "Can't repeat the past?" he says to Carraway. "Why of course you can . . . ." To Gatsby, to repeat the past is to suppress unwanted elements of it and to select only nice things from which to make an uncontaminated present. Grand this defiance of reality may seem; silly it nonetheless is. Indeed it is no more than "a promise that the rock of the world was founded securely on a fairy's wing," and it crumbles as soon as it encounters reality in the form of Daisy. As long as his life is controlled by his own unattained desires, Gatsby's vision remains safe; he continually recreates the present in the light of his own needs.

But as soon as Daisy's independent will enters the dream, Gatsby is forced to attach himself to the real world, to lose his freedom of action, and to pay the penalty for denying the past in having that past destroy the romantic present.

Gatsby's moral error is at least as clear as Kurtz's, and yet we give him our sympathy. Sneakingly we like Gatsby, while I defy anybody to *like* Kurtz. Partly this is because of Gatsby's adherence to the official American sexual code, the only moral code he does obey (whereas Kurtz has his native wife and indulges in "unspeakable rites"), but the major reason for the difference in our attitudes to the two men is the different reactions of Carraway and Marlow to their heroes' moral weaknesses. Where Marlow ends up loathing Kurtz, Carraway specifically tells us that he is not disgusted by Gatsby but by the mysterious "foul dust that floated in the wake of his dreams." Fitzgerald provides many obscure but pretty metaphors to evoke Carraway's ambiguous attitude to Gatsby's faults, and I think he is forced into metaphor because only metaphor will conceal the fact that the story as Carraway tells it is a paean to schizophrenia. Carraway is not deceived, of course, into admiring the superficialities of Gatsby's character and behavior; he represents everything for which Caraway professes an "unaffected scorn." And yet at the same time something makes Gatsby "exempt" from Carraway's reaction to the rest of the world. Carraway tells us that Gatsby's great redeeming quality is his "heightened sensitivity to the promises of life." Whether we criticize or praise Carraway for being sufficiently young to believe that life makes promises, we should notice at once that it is the promises—not the realities—of life to which Gatsby is sensitive, and that Carraway is in fact praising that very attempt to deny the past and reality whose failure he is recounting.

This flaw in Carraway's moral vision is illuminating because it shows that Gatsby stands in relationship to Carraway as Daisy stands to Gatsby. Gatsby represents the promises of life with which the rootless, twenty-nine-year-old, hazy-minded Carraway is as obsessed as is Gatsby himself. It is important in this respect to notice how closely Carraway's development is tied to Gatsby's and that, just as Kurtz's career is paralleled up to a point by that of Marlow, so does Carraway's reflect Gatsby's. It is not simply that Carraway becomes emotionally involved in Gatsby's affairs but that his attitude towards his own life is entirely dependent on his feelings about Gatsby. As one small example from many, his most lyrical expression of the rapture he feels for the East comes immediately after he has been convinced of the genuineness of Gatsby's romantic history. More important, his love affair with Jordan Baker is a second-hand impulse stirred by her revelations of Gatsby's love for Daisy. These are Carraway's words:

Unlike Gatsby and Tom Buchanan, I had no girl whose disembodied face floated along the dark cornices and blinding signs, and so I drew up the girl beside me, tightening my arms. Her wan, scornful mouth smiled, and so I drew her up again closer, this time to my face.

As though they were shadows of Gatsby's emotions, Carraway's feelings for the city and his love for Jordan both instantly collapse as soon as Daisy's infidelity to Gatsby is apparent, and he returns to the Mid-West, to what had previously seemed the "ragged edge of the universe" but has now become a haven. Gatsby's defeat brings down Carraway's dream as well.

In fact Gatsby himself is Carraway's romantic dream. The only difference between the world that Carraway despises and the man he admires is that Gatsby does things more spectacularly. In not seeing this, Carraway reveals that just like Gatsby he is willing to accept only those parts of reality which please him. He wants Gatsby to be different from the rest of the world. If we look at Carraway's behavior more closely, we may see that he shares others of Gatsby's failings, and that if Gatsby is no romantic hero, Carraway is even less the pleasant, anonymous, and highly principled character that he seems to be.

Were Carraway to characterize himself in a traditional phrase rather than metaphor, that phrase would be "man of principle." And yet his principles are challenged by the person who is presumably closest to him: Jordan Baker. Early in their relationship, Carraway and Jordan have a conversation which ends with Jordan saying, "I hate careless people. That's why I like you." After the sudden collapse of their affair, Jordan returns to this conversation in their last interview, when she accuses him of having thrown her over:

> "Oh, and do you remember"—she added—"a conversation we had once about driving a car?"
> "Why—not exactly."
> "You said a bad driver was only safe until she met another bad driver? Well, I met another bad driver, didn't I? I mean it was careless of me to make such a bad guess. I thought you were rather an honest, straightforward person. I thought it was your secret pride."
> "I'm thirty," I said. "I'm five years too old to lie to myself and call it honor."

Jordan is right about Carraway's character. This crisis of their affair reveals to her what she must have suspected before, that Carraway is neither as honest nor as high-principled as he might like to seem. It is interesting to note that she accuses him of the same "carelessness" that is the refrain in Carraway's attack on the Buchanans and the rest of the world. Her accusation suggests that at least in his dealings with her he has been as shabby as anyone else in East Egg.

And certainly his behavior with Jordan is no worse than the rest of his personal relationships, from the girl back home to Gatsby himself. Involved as he is with Daisy, Tom, Gatsby, and the Wilsons, he never acts well, just weakly. He fails to sense any obligation to avoid the flagrant dishonesty of his position and— far from feeling any qualms about playing either God or pander —he actually helps the others to continue activities which he later claims to regard as unworthy. His main principle is to say nothing. Most important is the final falsehood into which his loyalty to the dead Gatsby forces him. There is no intimation at all that at the inquest he feels his position of concealing the true facts to be in any way anomalous. Where we might reasonably expect some explanation of his attitude, he dismisses the event with the comment that "all this part of it seemed remote and unessential." He

simply prefers to conceal the truth rather than have the story
"served up in racy pasquinade" and praises Mrs. Wilson's sister
for "character" when she, "who might have said anything, didn't
say a word." Is his behavior here, or even his attitude, superior
to that of Tom, Daisy, Gatsby, or any other of the inhabitants
of the ashland? Let us not be deceived by his condescension
towards Wolfsheim's "gonnegtions" or his smugness about people
who cheat at golf.

Another significant episode occurs near the end of the novel,
when he encounters Tom for the last time. At first he avoids him
because he is convinced that Tom was the cause of Gatsby's
death. He says that he could neither forgive nor like Tom and
Daisy because of their talent for "smashing up things" and retreating into "their vast carelessness," a firm moral judgment in
words which we might expect from a principled man. But let us
look at the act that follows:

> I shook hands with him; it seemed silly not to, for I felt suddenly as
> though I were talking to a child. Then he went into the jewelry store
> to buy a pearl necklace—or perhaps only a pair of cuff-buttons—rid of
> my provincial squeamishness forever.

While shaking hands with Tom may be an urbane gesture to
avoid embarrassment, it is certainly not honest either to Tom or to
Carraway's principles, and to turn from recognition of the villainy
of Tom's behavior to dismissal of it as the behavior of a child is
not a sign of moral profundity or consistency. Carraway's honesty
is a matter not of principle, but of convenience. (Whether the
reader likes or dislikes men of principle is irrelevant—we are concerned only with Carraway's claims to be one.)

One could attack Carraway's nature further; to one who dislikes him, the opening and closing pages of the novel are a lexicon
of vanity. But the key issue is undoubtedly his honesty, because
that provides the basis of the reader's reaction to the novel. It is
here that he contrasts most strongly with Conrad's Marlow. For
example, both Marlow and Carraway are reticent about many
important matters, but when Marlow refuses to linger on a sub-

ject (such as the rites in which Kurtz participates) it is because
enough has already been said; more would be too much. Carraway's reticences, however, verge on falsehood. Instead of stopping short with just the right impression, they often succeed in
giving the wrong impression. The lie that Carraway acquiesces in
at the inquest and the complaisance he reveals in finally shaking
hands with Tom have as their motive no nobler desire than to
let sleeping dogs lie, whereas Marlow, who finds himself pushed
at the end of *Heart of Darkness* into an agonizing untruth, lies
because the truth would be infinitely more damaging and useless.
The truth about Mrs. Wilson's death could be damaging, but it is
more likely to be simply incommoding. We have, in any case, no
sign from Carraway that he even considered the problem.

Honesty can in the end be based only on some kind of powerful
drive, and this is something that Carraway does not possess. The
real nature of his principles appears if we contrast his own
estimate of his integrity with a similar statement by Marlow.
Long after the events which wrapped him inextricably in falsehood, Carraway writes, "Everyone suspects himself of at least one
of the cardinal virtues, and this is mine: I am one of the few
honest people that I have ever known." Marlow, on the occasion
not of a falsehood but of a minor false impression, says:

> You know I hate, detest and can't bear a lie, not because I am
> straighter than the rest of us, but simply because it appalls me. There
> is a taint of death, a flavor of mortality in lies—which is exactly what
> I hate and detest in the world—what I want to forget. It makes me
> miserable and sick, like biting something rotten would do. Tempera
> ment, I suppose.

The difference between Marlow's and Carraway's words is the
difference between a man who cannot deny reality and a man
who cannot face it. Both men feel deeply, but Marlow, at the cost
of real pain, has to push forward until he understands the meaning of what he feels, until he is honest with himself, whereas
Carraway stops short with whatever feeling he can conveniently
bear, dreading what further effort might uncover. Both men

record as much as they understand, but Marlow's honesty forces him to a much deeper understanding than Carraway achieves. To Marlow, feeling is part of the process that creates understanding, and honesty is his strongest feeling; to Carraway, feeling is the end product of experience, and honesty a matter for self-congratulation.

If the reader cannot accept Carraway's statements at face value, then the integrity of the technique of the novel is called in question. Rather than accepting what Carraway claims to be the effect of the events on his nature, the reader must stand further off and examine Carraway's development as though he were any other character, in which case a second vital weakness becomes obvious. Again like Gatsby, he never realizes the truth about himself, and despite the lesson of Gatsby's fate he fails to come to self-knowledge. There is a curious use of the conditional in Carraway's introduction to his story. He writes, "If personality is an unbroken series of successful gestures, then there was something gorgeous about [Gatsby], some heightened sensitivity to the promises of life." The reason for Carraway's hesitancy over a matter that should present no problem is that he himself is trying to contruct a personality out of a series of gestures such as the "clean break" with Jordan or the final handshake with Tom, behavior which results from his inability to decide what he should be doing or why he should be doing it. He is a moral eunuch, ineffectual in any real human situation that involves more than a reflex action determined by social pattern or the desire to avoid trouble with "*any*body." At one stage Carraway senses that something is wrong and suggests that Tom, Gatsby, Daisy, Jordan, and he all "possessed some deficiency in common," but he fails to see that the deficiency is the hollowness in their moral natures that leaves them prey to self-deception and "carelessness."

Consequently Carraway's distinctiveness as a character is that he fails to learn anything from his story, that he can continue to blind himself even after his privileged overview of Gatsby's fate. The defeat evident in his disillusionment is followed not by progress but by retreat. He returns not only to his safe environment in the Mid-West but also to the same attitudes from which he started. One cannot praise him for being disillusioned with the ashland life of the East. For him to be disillusioned with values that are, after all, transparently unworthy, is not as remarkable as the fact that he remains enamored of the person who represents those values in their most brilliant and tempting form. He refuses to admit that his alliance with Gatsby, his admiration for the man, results from their sharing the same weakness. Writing when he has had time to deliberate on Gatsby's fate, he says, "Only Gatsby . . . was exempt from my reaction—Gatsby, who represented everything for which I have an unaffected scorn." This is precisely the attitude which he held long before, at the height of his infatuation with Gatsby's dream. He has learned nothing. His failure to come to any self-knowledge makes him like the person who blames the stone for stubbing his toe. It seems inevitable that he will repeat the same mistakes as soon as the feeling that "temporarily closed out my interest in the abortive sorrows and short-winded elations of men" has departed. The world will not, despite his wishes, remain "at a sort of moral attention forever."

Because of the weakness of Carraway's character, the meaning of *The Great Gatsby* is much blacker than that of *Heart of Darkness*. In the latter Marlow progresses through his encounter with Kurtz to a greater self-knowledge; and even if we consider self-knowledge a pitiful reward to snatch from life, we must still admit that it has a positive value and that the gloom of the story is not unrelieved. Such cautious optimism is apparent only if we can see first that the narrator of *Heart of Darkness* is a reliable purveyor of truth, and second that he has come to greater self-knowledge. It is to the end of emphasizing these qualities that Conrad fashions the structure of the novel. The beginning of the work and the interruptions in Marlow's narrative have the purpose of reminding us at key points that the story is being refracted through Marlow's mind and that he is a character whose reactions are as important as his tale. The most emphasized of Marlow's qualities are his self-knowledge (we recall his Buddha-like pose) and the stress of his desire to fight his way through the material of his experience to reveal the truth. We can accept Marlow's recounting of the events only if we believe that, both as narrator and as person, his judgment is to be respected, and Conrad takes some of the novel out of Marlow's hands for exactly this purpose.

But we have seen that it is just here that Fitzgerald makes a major change in the structure of *The Great Gatsby*. There is little doubt that we are intended to see Carraway both as a reliable narrator and as a character learning from experience, but because we see only his version of the events and of his character, an objective evaluation is difficult. When we do attempt to be objective, we find that we have to impugn Carraway's honesty as a narrator and his self-awareness as a person. In this way Fitzgerald's change in technique makes *The Great Gatsby* a much more pessimistic novel than *Heart of Darkness*. If the story means (as Fitzgerald probably intended) that Gatsby's romantic dream is magnificent and Carraway's change a growth, then we have a somber but reasonably constructive view of life. But if our narrator turns out to be corrupt, if our Adam is much less innocent than we suspected, then despair replaces elegy. Had Carraway been defeated by the impersonal forces of an evil world in which he was an inffectual innocent, his very existence—temporary or not—would lighten the picture. But his defeat is caused by something that lies within himself: his own lack of fibre, his own willingness to deny reality, his own substitution of dreams for knowledge of self and the world, his own sharing in the very vices of which his fellow men stand accused.

The irony produced by a comparison with the superficially gloomier *Heart of Darkness* is the realization that while Marlow sees the events as typical and Carraway as crucial, in effect they are crucial for Marlow and typical for Carraway. Where Marlow gains an expansiveness of outlook from his experiences, we find Carraway saying that "life is much more successfully looked at from a single window, after all," surely a supreme expression of the ethical vacuity which brought about his sufferings in the first place. If the one person who had both the talent and the opportunity to realize his own weaknesses remains unchanged, then we have a world of despair. Perhaps in this light the final image of the novel gains a new felicitousness: "So we beat on, boats against the current, borne back ceaselessly into the past."

It is usually considered that Fitzgerald intended *The Great Gatsby* to warn us against the attempt to deny reality. My interpretation of the novel goes further to suggest that unwittingly, through careless technique and cloudy thinking, Fitzgerald in fact created a novel which says that it is impossible for us to face reality. One would like to think that Fitzgerald knew what he was doing, that in the opening pages he intended Carraway's priggishness and enervation to warn the reader against the narrator. Certainly there is enough evidence in the novel to support such a view, which can no more be completely disproven than can similar readings of *Moll Flanders* and *Gulliver's Travels,* but before we accept it we have to answer two questions: was the young Fitzgerald capable of such ironic perception, which would involve an extraordinarily complex attitude not just to his characters but to his readers and to himself as writer and individual? and if so, why did he choose deliberately not to make the irony clearer to the reader, especially with the example of Conrad in front of him? My own belief is that Fitzgerald achieved something other than he intended. Knowing that he always had difficulty in distinguishing himself from his characters (and admitted to being even Gatsby!), we can legitimately suspect that Carraway's failure is Fitzgerald's failure, and that Fitzgerald himself was chronically unaware of the dangers of romanticism. If Daisy is Gatsby's dream, and Gatsby is Carraway's dream, one suspects that Carraway is Fitzgerald's dream.

Much of *The Great Gatsby* is of course brilliant, and its historical position as one of the earliest American novels to attempt twentieth-century techniques guarantees it a major position in our literary hierarchy. But it is usually praised for the wrong reasons, and we should take care that Fitzgerald does not become our dream, as the recent spate of biographies and articles might suggest. The character of Carraway as Fitzgerald saw it, the innocent Adam in the school of hard knocks, appeals to our liking for sentimental pessimism; critics and teachers can overvalue romanticism as much as authors, and thus damage our literary tradition by mistaking delicate perceptions for sound thinking. Unless we wish to teach what Fitzgerald intended rather than what he wrote, unless we prefer an attractive exterior to an honest interior, unless we cherish a novel because we think it says the things we want to hear, then we should be very precise about the value of what the novel actually says. Ultimately, to withdraw our sympathy from Carraway, even to lower our estimation of Fitzgerald's skill, is not to depreciate but to change the worth of *The Great Gatsby*. It may serve to teach both readers and writers that careful technique is worth more to a novel than verbal brilliance, and that honest, hard thinking is more profitable than the most sensitive evocation of sympathy. We may no longer be able to read it as a description of the fate that awaits American innocence, but we can see it as a record of the worse dangers that confront American sentimentality.

John Simon

(b. 1925)

Of the many areas of everyday life wherein criticism provides a valuable service for the non-specialist in literature, one of the most immediate is the review of the dramatic production. The inveterate theatre-goer likes to identify beforehand the plays worth seeing, and afterwards, he likes to compare his appraisals with those of the established critics. In addition, he usually evinces great interest in the overall assessments of the entire season. He seeks to learn which plays, in the opinion of the best critics, are likely to win the prestigious annual awards and, more important, which plays are likely to survive their own time.

In the essay below, John Simon, theatre critic for The Hudson Review, *weighs the 1968–69 season in retrospect. He cites the plays which received the greatest acclaim and discusses them critically. In the process, Simon reveals acutely his own standards for the dramatic production as well as his concept of the theatre as an art form. In short, he invokes not only his critical theory but his explanation of the play as an entity in the sphere of art.*

Especially interesting is Simon's view of the responsibility of the artist to traditional practices and philosophies. While great or important works have sometimes been produced by the artist who departs from the tradition—as for example, Eugene O'Neill in the realm of drama—the art form itself may suffer, on occasions, from the treatment accorded it by individual artists. This latter situation is of special concern to Simon.

Of further interest is the author's comments on acting. As the most naive of theatre devotees knows, the interpretations of the actors—as individuals and as a cast—are the medium through which one meets the play itself. Hence arises the self-evident truth that the finer the actors' performances, the better the circumstances for judging the play competently; or to state the matter in other, more blunt phraseolog'', poor acting can obscure the finest of plays. Therefore, any criticism of a dramatic production must be a double undertaking; it must be a criticism of the play itself, and it must be a criticism of the persons responsible for the presentation.

John Simon, born in Yugoslavia, received his early education in Yugoslav, English, and American schools and his higher education at Harvard (A.B., 1946; A.M., 1948; Ph.D., 1959). After teaching at Harvard, the University of Washington, the Massachusetts Institute of Technology, and Bard College, Simon left the academic world to confine his efforts to writing. His most widely read books are Acid Test *(1963), a collection of essays and reviews in various arts, and* Private Screenings *(1967), a collection of film criticism. In addition, he has edited several volumes on individual authors and anthologies of verse and short stories— as well as producing numerous reviews, poems, and translations. Currently, he is preparing another collection of essays. His professional attachments of the moment are drama critic for* The Hudson Review *and* New York *magazine and film critic for* The New Leader.

Theatre Chronicle, 1968–1969

If Albee were not so arrogant, one would view his desperate stratagems with pity. When you have failed with every kind of play, including adaptations of novels and other people's plays, the last remaining maneuver is the nonplay. Finding himself in a box, Albee has contrived two interlocking nonplays, based, apparently, on a mathematical error: it is by multiplying, not by adding, minuses that you get a plus. *Box* and *Quotations from Chairman Mao Tse-Tung*, when run together like two ink blots of different colors, raise the Rorschach test to new dramatic heights.

Box is a fifteen-to-twenty-minute taped monologue piped into a darkened theatre with only the outlines of a large empty box gleaming in ultra-violet light on the black stage. As you gaze at this piece of hollow geometry for a *mauvais quart d'heure,* Ruth White's voice from the P.A. system flutteringly harangues you with platitudes and non sequiturs about life and art, including some impudent but prestigious references to Bach and to our arts slipping into mere crafts—as if this redundant message were necessary when we have *Box* before or (considering the placing of the loudspeaker) behind us. Albee's renowned command of language once again manifests itself in such hearty solecisms as "off of."

Lights go on as the box gradually fills up with a schematic setting: on the deck of an ocean liner, Chairman Mao stands erect, an old woman squats in a corner by her shabby suitcase, and a minister and a "Long Winded Lady" (as the program identifies her) lounge in deck chairs. There ensues what Albee no doubt thinks of as a fugue for speaking voices. The old woman recites a trashy piece of thirties doggerel, "Over the Hill to the Poorhouse," by one Will Carlton or Carleton, whoever he may be, about a poor, creaky critter whose ungrateful children consign her sunset years to the poorhouse. This is interrupted periodically by Chairman Mao (who strips off a rubber Mao mask to reveal beneath it—a Mao face; he is nothing but a walking set of Chinese boxes); he recites endlessly from his aphorisms. This is interrupted in turn by the Long Winded Lady, who relates her life with her husband, his death, her estrangement from her daughter, and her attempted suicide by leaping from just such an ocean liner. The clergyman responds to her with various more or less commensurate gestures, but never utters a syllable. This is, presumably, the Cagey element in the fugue. Mao paces about the stage and the entire auditorium; the old woman makes one slow symbolic trajectory toward an upstage perch; the LWL and the minister walk about a little. The three voices spell one an-

other, and are joined, toward the end of the play, by the taped
voice from *Box* interjecting some of its own previous pronouncements in what is supposed to be an ironically pregnant *stretto*.

But, alas, even though some members of the sparse audience
laughed relentlessly at the satiric depths they perceived in the
random juxtapositions of these unrelated voices, I felt doused
with discrepancy. Rather than as a fugue, the exercise struck me
as a piece of vocal *cadavre exquis*, without even the amusing
trouvailles bequeathed by Chance on that famous surrealist
parlor game. One can perhaps extract some quasi-meanings (like
teeth from a toothless mouth): the commonplaces of communism
vs. the banalities of the bourgeoisie; the parallel miseries of the
rich and the poor; the shibboleths of Mao's gospel vs. the silences
of the man of God. But these are not so much legitimate explica-
tions as counsels of despair. In a fugue, in any case, there is
development. Here, once the quartet is visually and vocally
presented, there is nowhere to go. The grandam recites her WPA
poetastery with ever campier emphases, and with increasingly
dogged repetition of the wretched verses; Mao, sprouting successively from opposite proscenium boxes, spouts the same
minimal maxims; the clergyman produces more and more D. W.
Griffithish faces and gestures. The one thing that moves on freely
is the LWL's narrative—but that is just what it is: a rambling, pet-
tifogging, pseudoliterate monologue of strictly nondramatic
verbiage.

We get the same ambitious, artificial, circumlocutory prose
Albee keeps elaborating in his later, sterile works. It consists of
false starts, emendations, indirections, apologies, and general
syntactic deviousness. One guesses that Albee imagines this to be
some wonderful cross between Beckett and Joyce; in fact, it is a
barren, puerile mannerism. It suggests a kind of doddering
pedantry that Albee might attribute to a particular character—if
it were not so often out of character, and if a good many of his
more recent favorite personages did not speak exactly, or in-
exactly, like this. And always that pathetic intellectual climbing of
the (insufficiently) self-educated: "They didn't know who Trol-

lope was!—that is a life for you," complains the LWL, and one winces for Albee. For behind such outcries we have come to recognize the genteel author's feelings of superiority over, and especially *against*, the unwashed that surrounded him, or that he chooses to surround himself with. Significantly, this motif is equally frequent in Tennessee Williams. And Trollope as status symbol! Next thing it will be Rupert Brooke.

But suppose it were the character that is being ridiculed. So much the worse for play and playwright; it would mean that they are suffering from delusions of being Beckett, who alone can get away with this sort of thing by virtue of much greater sensitivity to words and to the essential foibles of human nature. There is even a conscious or unconscious allusion to Beckett in the LWL's repeated references to falling and "all that falling," including, if my memory isn't playing Albeesque tricks on me, to falling *upward*. Typical of this monologue is a line like "that was more seeing than landing—if you like a pun," with that built-in escape clause yielding irritation rather than mitigation. Or take this, from an evocation of the LWL's husband: "His scrotum was large, and not only for small men. His penis also long and of a neat proportion . . . I cupped my hands around his lovely scrotum . . ." Balls, if you like a pun. Though, obviously, it is testicles that are large, "scrotum" is one of the few remaining words that have not been heard on the stage, and Albee wants to get there first with the absolute most. And, of course, it should be "for a small man"—or could this be deliberate catachresis? And who but a poor stylist would write "His penis also long and of a neat proportion," which is both fancy and vague. And who would describe a scrotum as "lovely"? Certainly not a woman. What need is there, above all, for this entire, here abbreviated, speech? But Albee's pretensions are large, and not only for a small man.

Shock value is always the last resort of the impotent. Indeed, when the taped voice joins in, pseudosignificance runs amuck as darkness engulfs the scene. Alan Schneider has made resolute but arbitrary attempts at moving the characters around a little, but to no great effect, except perhaps to make the "fugue" sound stereo-

phonic. Sudie Bond continues to play the one part she has played
ever since *The Sandbox* and *The American Dream,* and there may
be some perverse glory in having built a career on Albee's granny.
The parts of Mao and the minister are equally nonexistent, but
Nancy Kelly makes the LWL as amiable as possible. Ruth White's
taped voice babbles on almost as magisterially as Ruth White in
the flesh. As for Albee, where does he go from here? He could
perhaps eliminate the third dimension from his box, or have us
sit in a voiceless dark. We'll get to the grass roots of theatre yet,
even if it means burrowing underground like a mole.

Pretentiousness and spuriousness of a more commercial sort
can be had in *The Man in the Glass Booth.* Robert Shaw is a
remarkable actor, but as a playwright he is hopelessly hokey. (I
don't much care for his fiction, either.) We are asked to believe
here that New York's richest Jew, Arthur Goldman, who sits in a
glass-plated pleasure dome above Manhattan, most of which he
owns, and semi-humorously terrorizes everyone from his secretary
to remote strangers, suddenly transforms himself into one Colonel
Dorff, a dreaded former SS monster, and lets himself fall into the
hands of three Israelis who will take him back to Jerusalem to
stand trial. In the second act, we are asked to swallow Dorff's
black-humored ribbing of the Israeli interrogators, rejecting his
former secretary's offer to bear favorable witness, going into the
glass booth in the courtroom to spew forth Nazi sophistries and
eulogies, and insisting that the Jews would have done the same
had they been chosen by Hitler. Just as he is about to be sen-
tenced to death, and to his intense displeasure, he is saved by a
surprise witness who erupts from the audience. A Mrs. Lehmann
identifies the prisoner as indeed the Jew Goldman, a cousin of the
Nazi Dorff who happened to be the commander of the camp
in which she and Goldman were held. Dorff was finally torn to
bits by the inmates, and Goldman ran riot on a German-murder-
ing spree, to end up as a crazy American millionaire. His intention, as he now admits, was to show the world what an unre-
pentant and unreconstructed Nazi truly is, and thus become a
supreme object lesson.

Preposterous as this résumé sounds, it is far less so than the play itself. To raise only the most obvious of many questions, why doesn't anyone in the Israeli government know about Dorff's Orphic demise until Mrs. Lehmann, suitably near the end of the play, volunteers her climactic revelation? Defenders of this turbid confection will say that it isn't meant to be a piece of naturalism, that it is rather an absurdist black comedy. In that case, why all the realistic trappings, why all the elaborate explanations, why the close imitation of the Eichmann trial? So much for the absurdism. And the comedy? If you think hearing an apparent SS officer say, "Mind you, I've always liked kosher. We've got a kosher restaurant in New York killed more Hebrews than I did," is funny, then comedy it is. At another point, when Goldman envisions "the first Jewish-American pope," his doctor says, "Pope Hyman." Whereupon we get the following exchange: "I didn't know you was a wit.—I'm not.—Keep at it: everything is a matter of practice." If Robert Shaw ever makes it as a playwright, I shall be obliged to agree with this proposition.

Shaw is exploiting genocide and a highly controversial trial for a contrived tragi-farce that is supposed to say something about the interchangeability of personalities, about circumstances (if not, indeed, clothes) making the man, about the flimsy boundary between victim and executioner. But this antiquated and at the same time over-simplified notion, executed with a wit that is anything but Shavian, does not entitle Shaw to horse around with shattering immensities. The model for this charade seems to be Dürrenmatt, but the Swiss dramatist is, at his best, incomparably sounder and funnier. Yet Dürrenmatt, too, seems to think that madness is a great source of comedy, which it isn't. Goldman's ravings alternating with cutely demented wisecracks are too alienated and alienating to involve us emotionally, and the idea content, especially as filtered through lunacy, is too thin to stimulate thought.

Reviewers, even those unsympathetic to the play, tended to swoon over Donald Pleasence's performance. Now it seems to me that no actor who is always almost exactly the same is truly good;

no actor who becomes possessed by his role instead of possessing it is truly good; no actor who overemphasizes what is already overemphatic is even intelligent. If ever a part demanded playing against the grain, this Goldman-Dorff is it; Pleasence merely piles madness on more madness. Harold Pinter, who directed, has tried to infuse some of his characteristic understatements and silences; this may help the earlier scenes but hobbles the climactic trial scene, which could use some Kazan or Tony Richardson. Among the supporting players, Laurence Pressman is plausible as the meek but not unambitious secretary, the others are mired in their material.

This season's most interesting offering so far is *The Great White Hope*. Howard Sackler's play, transferred from Washington's Arena Stage, revised and partly recast, generates considerable excitement. Generating excitement is not nearly so good as generating art, but, in these lean times, may have to do. How nice if Sackler, who had the good sense to use Shakespeare and Brecht as his models, had come up with something worthy of them; unfortunately, the writing is only hard-working, competent but overambitious middlebrow stuff.

The play is the semifictionalized story of Jack Johnson, the first Negro heavyweight champion of the world. In the play, Jack Jefferson (could the name Johnson be too dirty a word for a white liberal to apply to his black hero?) wins the championship against mighty odds, and, to the despair of white America, seems unbeatable. Worse yet, he has a white girl friend; this, however, enables his enemies in and out of the FBI to frame him under the Mann Act. He beats a trumped-up three-year rap by escaping to Europe with Ellie, his girl, Goldie, his Jewish manager, and Tick, his Negro trainer. He defeats all contenders, but it becomes harder and harder for him to get fights or even to remain unmolested in any country for very long: in various ways, America continues to hound him. He performs in shabby nightclub acts and stoops to other indignities, but refuses lucrative offers to throw the championship in a rigged fight. When his mother dies back home and he can't even attend her funeral, Jack angrily leads his faithful band to Mexico, whence he hurls defiance across the border while, in dire financial straits, he keeps in training for a possible fight. His bitterness is so great that he ends by driving his devoted girl to her death. Broken by this as well as by the Mexican government's expulsion order (under U.S. coercion), Jefferson agrees to fight "the great white hope" who has finally been found and groomed against him; he agrees, furthermore, to lose in exchange for not only money but also the dropping of charges against him. The Negroes are still solidly behind him, but when he loses the big fight in Havana (apparently honest), they too reject him.

Many things seem wrong to me with this sprawling three-act and nineteen-scene play. My first objection may seem irrelevant, but I consider it extremely unfortunate that boxing should be made into a heroic and noble thing. This so-called sport, which strikes me as the ugliest and most anachronistic of pastimes, can hardly be squared with our supposed discouragement or blood lust and our curbs on most (unfortunately not all) sports involving similar cruelty to animals. The leading Swedish newspaper, *Dagens Nyheter,* in its campaign against boxing, keeps unearthing numerous deaths in or just after the ring, which elsewhere go unreported. Jack Johnson may be a perfect symbol of the black hero-victim, there may have been no other avenues to fame for Negroes in the early 1900's, and Howard Sackler may certainly not have *intended* to glorify prizefighting, but all this and Pindar notwithstanding, I find the central positive value of the play a profoundly distasteful one, which diminishes the work *ipso facto.*

Scarcely more attractive is the ideological oversimplification. The play's moral universe is about as simplistic and false as LeRoi Jones's, with this difference: there is a *tertium quid* between all those lovable Negroes and appalling whites: Ellie and Goldie, who are good though white, apparently because they are Jewish. The world, I fear, just isn't that black-and-Jewish-and-white. At least that notion strikes me as equally open to doubt as the one that performing a musical-comedy version of *Uncle*

Tom's Cabin, an eminently respectable pursuit in Siam, as Rodgers and Hammerstein have taught us, should, in a Budapest cabaret, be appreciably worse than beating or being beaten to a bloody pulp in the arena.

Next comes the problem of focus. By trying for a personal tragedy as well as a racial one, scope as well as intimacy; by including even a proleptic view of the future in the unlikely character of Scipio, a Black Panther *avant la lettre;* by further adding vignettes satirizing the faults of various nationalities; by trying to write in high and low style successively when not simultaneously, Sackler finds himself in the position of the man who wants to paint a giant fresco and illuminate an initial both at once. Shakespeare could do it, true; but he could do anything. Brecht could do it, sometimes. Sackler cannot do it, or at least not smoothly and compellingly.

There are also some disturbing evasions. We never see the crucial events, the prizefights, which remain offstage. But the same holds true for such diverse masterpieces as *Oedipus Rex* and *Penthesilea,* for example. There, however, we have the dramatic poetry of Sophocles and Kleist to compensate for the lack—even to surpass the actual events in the most brilliant representation. Sackler's last scene, with fight fans reporting the bout from the top of a ladder in barely comprehensible shouts, falls flat. More crippling, however, is the cop-out: did Jefferson throw the fight or lose it fair and square? Sackler seems to be too much in love with his hero to accept either alternative; he leaves the matter hanging, and when the now victorious challenger is carried on stage, his face is one bleeding gash, as if a bomb had carried off most of it, whereas Jack's still has a human shape to it. At this point, Sackler has definitely thrown *his* fight.

But the main weakness of the play is its attempt at poetry. No viewer, myself included, could begin to smell blank verse behind what is heard at the Alvin Theatre. Yet on consulting the printed text, there it suddenly is. This is the school of blank verse extending from T. S. Eliot to Rolf Hochhuth, noted for the unnoticeableness of its pentameters. Which raises the legitimate question: why bother at all? Is anything gained by the meter in this passage typical of most of the play:

> Why, it juss like whut Presden Teddy say,
> Square Deal for Evvybody!—come on, les treat em right,
> git some chairs out here, they gonna stay, OK,
> no use they standing, some old-timie folks
> long with em here . . .

But observe that even in the rarer, more poetic passages, as in this meditation by Cap'n Dan, a former champion and now Jack's nemesis, nothing much is achieved:

> Now you'll say, Oh, that's only your title in sports—
> no, it's more. Admit it. And more than if one got to be
> world's best engineer, or smartest politician,
> or number one opera singer, or world's biggest genius
> at making things from peanuts. No calamity there.
> But Heavyweight Champion of the World, well
> it feels like the world's got a shadow across it,
> Everything's—no joke intended—kind of darker,
> and different, like it's shrinking . . .

I cannot help feeling that it is *lèse-majesté* to haul dramatic blank verse out of its mausoleum for such street-corner turns. And it's no use saying that that is what such people sound like. Fine, but let them sound like that in prose, where they belong.

Nevertheless, the play has energy and variety. It knows when to hurtle and when to sashay forward, there is humor in it, and it does generate a growing sense of entrapment and doom. The Negro speech patterns are accurate and flavorous, and the protagonist, for one, does emerge a full and appealing human being. The other parts, even when they are no more than stereotypes, are at least swirlingly animated stereotypes. The device of addressing the audience is positively run into the groundlings, but some of the text's more awkward speeches are mercifully cut in the stage version. Sackler has at any rate sketched in a historical play conceived in the grand style; some credit is due for the very boldness of his concept.

The production is better than anything currently on view in New York. Edwin Sherin, the director, has coaxed every spark to be had out of rapid movement, lightning transitions, connecting music and disconnecting voices shrilling and sputtering. His one fault is to have driven his actors to shouting overmuch; given the initial problem some of them have with diction, a goodly proportion of lines never makes it comprehensibly across the footlights. This, regrettably, goes most for James Earl Jones. Otherwise, his Jack Jefferson is a magnificent creation, so much so that the play is unimaginable without Jones. Physically, he is just the shiny-pated, swift-footed, barrel-chested, debonair giant Johnson must have been; quick-witted, too, and jovial, charmingly embodying that real or imagined animality that white men fear for real or imaginary reasons. His emotional range is no less colossal: from bubbling badinage through ironic jabs to overwhelming grief at the death of his girl—human, animal, titanic—Jones encompasses everything with the precision and ease of a master. Particularly fine is his timing: the entire performance is paced with the sensitivity to tempo and inflection of a virtuoso *lieder* singer. His breakdown over Ellie's body is as unbearably moving a piece of acting as I have ever seen.

Barely if at all behind him is Jane Alexander as Ellie. A *jolie laide* if ever there was one, she plays the part with an endearing firmness and modesty—almost a primness, if you can imagine primness as the vehicle for tenderness, warmth, and passionate resolve. Whether she is quietly defending her relationship against various legal bloodhounds or feverishly clinging to it in the face of her lover's seemingly brutal rejection, she maintains (along with flawless diction) a sturdy grip on the human dignity of the part. It is Miss Alexander's triumph that without the slightest bid for our sympathy she has us loving her, suffering with her, mourning her. There is something virginal about her acting: every gesture and utterance comes as a first awakening, an emergence from deep, shy reserve into daylight, exaltation, and pain.

Most of the supporting parts are at least capably handled. Even such often erratic actors as Lou Gilbert, George Mathews, and Jon Cypher give performances to be relished, and some of the briefest appearances manage to register. Equally to be commended are Robin Wagner's efficiently spare sets, David Toser's sensibly restrained costumes, John Gleason's graphic lighting, and Charles Gross's suggestively arranged musical underpinnings. Even the playwright deserves, after all, a lefthanded salute.

No such salute is due Joseph Heller's rather self-indulgent antiwar and anti-universal indifference play, *We Bombed in New Haven,* a belated foray into Pirandellism covering ideological and technical ground that is already flyspecked with footprints. While Ron Leibman and Anthony Holland give incisive performances, Jason Robards is perfunctory and Diana Sands (despite the obligatory chorus of critical acclaim any Negro actor is nowadays assured of) bad as usual. Two Pinter one-acters written for television would just manage to squeak by on stage, if only they were better performed. In *The Tea Party* (a needlessly obscure and basically empty play), Valerie French is as sexy as she is good, and John Tillinger is amusing though too unmenacing; but the others, with one painful exception, are only bearable. In *The Basement* (a rather more obvious and basically empty play), all three performances are shoddy. Ed Wittstein's sets, as always, perform as trickily and delightfully as trained poodles, but it is bad business for dramatic design to be outclassed by set design.

The most controversial event of the fall was The Living Theatre's limited engagement in Brooklyn, a place noted for its poor diction and turbulent streets. The Becks now practice revolutionary street theatre, and whether their offerings are based on Sophocles and Brecht, Mary Shelley, or their own and other people's improvisations, it all comes out a cross between Artaud and agit-prop, between slimy calisthenics and maniacal group therapy for performers and audience. Everyone must by now be directly or indirectly acquainted with these subverbal protest meetings against practically anything, these combination happenings and live-ins with poorly simulated sex, crudely mimed revolt, clouds of incense and pot, performers wallowing in the aisles and spectators rushing up on the stage. There is mutual heckling by actors and audience, alternating with performers imitating animals, platonic orgies, pseudonudie shows; there are swirlings, seethings, bellowings, mass possession by demons, anything but theatre. Long hours of dullness punctuated by an occasional clever stage image or an apt wisecrack from someone in the audience. How strange that so much bustle can add up to such boredom.

For a cogent, systematic, and justly severe dissection of The Living Theatre, everyone should read Eric Bentley's masterly critique in *The New York Times* of October 20. Bentley makes clear how confused and destructive the LT's politics are, how sterile their acting techniques, and how the glory of the theatre is to have risen from ritual, not to lapse back into it. My purpose here is merely to report a few typical symptoms; I undertake no complete nosography.

At the Sophocles-Brecht *Antigone,* antitranslated by Judith Malina, we hear: "As for me, I'm following the custom and burying my brother, and if they kill me for it, so what." Or: "And further, if I had left my mother's dead son lie unburied, that would have made me unhappy." Miss Malina speaks and acts these lines as execrably as the rest of the company acts and speaks, but you may be sure that they are accompanied by several actors impersonating ravening vultures to perfection. Words here are few in number and feeble in meaning, but the former is compensated for by endless repetition, the latter by frantic shouting. The Polynices of the evening, a chap who calls himself Echnaton and looks like the first syllable of that venerable name, used Unilateral Disarmament buttons to button his fly with. It is hard to say whether the cause of peace or of its near-homonym is worse served by this maneuver .

At *Mysteries and Smaller Pieces* the public got a splendid chance to display its imbecility. At one point several performers squat downstage facing the audience and produce a series of snorts and sneezes. The spectators respond with hurricanes of laughter and applause. During one phase of the evening, large numbers of spectators made a pilgrimage to the stage, formed an enormous circle with the performers, and proceeded to hum and sway, sway and hum. Several reviewers with reputations participated in this ritual. One young girl hobbled up on the stage on crutches. I am sorry to have to report that no miracle occurred; she had to hobble back to her seat. Rather like Lisieux, I imagine.

At *Paradise Now*, Julian Beck *en* (partial) *deshabillé* chants, "If I could drive you out of your wretched minds," and it occurs to me that the procedure here is not really therapy, not really exorcism, but, if I may coin a word, inorcism. The point is to infect as many people as possible with the demons, gripes, hatreds, foaming fits and brimming frustrations of the LT: if all become equally crazy, all will be equally sane.

Let me illustrate. At one point various voices from the stage yell out: "Fuck the Jews! Fuck the Arabs! Fuck means peace!" A spectator sagely corrects: "Fuck means a piece of arse." But note the LT's typical aggression. Is this pacification? Is this a political program? Is this comic theatre? Why should Jews or Arabs, or even hyenas in heat, submit to the embraces of the unwashed, unsightly, uncivilized, untouchable members of the LT? And, significantly, the entire ensemble now howls in chorus: "Kill! Kill! Kill!" In the name of peace, of course. And there are four-and-a-half hours of this, without intermission or even remission.

But the laughable, frightening, pathetic thing is that numerous reviewers and critics, some of them even vaguely respectable, should have taken this seriously, should have waxed enthusiastic and emitted fulsome encomia. I am glad that there is a Bentley left to call a spade a spade, but it's a Milton that should be living at this hour. Except that, struck down by the deafening torrent of mindlessness and hysteria, he too would end up a mute, inglorious Milton.

For Further Reading

Bower, Reuben and Poirier, Richard, eds. *In Defense of Reading: A Reader's Approach to Literary Criticism,* New York, Dutton, 1963.

Buck, Philo M. *Literary Criticism: A Study of Values in Literature,* New York and London, Harper and Brothers, 1930.

Crane, Ronald S. *Critics and Criticism, Ancient and Modern,* Chicago, University of Chicago Press, 1953.

Daiches, David. *Critical Approaches to Literature,* Englewood Cliffs, Prentice-Hall, 1956.

Foster, Richard J. *The New Romantics: A Reappraisal of the New Criticism,* Bloomington, Indiana University Press, 1962.

Frye, Northrop. *Anatomy of Criticism,* Princeton, Princeton University Press, 1957.

Matthiessen, F. O. *The Responsibilities of the Critic,* New York, Oxford University Press, 1952.

Pritchard, John Paul. *Criticism in America,* Norman, University of Oklahoma Press, 1956.

Richards, I. A. *Principles of Literary Criticism,* New York, Harcourt, Brace and Co., 1925.

Stovall, Floyd. *The Development of American Literary Criticism,* Chapel Hill, University of North Carolina Press, 1955.

Sutton, Walter E. *Modern American Criticism,* Englewood Cliffs, Prentice-Hall, 1963.

Welleck, René. *Concepts of Criticism,* New Haven, Yale University Press, 1963.

Wimsatt, William K. and Brooks, Cleanth. *Literary Criticism: A Short History,* New York, Knopf, 1957.

Winters, Yvor. *The Function of Criticism,* Denver, Swallow, 1957.